Bertolt Brecht

bertolt brecht

Political Theory and Literary Practice

Edited by

betty nance weber

and

hubert heinen

the university of georgia press
Athens

Copyright © 1980 by the University of Georgia Press
Athens, Georgia 30602

All rights reserved

Set in 10 on 13 point Garamond Book type
Printed in the United States of America

Library of Congress Cataloging in Publication Data

International Brecht Society.
    Bertolt Brecht, political theory and literary practice.

    "Essays . . . first presented at the fourth congress of the
International Brecht Society, November 17–20, 1976, in
Austin, Texas."
    Includes index.

    1. Brecht, Bertolt, 1898–1956—Political and social
views—Addresses, essays, lectures.   I. Weber, Betty
Nance, 1943–1979 II. Heinen, Hubert. III. Title.

PT2603.R397Z7117 1980   832'.9'1208   79–21646
ISBN 0–8203–0506–5

For all those colleagues and friends who journeyed
to the Fourth Congress of the International Brecht Society

Me-ti said: It's really awful. Rumors are being spread everywhere that I said the most ridiculous things. And, between you and me, the unfortunate truth is that I did say most of them.

Me-ti

Contents

IV: Uses of Poetry

Afterword

Notes on the Contributors

Index

Acknowledgments

These essays were first presented at the Fourth Congress of the International Brecht Society, 17–20 November 1976, in Austin, Texas. The contributors were patient and cooperative in adapting the original presentations so that they could be integrated into a productive dialogue. We are grateful to the American Council of Learned Societies and to the Suhrkamp Verlag for making the invitation of several speakers from abroad possible, to the University of Texas at Austin, especially the Department of Germanic Languages, the College of Humanities, and the Graduate School for generous support of the congress and this volume. We also appreciate the contributions from the colleges of Fine Arts, Social and Behavioral Sciences, Natural Sciences; the Division of General and Comparative Studies, the LBJ School of Public Affairs, the Graduate School of Business, the School of Communication; the departments of Slavic Languages, Philosophy, and Drama; and Delta Kappa chapter of Delta Phi Alpha. We owe special thanks to Nelda Keck, Jennifer Oppenheim, and the staff of the Department of Germanic Languages for their assistance with the congress and the preparation of this volume.

Klaus-Detlef Müller's article, "*Me-ti*," was first published in the *Brecht Jahrbuch* (1977) and is reprinted here by permission of Suhrkamp Verlag, Frankfurt. Margareta N. Deschner's article, "Wuolijoki's and Brecht's Politization of the Volksstück," is based in part on an article that appeared in the *Brecht Jahrbuch* (1978); permission to use that material is also gratefully acknowledged. The editors wish to thank the following publishers and individuals who have granted rights to reproduce and translate the quotations from contemporary German poetry that appear in this volume: Michael Hamburger, for permission to quote from translations of the works of Kurt Bartsch, Heinz Kahlau, and Reiner Kunze published in *East German Poetry: An Anthology* (New York: Dutton, 1973); Günter Kunert, for permission to quote in translation from *Das kleine Aber: Gedichte* (Berlin: Aufbau-Verlag, 1975); Carl Hanser Verlag, Munich, for permission to quote in translation from Günter Kunert's *Verkündigung des Wetters* (1966); Verlag Kiepenheuer and Witsch, Cologne, for permission to quote in translation from Wolf Biermann's *Für meine Genossen* (1975); Suhrkamp Verlag, Frankfurt, for permission to quote in translation from Hans Magnus Enzensberger's *Blindenschrift* (1964), *Landessprache* (1969), *Gedichte 1955–1970* (1972), and *Mausoleum* (1975), from Bertolt Brecht's *Gesammelte Werke in 20 Bänden* (1967), and from Thomas Brasch's *Kargo* (1978).

Note on Translations and Citations

Theodore Fiedler, Douglas Kellner, Antony Tatlow, and Betty Nance Weber provided English translations for all German quotations in their essays; Margareta Deschner, for all Finnish ones; George Lellis, for all French ones. Otherwise, except as noted, the English translations were done by Hubert Heinen.

Unless otherwise noted, all quotations from Bertolt Brecht in this study are taken from *Gesammelte Werke in 20 Bänden* (Frankfurt: Suhrkamp, 1967) and are cited parenthetically by volume and page number; e.g. (12: 375). References to materials from the Bertolt-Brecht-Archiv (BBA) are cited according to portfolio and page number. See Herta Ramthun, *Bestandsverzeichnis des Bertolt-Brecht-Archivs*, 4 vols. (Berlin: Aufbau, 1969–73).

Introduction

Introduction

Although Bertolt Brecht has been a major figure in German and, indeed, international literature and theater for almost half a century, the scope of criticism available on his work in English and in English translation is limited. Several surveys of his life and work serve as introductions and numerous articles in scholarly journals address specific issues, but only a few collections of essays provide easily accessible interpretations. The majority of these volumes were published in the early and mid-sixties and precede significant findings that have appeared in German in the last decade. Moreover, the Brecht Archives have yielded many valuable texts and documents that early studies could not consider. In view of Brecht's increasing importance for American theater and literature, there is a need for studies that not only introduce the poet and his work but also convey the richness of interpretation and analysis in contemporary criticism.

This volume, assembled on the occasion of the eightieth anniversary of Brecht's birth, reflects the ongoing dialogue about the genesis of Brecht's works and their impact on contemporary literature, theater, and film. The essays focus on an aspect of Brecht's work, namely the function of political philosophy and practice, that has received relatively little attention or has been disputed in major English-language biographies and collections now available. This aspect, which is still a controversial subject in German-language scholarship, is all the more important because it permeates Brecht's literary career. The essayists treat Brecht's confrontation with Marxism and its political manifestations, the influence of his work on theater and film, or the uses his literary descendants make of his political commitment.

The volume is structured to proceed from Brecht's involvement with the political history of this century, considered by Iring Fetscher in his foreword, to the involvement of postwar generations with the poet and his political legacy, discussed in an afterword by Frank Trommler. The first section of essays, "Political Theory and Practice," examines Brecht's concern for political theory and history as they inform his literary production. Antony Tatlow proposes "critical dialectics" as a concept with which one can analyze Brecht's "position and the function of his art." This concept is developed from a reading of *Me-ti*, a posthumously published collection of aphoristic anecdotes "in the Chinese manner on proper rules of behavior." Douglas Kellner and Klaus-Detlef Müller investigate the genesis and structure of *Me-ti* and reveal its primary importance for an understanding of how Brecht deals with the difficulties and discrepancies within the Marxist movement. *Me-ti* is viewed, in these essays, as a political testament because Brecht explicitly identifies figures and events in revolutionary history. Betty Nance Weber suggests that Brecht's political testament is also to be found in less explicit works: the "classic masterworks" of the exile period, which were, indeed, in their inception commentaries on revolutionary history in Russia.

In the second section of the essays, "Production," experiences with staging Brecht works in a variety of circumstances are discussed. Efim Etkind and Henry Glade describe Brecht's impact on the Soviet Union in the 1950s and 1960s. Etkind, a preeminent Brecht translator who witnessed this era, conveys the excitement of the intelligentsia who discovered in Brecht a vehicle for reviving long-decried native traditions from the 1920s. Glade, who is concerned with the symbiosis of dramaturgical intent and political statement, delineates the three phases of Brecht's reception on postwar Soviet stages. Ian McLachlan and Wolfgang Storch, as participants in the production process, give accounts of how two theater groups in the West attempted to relate "the relevance of a revolutionary play for a nonrevolutionary audience." On the one hand, McLachlan's group introduced a difficult and much disputed Brecht text, *The Measures Taken*, to a proletarian audience in Peterborough, Ontario. On the other hand, the *Schaubühne am Halleschen Ufer* in Berlin, working with Storch as dramaturge, approached an audience for whom Brecht plays are standard fare with the world premiere of the unpublished fragment *Fatzer*.

In the second half of the volume the focus is shifted to Brecht's impact on individuals. In the third section, "Alteration of Aesthetic Values," Margareta Deschner and George Lellis investigate the changes that issue from a confrontation with Brecht's theories. For Hella Wuolijoki, who offered Brecht refuge during his exile in Finland, the personal/intellectual confrontation profoundly altered her understanding of the *Volksstück*. Lellis traces meticulously how the study of Brecht's aesthetic theories has indeed changed the course of film history.

In the final section of the volume, "Uses of Poetry," three essayists discuss German poets for whom Brecht's work is an almost overwhelming literary inheritance. Richard Rundell and Theodore Fiedler analyze the difficulties encountered by poets from the German Democratic Republic in which Brecht is an officially proclaimed socialist classic. Rundell treats the reception of Brecht's poetry in the 1960s; Fiedler, in the 1970s. For the Federal Republic of Germany, where Brecht's work prevailed despite official disfavor, Hans Magnus Enzensberger's reception is treated by Wulf Koepke as representative of contemporary political poets.

With this series of essays an English-speaking audience is brought to the mainstream of controversy about Brecht's work. Despite the enormous amount of research that has been done in German-language scholarship, there is still much to discover. The man himself is often misunderstood and there is even greater confusion on what is meant by the term *Brechtian*. What, indeed, is Brechtian about Brecht's work and his legacy? To write a poem or produce a play in a Brechtian style is not necessarily Brechtian. His techniques and forms, vocabulary and images were always a response to a specific historical situation and to "quote" them may be to distort their purpose. Brecht sought modes of expression that could convey his confrontation with the major issues of his lifetime, issues that are still at the center of political history. Giving artistic form, finding the uniquely appropriate aesthetic expression for a particular moment is genuinely Brechtian in contrast to echoing Brecht's stylistic devices.

Brecht himself has given an indication of the proper use of his works. In a parable about a teacher and two pupils in his *Tui Novel* he shows why one pupil learns and the other does not. As the teacher describes the surroundings, the unsuccessful pupil observes them, while the successful one observes the stance of the teacher (12: 602–4). The importance of Brecht's work lies not in the costumes his ideas are clothed in, for these are historically determined, but in the attitudes with which and the purpose for which he presents them. These essays can help us refine our awareness of the complexity of what is Brechtian and achieve a more sophisticated appreciation of Brecht's significance.

The heated debates that still rage about Brecht's political commitment and the value of individual works should not distract our attention from the larger question: how can we use an investigation of Brechtian thought to arrive at viable models for behavior? The concentration on Brecht, politics, and literary expression both focuses discussion and expands the possibilities for confronting the major issues of our time in artistic form.

BETTY NANCE WEBER
HUBERT HEINEN

In Memoriam
Betty Nance Weber 1943–1979

Since 1956, when I was introduced to songs and plays by Brecht while struggling to learn the fundamentals of German, I have been interested in and have tried to interest others in his works. For over a decade I have been especially fascinated by Brecht the poet, and have regarded his poem "The Doubter" (9: 587–88) to be both a key to his works and their development and to be a stimulating model for collaborative creativity. I was delighted when Betty Nance Weber came to the University of Texas in the early seventies and I had someone with whom I could share ideas. Betty and I frequently differed in our attitudes toward and approaches to life and literature, but our very differences were helpful to both of us as we tried to express our thoughts.

Our work together in organizing the Fourth Congress of the International Brecht Society was both exhilarating and sobering. More often than not the initiative for seeking speakers, funding, accommodations, and an ideological base came from Betty, whose energy and enthusiasm overcame virtually all obstacles. We had to formulate descriptions of what we were doing, and in the process we discovered that we worked best together when we were restating what the other wanted to say.

As we planned this volume and began to edit the essays we had selected for it, we developed a method of working which was intentionally shaped by Brecht's collaborative practice. One or the other of us made a preliminary decision about how each essay should fit our overall theme and whether any extensive revisions seemed necessary. One of us would prepare an "editor's draft" and read it aloud while the other listened.

After each sentence we asked each other if it was clear what was being said, and if it was necessary to say it. We often decided to delete passages, to rephrase sentences, and even to restructure arguments, which meant that our first editor's draft needed to be reworked to remove redundancies and awkward sentences that our piecemeal revisions had created. At this stage we generally switched the roles of reader and listener. When we sent the results of our collaborative efforts to the various authors, our suggestions for revisions sometimes elicited cries of anguish and distress—with considerable justification. We were striving for a consistent style for diverse presentations (though some were so sharply profiled that we did little more than standardize citations) and did miss the point, muddy an author's limpid syntax, or introduce an inconsistency from time to time. Our long-suffering authors were very cooperative, however, in leading us back to what our method had caused us to discard. Our impertinences in emendation were met with forebearance and understanding.

We both felt that our exercise in collaboration, though it had been extremely time-consuming and had on occasion caused more work than reward, was valuable in itself, and were looking forward to more such endeavors. Betty's untimely death, which occurred after the editorial work on the volume was essentially complete, was a tremendous shock to me, as it was to her family and her many other friends, and it was a great loss to Brecht studies.

I found and find the thesis of her essay in this volume uncomfortable; I enjoy a simple reading of *Galileo* more. Betty's earlier expressions of her thesis that Brecht consciously echoed the political history of the first third of the twentieth century in his "classical" plays written in exile (in her book on the chalk circle material as well as in talks and discussions) have been bitterly attacked by those for whom the political implications are unpleasant as well as those for whom the notion that literature has political implications is disquieting. A consistent objection even by scholars without an ideological ax to grind is that many of the parallels she notes are farfetched. However, as she worked with the material, Betty found more and more evidence that Brecht created such parallels. Why he did so, and what his having done so was supposed to mean at the time and can mean today, are questions Betty was only beginning to answer. Let us hope that Brecht scholars will address themselves to them, rather than to quibbles about individual parallels. Preconceptions about ideo-logical orthodoxy and an ideology of literature as autonomous and self-referent are inappropriate approaches to Brecht in any case. Betty's efforts will certainly serve to prevent us from "removing the contradic-tion" from our understanding of Brecht, even if she did not live to finish her investigations, and perhaps they can cause us to say, "we looked at each other and / Started over again" (9: 588).

HUBERT HEINEN

Foreword

Bertolt Brecht and Politics

Iring Fetscher

No one is born as a political or an unpolitical human being. In his school years Brecht appears to have been an ecstatic individualist, an anarchial artist. The events that led to a political consciousness in Brecht were the First World War, a brief experience as a medic, and the revolution in Germany. But even in these situations he remained an observer—often a cynical observer, occasionally a critical and skeptical one, but never an active participant. Neither the revolution in the imperial capital, Berlin, nor the Workers' Council government in Bavaria provoked in him more than a certain natural, even though distant, interest. He was fascinated by people and by their violence. He reacted emotionally and with moral, not political, consciousness. He was appalled by the worthlessness of the Rhinelanders in the occupied territory of Germany and by the inactivity of those who were tired of war.

The quick successes of plays and poems and the relative stability of the Weimar Republic also may have hindered the development of his political consciousness. But Brecht did not wait until the outbreak of the world economic crisis to become a Marxist. He has reported that a theoretical problem prompted him to read Marx's *Das Kapital* in 1926. In order to write a play that would be set in Chicago, he needed the commodities market as a background. How this market functioned was a question that neither market specialists nor grain dealers could explain to him. It appeared to be as irrational as many of the things that human beings do. There had to be, however, an explanation. Thus came Brecht to Marx.

In *Saint Joan of the Stockyards* the newly found teachings are used descriptively. Central to the piece are two themes: the radical rejection of religion as the opiate of the workers and the rejection of mere charity as a means that does not lead to liberation from servitude and exploitation. In subsequent years Brecht repeatedly treated the awakening consciousness of social incongruities in the minds of proletarian or even

bourgeois women. In the plays *The Mother* and *The Rifles of Señora
Carrar*, the learning processes are demonstrated by which individuals
overcome their own limitations. While Saint Joan dies in the resigned
recognition that she had acted incorrectly, the mother develops into a sly
combatant in the class struggle, and Señora Carrar supports the republi-
cans by handing over her weapons for their cause.

Brecht looked upon the developing Nazi barbarism and the split of the
German workers' movement into Social Democrats and Communists—as
did many other leftist intellectuals—with agitated concern. In vain, he
put his hope for a time in a cooperation of the two. But the influence of
the communist theory that Fascists and Social Democrats were "twin
brothers" (a theory that Brecht never advocated himself) was great
enough to move him to view the Social Democrats with the utmost skepticism. For the remainder of his life Brecht gave critical allegiance to the
communist movement, to which his hopes, like those of other bourgeois
intellectuals, were linked. In spite of his tendency to dress and act like a
proletarian—which probably had more to do with his bohemian background than with his political convictions—Brecht never claimed to be a
proletarian. He never claimed any other role than that of a bourgeois
who sympathized with the cause of the working class. This stance made
possible, on the one hand, his artistic freedom, which he could have
hardly maintained within the Party during the Stalin era, and, on the
other hand, the sophistication that is characteristic of his plays and
poems in contrast to the works of party-line Communists.

Bertolt Brecht was, however, not only a passive observer of the struggle of the revolutionary workers' movement and a sympathizing reporter.
He also wanted, in his own way, to take part in this movement. During
the last years of the Weimar Republic he attempted, with his learning
plays, to support the development of class consciousness and disciplined
struggle. He addressed himself directly to workers' choruses and amateur
theater groups. For all practical purposes he had given up on a bourgeoisie that had celebrated his *Threepenny Opera* without comprehending that it was applauding its own cynicism. It was not until the exile
period, when he was forced to address an audience that was indeed anti-
fascist but still not completely proletarian (to the extent he had an
audience at all), that his pieces were intended to bring convincing arguments to a bourgeois public. This view is supported by the fact that these

pieces were great successes in the postwar period—especially in the Federal Republic and for West German bourgeois intellectual audiences who made up a considerable part of the audience for productions by the Berliner Ensemble in East Berlin. In these plays—*The Caucasian Chalk Circle, Mother Courage and Her Children, The Good Woman of Szechwan*, and *Puntila*—problems are presented which the sensitive bourgeois individual in a capitalist society understands: the fatal danger of goodness (*The Good Woman of Szechwan* and *The Chalk Circle*), the necessity for wearing a mask for one's character (*Puntila* and the fragment *The Curious Illness of Henri Dunant*), and the impossibility of being a capitalist entrepreneur and being good at the same time, the incompatibility of making war profits and surviving if one has no "giant-size spoon" (*Mother Courage*). A bourgeois audience can empathize with all these issues. But Brecht did not want such an audience to enjoy, in a self-assured and sentimental manner, its own moods in the theater. He wanted the audience to learn, to comprehend that only through a revolutionary alteration of society can the incongruities be overcome, the incongruities under which we still suffer. Usually, in the theater, this effect was not achieved. The liveliness of the characters, the richness of the language, the sophisticated dramaturgy, and the brilliance of actors made it possible to react to these pieces as culinary art—even though the playwright denounced such a stance very loudly. All of his theatrical provocations were enjoyed by a satiated postwar public simply as additional spice.

The theory of the V-effect, the estrangement effect, originated very early in Brecht's work from the recognition of the necessity for restructuring the theater: the actor was to stand "beside the character portrayed"; identification and empathy were to be hindered in order to make the audience free to criticize the actions and positions that were shown. Good Brecht disciples were able to approximate this ideal, but the reactions of audiences that had ossified through generations were not so easily or quickly revised.

For Brecht it would be ideal, as he wrote in his notes on theater, the "Small Pedagogy," and in other essays, if the distance between audience and actors, audience and stage, would disappear altogether. The learning plays were supposed to be opportunities for learning for those who were playing, those who would estrange their own roles, exchange their roles, and in so doing experience in their own playing the problems of the struggle. There is no doubt in my mind that Brecht envisioned with this kind of theater a higher form suitable for the mission of the revolutionary workers' movement. Plays could then be the means for rehearsing and practicing correct revolutionary action. They could make the lessons of history more comprehensible and encourage assuming the "correct stances."

Even before he became a revolutionary socialist, Brecht was a "theoretician of struggle." He was fascinated by it, and Marxism became an aid in replacing his early preoccupation with combat as an absurd phenomenon of nature with meaningful, historically explicable striving. Repeatedly he demonstrated an awakening consciousness of a necessity for confrontation and for the beginning of struggle itself. He was less fascinated by victory and construction—especially in the unheroic and unexpected form they would later take in the German Democratic Republic. He even had difficulty in repeatedly convincing himself that a revolution from above was better than no revolution at all.

This attitude probably underlies his skepticism toward the leading politicians of the DDR, even though he never revoked his allegiance to that state. This distance was to become apparent again in his analysis of the events of 17 June 1953 (the workers' uprising). In his opinion the uprising was "the grand opportunity," an opportunity that the Socialist Unity party had missed. Making contact with the actively struggling class that had finally emerged from its passivity could have ushered in a new epoch. Instead of rising to this occasion, the party leaders hid behind Soviet tanks. Development by bureaucrats under a "leadership from above" was not to Brecht's liking; he had read Rosa Luxemburg well. A true revolutionary movement learns more from its own mistakes than from the leadership of a central committee, be it ever so competent. While the feisty revolutionary playwright, despite all the absurdities of the mass strike of 17 and 18 June, recognized the encouraging fact that German workers finally had risen up, the ex-communists, who in the meantime had become bureaucrats, saw from their vantage-point at the top of the state hierarchy only a threat to their privileges. These people were—as Brecht had already noted during the exile period—enemies of "production," that is, of the activities that do not correspond to their bureaucratic notions. This was true not only for art and literature (Brecht defended, among other works, those of Ernst Barlach and the *Faust* of his friend Hans Eisler) but also apparently for the politics of the workers.

Bertolt Brecht was not suited for the role of the official state poet, a role that he magnanimously ceded to Johannes R. Becher (whom he privately scorned). Brecht's "Children's Rhymes," which well could have become the national anthem, apparently were too modest for party leaders:

> Spare neither charm nor effort,
> Neither passion nor reason,
> To make a good Germany flourish
> As any other good land.

This is a sort of a counter-hymn to "Deutschland, Deutschland über alles." There is no longer the wish to excel, to be better than, or to conquer; there is merely the hope for peaceful coexistence. The love of one's own land is juxtaposed to the love, as a natural phenomenon, of other peoples for their lands:

> And it appears to us to be the best
> Just as theirs appears to other peoples.

Bertolt Brecht was a political writer. This is true at least for those works written after 1927. It is possible to admire the grandness of his linguistic facility without recognizing his political convictions and intentions. But it is impossible to understand his plays (and many of his poems) without knowing the form of Marxism peculiar to Brecht, a Marxism that derives from his own studies and the influences of friends such as Karl Korsch. The following essays show several aspects of this Marxism and its influence on Brecht's theater. Brecht was the sort of intellectual writer one rarely encounters. He was well aware of the fact that he was opposing the traditional cliché of the artist as an ethereal eccentric with his literary work. The cliché against which Brecht reacted is still an important determinant in the cultural life of Germany, as is illustrated by the reception that Peter Handke and Hermann Hesse have sought and found.

But even as a Marxist theoretician Brecht was a practical writer, whose reflections on theories and relationships were never divorced from the possibilities of the theater (as his basic reality) or political exigencies (of the Soviet Union, of the Second World War, of the danger of war during the period of the cold war). For this reason he felt a closer affinity with the Marxist revolutionaries (such as Rosa Luxemburg, Lenin, and Trotsky) than with the pure theoreticians, among whom he had good friends. In his short report *Reason and the Poet*, Fritz Sternberg describes Brecht as a very difficult pupil in his Berlin years: his questions were often more concrete than the thought processes of the lecturer permitted.[1] Brecht wanted to make practical what he had heard. He was interested only in the kind of thinking that converts into action. This attitude separated him from the professors of the Frankfurt school whom he would encounter in California. Long before Herbert Marcuse, in connection with the student movement, came to a certain "praxis orientation," Brecht recognized him as a kindred spirit. He considered the others "Tuis," intellectuals who theorize for a living without the will or the ability to convert their thought into action. On occasion Brecht accused them of simple opportunism, when actually they were cultivating the critical spirit in an ivory tower. There may be an element of self-hatred in this particular polemic. Brecht's enthusiasm for competitive sports and for political struggle did not induce him to take an active role in, for example, the civil war in Spain as did many of his friends, such as Ruth Berlau. His reasons for not joining in the conflict were sound: with a pen he could be of more use than with a machine gun. But perhaps he privately envied those who participated in the physical struggle.

In a brief prefatory note one cannot comment on and resolve all the contradictions of the writer and the struggler Bertolt Brecht. It would be strange if there were no such inconsistencies in his character and in his work, both of which evolved in a time of war and class struggle, in a time of social incongruities and moral conflicts. Such inconsistencies can be resolved only when "humans befriend other human beings." When we remember Brecht "with forbearance," then we know we also require such forbearance. To list only a few of the paradoxes that Brecht was unable to resolve: his readiness to learn from all collaborators and to form a productive theater collective versus his dictatorial style of leadership; his assumption in principle (which he never articulated) of the equality of the sexes versus his cliché-ridden image of women in most of his pieces; his allegiance to Rosa Luxemburg's concept of self-learning and self-activity as a basis for revolution among the masses as they become emancipated versus his willingness, in spite of all criticism, to accept Lenin's elite concept of the Party hierarchy and to justify Stalin's deformed dictatorship of the Party; his silence about the Moscow trials versus his skepticism concerning the justification of many of the sentences; his courage versus his ability to conform more than was necessary for survival; his honesty versus his sly cunning. Without these incongruities and contradictions Brecht would not have been a child of our age.

Translated by Betty Nance Weber

Note

1. Fritz Sternberg, *Der Dichter und die Ratio: Erinnerungen an Bertolt Brecht* (Göttingen: Sachse and Pohl, 1963), p. 12.

Part One
political theory & practice

Critical Dialectics

ANTHONY TATLOW

I wish to bring apparently incompatible planes into relation. We need to make some terminological differentiation to encompass Brecht's fundamental position and the function of his art. Constant employment of the same vocabulary for divergent purposes blurs crucial issues. I propose critical dialectics.

We are reminded of Brecht's own wryly deprecatory epitaph:

> I need no gravestone, but
> If you need one for me
> I would like to see written:
> He made proposals. We
> Accepted them.
> Such an inscription would
> Honor us all. (10: 1029)

In fact, he received from the funeral address by Lukács onward that potentially injurious public honor: daily embalmment, being preserved unchanged but lifeless.

At the 1974 Montreal meeting of the International Brecht Society, Iring Fetscher thought to detect a "certain Rousseauism" in Brecht, describing it as "a theoretical weakness." I wish to pursue this question for it leads to the center of my inquiry. I doubt whether Rousseau himself was the cause of any such debilitation. Brecht mentions him only once, on the question of technique and the novel of education. It is certain, however, that Brecht did associate the assertion of natural human qualities with Chinese philosophy. For some this may push the whole matter to the outer limits of tolerable discourse, but that does not obviate the problem. Brecht's attitude toward those embarrassingly Wise Men of the East is nicely caught in *Me-ti, The Book of Twists and Turns*:

> Me-ti said: When one finds pieces of bronze or iron among the rubble one asks: what kind of tools were those in olden days? What were they used for? From weapons, one deduces battles; from ornamentation, trade. One per-

ceives all kinds of predicaments and possibilities. Why does one not do the
same with the thoughts of olden times? (12: 563)

I do not now contemplate a ritual evocation of assorted Confucian virtues, which Brecht himself viewed with suitable skepticism. There are,
naturally, parallels in Western philosophy; Hegel, for example, held that
the individual and the common good must be made to coincide. Were
these entirely Chinese ideas, we would suspect them, but Hegel did not
speak with the memorable clarity of the Chinese.

In "Estrangement Effects in Chinese Acting" Brecht states the usual
Marxist position on innate human qualities; they are properties of the
bourgeois *theatrum mundi*, whereas in reality human beings are vari-
ables of their milieu, which itself must be understood in terms of relations between humans. We know how Brecht integrated into his work
Chinese anticipations of such perceptions.[1] But there is something more
intriguing here than the counterweight for Marxist abstractions of parabolic Chinese specificities, in spite of their usefulness. Like many other
left-eyed and right-handed people, Shen Te turns into Shui Ta. Create the
conditions that will enable people to be good, said Mencius, and Brecht
plucks this out of any stabilizing Confucian context.

We could dismiss assertions of natural qualities as so many phrases in
the "language of slaves," Brecht's acidulous concession to the policies of
the United Front. But such affirmations are not confined to the public aspect of his work, nor did they end in 1945. We could propose them as
part of a utopian perspective, but this surely slackens the present tensions they generate.

Let us look for the evidence beyond the "public" plays, also beyond
the more private poetry, to writings published posthumously in which
Brecht speculated, both directly and in characteristically Chinese anec-
dotal refraction, on problems as they occurred to him. I refer to *Me-ti*
and the *Work Journals*.

> There are few occupations, said Me-ti, which so damage a person's morals
> like the occupation with morals. I hear people say: one must love truth, one
> must keep one's promises, one must fight for the good. But the trees do not
> say: one must be green, one must let the fruit drop vertically, one must rustle
> the leaves when the wind passes. (12: 504)

Such affirmation of congruence is redolent of Chinese perceptions; the
implications concern us presently.

Discussing in 1941 the crisis in drama, the need to create complex, developing figures, the collectivization of human beings through deprivation, and behaviorist psychology's reflection of society's instrumentalization of the individual, Brecht observed:

> On the other hand, the demolition, explosion, atomization of the individual psyche is a fact, i.e., it is not only an erroneous habit of observation, if one determines the strange centerlessness of individuals. But absence of center does not mean absence of substance. One simply faces new entities which must be newly defined. . . . The new entity also reacts *and acts* in an individual manner, uniquely, "unschematically." [2]

This qualified imputation of substance not only implies a very wary teleology, it also demands a differentiated aesthetic, and this brings us to the question of the relationship between such an imputation and Brecht's dialectics.

Considering the role of his theater in the last years, Hans Mayer observes ironically that Brecht finally came to the position of the despised "Frankfurt Tuis," [3] that his work was ultimately not far removed from the position of Adorno's negative dialectics. Mayer quotes Brecht:

> He seriously considered the question whether his plays, mostly set in a capitalist society, could offer anything more to the new readers. Perhaps they can contribute nothing or little to the solution of the direct pressing daily problems. That is his fear.
> But his hope is that daily problems can perhaps be better approached if they are considered in relation to the problems of the century. And the great problems surely stand in the brightest light during the greatest battles, the great revolutions.

Mayer concludes, "Brecht asks himself with such sentences the question whether his Marxist art is not inseparably tied to the process of transition from capitalism to socialism. Therefore that its relevance must disappear with the beginning of the new society." [4] We need to remember that Brecht wrote his words for a Russian translation of twelve plays published in 1956. He therefore studiously avoided any reference to the relationship between style and stimulation, in other words, to the whole thrust of his theater, finding it more politic to remark on the context of the plots.

The characteristic withholding of conclusions in Brecht's theater distinguishes it immediately from what I want to call positive dialectics and suggests their opposite. But those conclusions are anticipated; we also have the excluded middle.

There is a simple explanation for Adorno's attitude toward Brecht: Stalinism. It lies behind the bitter accusation of infantility, behind the supposition of grave political naiveté beneath the aesthetic surface, also behind the sarcastic rejection of the "gesture of wisdom" and its idyllic rusticity. Missing completely the Chinese reverberations in Brecht's thought which presuppose the potentiality, the essentially relative condition of qualities, Adorno treats him like a purblind Platonist, culminating in the charge that he is an "existential ontologist."[5]

Though some of his expectations apply to Brecht, the crucial distinction lies in Adorno's practically absolute separation of the work of art from any intervention in process. So he extols those works that through their form "resist the course of the world which continually points the pistol at the breast of human beings."[6] Is there not a greater danger here that this "anti-system," by virtue of its withdrawal and rigorous adherence to the first step of negation, by virtue of default, will merely have the effect of constituting that with which he reproached Heidegger's ontology: affirmation of that which is?[7] I find Heiner Müller's comment apposite: "Whoever does not want to engage himself will be engaged, possibly against his interests as person and author."[8]

Brecht was too close to Benjamin's theories on the organizing function of art, which takes precedence over any autonomous function a work of art may possess, for us to assign to him the abstractions of negative dialectics. Yet positive dialectics constituted another trap. Let us recall the fundament of this problem. The mechanical transcript reflection theory concealed potent distortions. Lenin later modified slightly his position but statements like "Historical materialism recognizes social being as independent of the social consciousness of humanity,"[9] when translated into simpler political terms, could be taken to mean that individual consciousness was comparatively unimportant since history was marching anyway. In its crudest form, this could be seen as a sanction for what Stalin once euphemized as "revolution from above."[10] Hence the inculcations of positive dialectics, all the heroics and excitations of revolutionary romanticism, that swift slide into the idealities of socialist realism. Though the style is markedly different from its European equivalents, containing the potentiality for interesting developments, Chinese drama since the Cultural Revolution has consistently projected images of idealized exempla: monsters and gods.

We can hardly dispute Adorno's description of the compatibility between what he refers to, perhaps misleadingly, as critical or socialist realism, with its aversion to the alien and alienating, and authoritarian systems of coordination.[11] Stalinist stagnation led, as Brecht recognized, to a pursuit of the "harmonious" and the "intrinsically beautiful" in the theater (17: 1154). The original critical thrust had foundered in affirmation; hence Brecht's hopes for a revival of dialectics as a result of the Chinese impulse. His observations on China during the last years are extraordinarily revealing.[12] We even find for a comparable purpose the same terminology in Brecht and Mao Tse-tung. Both appeal to the wisdom of the masses, not as ritual invocation but as a form of assault on the bureaucratic inhibition of individual consciousness.

This impetus from China in the early 1950s was largely responsible for Brecht's proposal to change the description of his theater from "epic" to "dialectical." So much for any supposition of the cessation of contradiction: "The changeability of the world insists on its contradictoriness. There is something in things, people, events, which makes them what they are, and at the same time something which makes them different" (16: 925). Such insistence on the prevalence of contradiction *in* people is crucial for the sustentation of critical dialectics.

Brecht's reaction in the 1930s to Fadeyev's demands for uniformity of style was to reject the ideal images and the almost mystical character of their evocation, the great stress on feelings. Brecht's alternative proposal: "The critical element in realism must not be suppressed. It is decisive. Even if it were possible, mere reflection of reality would not serve our ends. Reality must be criticized by giving it shape, it must be criticized realistically. For the dialectician the decisive element is the critical factor, herein lies the tendency" (19: 446). In the 1950s he was saying exactly the same thing, complaining that some people were trying to distinguish between the earlier critical realism—the nineteenth-century Russian version—and socialist realism by turning the latter into an "uncritical realism" (19: 545). On the contrary, socialist realism must be critical, and this means, among other things, that it must show the contradictions *in* people. Chinese drama during the Cultural Revolution and until the fall of the Gang of Four would have disappointed Brecht, for it constituted a redogmatization of the newly found dialectical process: the villainous bourgeoisie and the ever-victorious proletariat.

For obvious reasons Brecht preferred to adopt the term *socialist realism* and subvert it from within. But critical dialectics delimits his position from the prescriptive positive and the recusant negative varieties and inhibits misapprehension of the social realist label.

Critical dialectics implies a realistic recognition of the complexities of character: "The brave man is not always brave: sometimes he defaults. In him live cowardice and courage and courage triumphs, but not always" (10: 908). This, in turn, depends upon accepting human potentiality and consequently a relative ethic. Critical dialectics implies stimulation of the ability to perceive contradictions, also an appeal to an active consciousness, to the "wisdom of the people." Inevitably there is a tension between "creating the necessary conditions" and stimulating consciousness—that is, indeed, "the simple, which is difficult to create" (2: 852).

Critical dialectics also draws attention to its own evident present relevance. I quote B. K. Tragelehn of the Berliner Ensemble, interviewed in 1976: "And in spite of all political criticism of Lukács, his aesthetic ideas are still dominant. The work of art is considered an enclosed, organic entity which is a representation or a graphic reproduction of a predetermined social totality." [13]

Brecht's critical dialectics does not supply models for emulation, presupposing closed totalities, but stimulation for intervention. In his view, dialectics enabled interventionary thought. In his notes on dialectics he says that one should never make portraits complete (20: 169). He rejects the "unfortunate representation" of "only one motive" in place of what he calls the "whole sheaf of motives" (20: 157).

Dialectics remains an abstract process unless it involves a certain form of intervention and this, in turn, will fail unless it can create the conditions to enable people, to use the shorthand, to be good. If the evident vitality of Brecht's thought suggests a form of failure, it also implies a form of success.

Following Richard Wilhelm's translations, Ernst Bloch sees Taoism in a theological perspective. [14] Brecht did not really share Blochian longings and his own perception of the dialectical quality of Taoist thought is remarkable, implying potentiality and a relative ethic together with the perception of naturality, without which potentiality cannot be posited. As one illustration of this concatenation in Brecht's poetic, rather than theoretical, work we may take the customs man in the poem "Legend of the Origin of the Book Tao Te Ching." In the West organicism has always connoted political conservatism, perhaps because it never shed its theocentrism or the Platonic heritage. But Chinese organic naturalism knew neither. The powerful Taoist element in Sung dynasty neo-Confucianism presupposed a radically different concept of totality, which originally did not connote hierarchy and subservience, neither on the material nor on the social level. To be sure, the Confucian scholar-administrators well understood how to transform it into a defense of hierarchical structures, and Brecht's skeptical response to Confucianism derived from a recognition of the strength and universality of such an impulse. Socially, the constant Taoist flux anticipated the cohesion of equals, while energies constantly interchanged pattern and matter in the ceaseless rhythm of the cosmos, concepts that would seem congruent with the image of reality in modern biochemistry and nuclear physics.

Marxism is a critical theory, not immobilized dogma. Might not the exploration of such modes of thought regain for socialist literature that vitality of natural image which Brecht, under his circumstances, felt constrained to refuse, and against whose absence he had already begun to react in his last poems? Such a recovery would of course depend upon a fresh perception of our relationship to the natural world and upon a rejection of the scientifically meaningless and psychologically debilitating, traditionally "Western" sense of alienation from it, once the "Marxist" variation of this particular form of alienation has been understood as a response to the ideology of a self-serving conservative organicism.[15] In a nutshell: class struggle has nothing to do with any struggle against nature. The Chinese conviction of the congruence between natural and social process may have an interesting intellectual and political future as well as a revealing past.

We recall the characteristically Western body-state analogy in *Coriolanus*, when Menenius would persuade the plebs that they are the toes and fingers and somebody else the nourishing stomach. Here is the Taoist equivalent: "The hundred parts of the human body . . . all are complete in their places. Which should one prefer? Do you like them all equally? Or do you like some more than others? Are they all servants? Are these servants unable to control each other, but need another as ruler? Or do they become rulers and servants in turn? Is there any true ruler other than themselves?"[16]

Notes

1. For a fuller discussion of these matters see my study *The Mask of Evil: Brecht's Response to the Poetry, Theatre and Thought of China and Japan—a Comparative and Critical Evaluation* (Berne: Lang, 1977), especially pp. 347–475. In *Me-ti* Brecht refracts attitudes he encountered in the historical Me-ti (Mo Tse), but he also shows his response to Taoism.

2. *Arbeitsjournal* (Frankfurt: Suhrkamp, 1973), 1: 270.

3. "Tui" was Brecht's disparaging term for the merely speculating intellectuals.

4. Hans Mayer, *Brecht in der Geschichte* (Frankfurt: Suhrkamp, 1971), p. 240. See "An die Sowjetleser," BBA, 94: 1–2.

5. Theodor W. Adorno, *Noten zur Literatur* (Frankfurt: Suhrkamp, 1974), p. 422.

6. Ibid., p. 413.

7. Theodor W. Adorno, *Negative Dialektik* (Frankfurt: Suhrkamp, 1973), pp. 73–79.

8. See Heinz Klunker, "Fluchtpunkte des DDR-Theaters," *Theater 1974, Sonderheft der Zeitschrift Theater heute*, p. 21.

9. Lenin, *Collected Works* (Moscow: Progress Publishers, 1968), 14: 326.

10. H. B. Franklin, *The Essential Stalin: Major Theoretical Writings, 1905– 1952* (Garden City, N.Y.: Anchor, 1972), p. 426.

11. Adorno, *Negative Dialektik*, p. 412.

12. For the evidence, I refer to *The Mask of Evil*, pp. 500–527.

13. See *Theater 1976, Sonderheft der Zeitschrift Theater heute*, p. 95.

14. Ernst Bloch, *Das Prinzip Hoffnung* (Frankfurt: Suhrkamp, 1959), 2: 1438ff. Since Taoist thought can be considered as a natural response to the bureaucratic distortions imposed by the Asiatic mode of production and since the legacy of that mode is now held responsible for the deflection of democratic process in those societies modeled on the institutions of the Soviet Union, it could well be that the Taoist critique might help to overcome the failings that plague the social models in postcapitalist societies. For further speculation on some aspects of Brecht's response to Taoism, I refer to my article: "Peasant Dialectics, Reflections on Brecht's Sketch of a Dilemma," *New Asia Academic Bulletin*, Hong Kong, 1 (1978): 277–85.

15. Marx is full of surprises for the unwary. For example: "Atheism, as a denial of this non-essentiality (of nature and of man) no longer makes sense, for atheism is a negation of God and through this negation posits the existence of man; but socialism as socialism no longer needs any such mediation; it begins with the theoretical and practical sensual consciousness of man and of nature as essence." *Marx-Engels Gesamtausgabe* (Berlin: Marx-Engels Verlag, 1932), 3: 125; see also Marx-Engels, *Collected Works* (London: Lawrence and Wishart, 1975), 3: 306.

16. *Chuang Tzu*. Ch. 2. For this translation, see Joseph Needham, *Science and Civilisation in China* (Cambridge: at the University Press, 1956), 2: 52.

Brecht's Marxist Aesthetic:
The Korsch Connection

Douglas Kellner

In the voluminous literature on Bertolt Brecht, the impact of the version of materialist dialectic advocated by Brecht's Marxian "teacher" Karl Korsch on Brecht's work has not been adequately clarified.[1] Not only did Korsch strongly influence Brecht's conception of Marxian dialectics, but the Marxian ideas that were most fruitful for Brecht's aesthetic practice were precisely the ideas shared by Brecht and Korsch in their conception of materialist dialectics and revolutionary practice. Brecht used the Korschian version of the Marxian dialectic in both his aesthetic theory and practice, in a way that is central to his work, and not incidental as it is sometimes claimed to be.[2]

Korsch and Brecht

In the 1920s Brecht began serious study of Marxism while attempting to write a play on the stock market (the fragmentary *Joe Fleischhacker*) and shortly before working on *St. Joan of the Stockyards*. When he could not find anyone to explain the workings of the capitalist economy, he began to read Marx's *Das Kapital* and became increasingly interested in both the Marxian theory of society and the dialectical method of analyzing society and history.[3] To help him in his study of Marxism, Brecht sought the acquaintance of people who could teach him its fundamental ideas and method. At the time, Karl Korsch was one of the leading Marx scholars in Germany and was also one of the most active militants in the communist movement.[4] After serving on the ill-fated socialization commission following the November revolution, Korsch joined the Independent Socialist party (USPD) and then the Communist party (KPD) in 1920. He served as justice minister in a short-lived left coalition in Thuringia in 1923, became editor of the communist journal *Internationale*, was on the Central Committee of the German Communist party, and represented the communists in the Reichstag. In 1926 Korsch was one of the first victims of Stalinism and was expelled from the movement to which he was deeply committed and which he had loyally served. Thereafter he moved into the forefront of the Left Opposition and developed one of the sharpest critiques of the Stalinization of the Soviet Union, the Comintern, and the German Communist party. He worked with a variety of left oppositional groups and taught courses on Marxism at the Karl Marx School and in small study groups in Berlin. Brecht joined these courses and Korsch's study group and from then on titled Korsch "my teacher" of Marxism.[5]

From the beginning of his involvement with the communist movement in the early twenties, Korsch saw the Marxian dialectic as the theoretical core of Marxism. He characterized the Marxian dialectic by the principles of historical specification, critique, and revolutionary practice. The principle of historical specification articulates Marx's practice of comprehending "all things social in terms of a definite historical epoch."[6] For Korsch, Marx's achievement was his analysis of historically distinct and specific features of capitalism and bourgeois society, and his development of a method that enabled one to analyze distinct social formations critically and to transform them radically. Bourgeois political economy and theory, on the other hand, dealt with the forms of bourgeois society as if they were universal, eternal, and unchanging relationships, rather than historical forms of a system that was full of contradictions and subject to radical transformation. Problems of economy, politics, and culture cannot be solved through a general abstract description of "economics as such," but requires "a detailed description of the definite relations which exist between definite economic phenomena on a definite historical level of development and definite phenomena which appear simultaneously or subsequently in every other field of political, juristic, and intellectual development."[7]

For Korsch, the Marxian dialectic is a *critical dialectic* that aims at the critique and transformation of the existing bourgeois order. The Marxian dialectic sees reality as a process of continual change and is interested in those contradictions and antagonisms that make radical transformation possible. Above all, Marxian dialectic integrates critical theory with *revolutionary practice* which would emancipate the working class and construct socialism. Korsch summarizes his description of the basic principles of Marxism in *Karl Marx*, a book written in part while Korsch was a guest of the Brecht family in exile:

> Marxian theory, viewed in its general character, is a new science of bour-
> geois society. It appears at a time when within bourgeois society itself an
> independent movement of a new social class is opposing the ruling bour-
> geois class. In opposition to the bourgeois principles, it represents the new
> views and claims of the class oppressed in bourgeois society. It is, so far, not
> a positive but a critical science. It "specifies" bourgeois society and investi-
> gates the tendencies visible in the present development of society, and the
> way to its imminent practical transformation. Thus, it is not only a theory of
> bourgeois society but, at the same time, a theory of the proletarian
> revolution.[8]

Brecht's theoretical writings show that he agreed with Korsch on these issues and that he developed his conception of dialectics while working in Korsch's seminars and discussion groups.

Epic Theater:
Materialist Dialectics, the V-Effect, and the Politics of Separation

In his epic theater built on the principles of historical specification and critique, Brecht sought to illuminate the historically specific features of an environment in order to show how that environment influenced, shaped, and often battered and destroyed the characters. Unlike drama-tists who focused on the universal elements of the human situation and fate, Brecht was interested in the attitudes and behavior people adopted toward each other in specific historical situations. Thus, in *Mahagonny* and *The Threepenny Opera* he was interested in how people related to each other in capitalist society; in *Mother Courage*, how tradespeople re-lated to soldiers and civilians during war in an emerging market society; in *The Measures Taken*, he depicted revolutionary relationships in the struggle in China. Brecht called this practice "historicization" and be-lieved that one could best adopt a critical attitude toward one's society if the present social arrangements and institutions were viewed as histor-ical, transitory, and subject to change.[9] Brecht intended that epic theater show emotions, ideas, and behavior as products of, or responses to, specific social situations and not as the unfolding of the human essence.

The primary theatrical device of epic theater, the *Verfremdungseffekt* was intended to "estrange" or "distance" the spectator and thus prevent empathy and identification with the situation and characters and allow the adoption of a critical attitude toward the actions in the play.[10] By preventing empathetic illusion or a mimesis of reality, epic theater would expose the workings of societal processes and human behavior, and would thus show the audience how and why people behaved a certain way in their society. For example, the greed in *Mahagonny* and *The Threepenny Opera*, Mother Courage's sufferings, or Galileo's persecution were to be understood as historically specific constituents of a social environment. As Walter Benjamin stressed, the response to epic theater should be: "Things can happen this way, but they can also happen a quite different way."[11] The strategy was to produce an experience of curiosity, astonishment, and shock: "Is that the way things are? What produced this? It's terrible! How can we change things?" This attitude was also fostered by a "montage of images" and series of typical social tableaux that Brecht called "gests."[12] He wanted his spectators to work through these examples, to participate in an active process of critical thought that would provide insights into the workings of society, and to see the need for and to implement radical social change.

Brecht's epic theater broke with the "culinary theater" that provided the spectator with a pleasant experience or moral for easy digestion. He rejected theater that tried to produce an illusion of reality and that reproduced the dominant ideology, just as Korsch rejected the identification of bourgeois ideologies with reality. Brecht appropriated Korsch's theory that ideology was a material force that served as an important tool of domination; they both saw ideology as a deluding force from which people should be emancipated.[13] Hence Brecht's practice of ideology-demolition and intervening thought is an application of Korsch's principle of ideology-critique and intellectual action.[14] Thus both Korsch and Brecht viewed intellectual action as well as aesthetic theory as important moments in revolutionary practice (along with economic and political action).

In order to produce a revolutionary theater, Brecht argued for a "separation of the elements" or a "politics of separation."[15] In the important *Mahagonny* notes, Brecht distinguished his separation of words, music, and scene from the Wagnerian *Gesamtkunstwerk*, which fused the elements into one seductive and overpowering whole in which word, music, and scene work together to engulf the spectator in the aesthetic totality.[16] In his "radical separation of the elements," each aesthetic component retains its autonomy and "comments" on the others, often in contradiction, to provoke thought and insight. For instance, in *The Three-penny Opera*, first Mac and Polly, and then Mac and Jenny sing of love and romance, but the scene is first a warehouse full of stolen goods and then a brothel, and the plot is one of deception and betrayal, thus shocking one into reflecting on the bourgeois ideology of love. In Brecht's film *Kuhle Wampe*, romantic organ music is played as a young unemployed youth returns home after another futile search for work, evoking a poignant contrast between music and image. Contradiction between the elements, Brecht believed, would prevent identification and passive immersion and would provoke critical reflection. Each aesthetic medium retains its separate identity, and the product is an "aggregate of independent arts" in provocative tension.

Brecht's theory of aesthetic production is congruent with Korsch's model of the workers' councils as the authentic organs of socialist practice.[17] For just as Korsch urged a democratic, participatory activity of coproduction in the spheres of labor and politics, Brecht urges the same sort of coparticipation in his aesthetic production. Brecht worked whenever possible in collectives in which a team of co-workers collaborated on production. He was especially attracted to radio and film as exemplary of the highest development of the forces of production and as involving a new kind of collective work.[18] He saw his co-workers as important participants in the creative process, all of whom were encouraged to contribute to the production of the work of art. Such a revolution in the concept of creation, rejecting the notion of the creator as the solitary genius, was intended to alter aesthetic production radically, much as the workers' councils were intended to revolutionize industrial and political organization, thus providing a model for socialist cultural organization.

Both Brecht and Korsch stress the primary importance of production in social life and see socialism as a constant revolutionizing of the forces and relations of production. Thus, in opposition to such critics as Georg Lukács, Brecht defended the need to innovate, experiment, and produce new aesthetic forms. He argued that since the apparatus of aesthetic production was not yet controlled by artists and did not work for the general good, revolutionary artists should strive to change the apparatus. One had to develop "the means of pleasure into an object of instruction, and to convert certain institutions from places of entertainment into organs of mass communication."[19] Brecht's art aimed at a *radical pedagogy* that would provide political education, cultivate political instincts, and provoke revolutionary political practice.

The Learning Plays as the Model of Brechtian Revolutionary Theater

Parallel to his work on epic theater, which he feared might be as "culinary as ever,"[20] Brecht developed a new type of play, the "learning play." Here, too, Korsch's influence is pronounced, for, as Hans Eisler has noted, these plays resemble political seminars.[21] Brecht described them as "a collective political meeting" in which the audience is to participate actively (18: 132). One sees in this model a rejection of the concept of the bureaucratic elite party where the theorists and functionaries are to issue directives and control the activities of the masses. In these plays, correct doctrine and practice would be discovered and carried out through a participatory, collective practice rather than through hierarchical manipulation and domination; that is, they were to function as Korsch had envisioned the operation of the workers' councils.

The "learning plays" were conceived by Brecht as the model for the "theater of the future." They exemplified materialist aesthetics, whereas his epic dramas were seen as "compromise forms." The "technical regression" of the latter (*Galileo*) was necessitated by conditions of production in exile and then in the early years of the DDR.[22] The learning plays were his most explicitly political plays and his most radical attempt to politicize art. In his "theory of pedagogy" for a socialist future, he wrote:

> Pleasure in observation alone is harmful for the state just as pleasure in action alone. Insofar as young people while playing perform actions that are derived from their own observations, they will be educated for the state. This sort of playing must be invented and performed in such a way that it is useful for the state. It is not beauty that is decisive for the value of a sentence or a gesture or an action, but whether it is useful for the state when the players speak a sentence, perform a gesture, or carry out an action. (17: 1023)

The learning plays were superior to epic theater, in Brecht's view, because they were more effective pedagogically, both for the artistic producers and for the audience who were to participate in more direct and creative ways in the aesthetic experience. The actors and audience were to distinguish social from asocial behavior by imitating ways of behaving, thinking, talking, and relating. Within a single play the actors frequently exchanged roles so that they could experience situations from different points of view. The learning plays confronted them with situations such as sacrificing oneself for the good of the public (*Lindbergh's Flight, The Baden Learning Play of Consent*) or egotistically putting oneself above all else (*Fatzer, Baal the Asocial*). There would often be contradictory models of service or exploitation (*The Exception and the Rule*), social consent or refusal (*The Yes-sayer and the No-sayer*), and effective or ineffective revolutionary practice (*The Measures Taken*). Brecht called this practice the "grand pedagogy" which would turn actors/audience into statesmen and philosophers. Whereas the "lesser pedagogy" of the epic theater merely "democratized the theater in the pre-revolutionary period," the "grand pedagogy" completely transforms the role of the producers and "abolishes the system of performer and spectator."[23] Brecht intended his learning plays for schools, factories, or political groups; actors and audiences could read, improvise, and alter the plays at will as Brecht himself had done with many groups.

Thus, in Brecht's concept of emancipatory pedagogy and revolutionary theater, the learning plays are not concerned with advocating specific doctrines, handing down a teaching for easy consumption, functioning as propaganda. Rather, the plays are to engage a small audience in a process of learning.

For example, *The Measures Taken* confronts the audience with basic questions of revolution: violence, discipline, the structure of the party, the relation to the masses, revolutionary justice, and so on. There is no "correct doctrine" set forth; the actors are to present a scene and then discuss it with the audience. Like Korsch's model of the workers' councils there is to be no established hierarchy; rather there is to be democratic participation in coproduction. The people are to establish the principles of revolutionary practice, strategy, and tactics, and not the party elite theoreticians or bureaucrats. Moreover, the task of the revolutionary artist here is not to make palatable party doctrine for easy assimilation, but to encourage revolutionary thought and critique. This stance was clearly a threat to bureaucratic party functionaries, and they have consistently opposed Brecht's work.

Brecht saw his learning plays as a series of "sociological experiments," as "limbering-up exercises" or "mental gymnastics" for dialecticians.[24] He thought that the learning plays would radically revolutionize the theater apparatus. Thus they should not be seen as minor works as many critics have suggested. Brecht did in fact return to epic theater with the advent of fascism and conditions of exile, for the learning plays were viable only in contexts where there were political groups who could perform them and an audience who could relate them to revolutionary practice. In his last years he again turned his attention to the learning play and suggested that *The Measures Taken* should be considered as the model for a revolutionary theater of the future.[25]

Me-ti: Materialist Dialectics in Literature and Brecht's Political Contradictions

During the exile period, Brecht was forced to develop new aesthetic forms. One such experiment, the *Me-ti* novel, embodies the principles of his materialist aesthetics in the prose domain, while articulating the political conflicts of the times and unfolding the contradictions and ambiguities in Brecht's political position. Brecht was drawn at once to the ideas of democratic socialism espoused by Luxemburg and Korsch and to the authoritarian communism of Lenin and Stalin.[26] A tension between Brecht's work and orthodox Leninism in both politics and aesthetics surfaced in the hostility of the German Communist party to his work, and in the polemics with Lukács over the official aesthetic doctrine of Socialist Realism.[27] Although Brecht had an ambivalent position within the communist movement, he presented himself as an orthodox Marxist, a fervent devotee of Lenin, and publicly defended communist orthodoxy in the Stalin period. The private Brecht was torn by ambivalences and doubts concerning Stalinism and developments in the Soviet Union. These doubts, which Brecht confided to Marxian heretics such as Korsch and Benjamin, found literary expression in *Me-ti*, one of the most important sources for measuring Karl Korsch's influence on Brecht and Brecht's political contradictions (see Müller's essay in this volume for another interpretation of the importance of *Me-ti*).

There are formal similarities between the *Me-ti* novel and Brecht's learning plays. Both provoke thought and discussion of revolutionary theory and practice, rather than simply promulgate ossified doctrines or a party line. The main topics of *Me-ti*, "the grand method" (dialectics) and "the grand order" and "the grand production" (socialism), are presented in the form of aphoristic debates in which Leninism, Stalinism, and the construction of socialism in the Soviet Union are measured against the ideas of Marx and Engels, Korsch, Luxemburg, and Trotsky. The reader is forced to think through the opposing positions of the Marxian classics and contemporary Marxian theorists and to evaluate events in the Soviet Union. Although Brecht inserts himself in the aphoristic dialogues, he does not represent a privileged point of view, nor does Me-ti, Mi-en-leh (Lenin), Meister Ko (Korsch), or any of the other participants. The readers of this literary experiment are thus co-workers who contribute their own thought to produce revolutionary critique and reflection on Marxian theory and practice.

Throughout *Me-ti*, Brecht applies the materialist concept of history to the history of historical materialism, as Korsch did earlier.[28] Like Korsch, Brecht analyzes how later Marxian theories and practice realized or failed to realize Marx's ideas, which in turn were critically appraised in terms of the results they produced (or failed to produce). A single passage, "The Opinion of Philosopher Ko Concerning the Construction of the Order in Su" (12: 537), reveals the complexity of the situation Brecht was analyzing when he related Marxism to the developments in the Soviet Union. He indicates that Lenin "created a powerful state apparatus for the construction of the *grand order*, which must necessarily become a hindrance for the grand order in the foreseeable future." Here Brecht is referring to Marx's doctrine of the withering away of the state in the transition to a higher stage of socialism. He then refers to Korsch's critique that "the orderer would be a hindrance to the order," in reference to Korsch's belief that the Stalinist bureaucracy would prevent the development of an emancipatory socialism. Brecht also advanced Korsch's position that "actually the apparatus always functioned very badly and continually putrified, throwing off a sharp stink." Further, Brecht cites Korsch's position that the power struggle between Stalin and Trotsky portended a surrender of Leninism, and that Trotsky merely "proposed rather doubtful reforms." The conclusion that "those principles proposed by Ko showed a clear weakness where Mi-en-leh's principles were

strongest, but Ko characterized excellently the weaknesses of the principles of Mi-en-leh" indicates that there are serious weaknesses in Leninism
and suggests that there were sharp tensions in Brecht's political views.

While Brecht did not accept all of Korsch's sharp attacks on the Soviet
Union, Leninism, and Stalinism, he continually reflected on Korsch's
views and frequently incorporated them in *Me-ti*:

THE TRIALS OF NI-EN [STALIN]

Me-ti expressed his disapproval of Ni-en because in his trials against his enemies in the association he demanded too much confidence from the people. He said: When someone asks me to believe something which can be
proven (without furnishing me the proof), it is tantamount to my being
asked to believe something which cannot be proven. I will not do it. Ni-en
might have benefited the people by removing his enemies inside the association, but he did not prove it. By conducting trials without proof he has done
damage to the people. He ought to have taught the people to demand proof,
especially from a man who in general is so useful. (12: 538)

AUTOCRATIC RULE OF NI-EN

Me-ti spoke with Kin-jeh [Brecht] about Ni-en, who exercised autocratic
rule. Me-ti said: Mi-en-leh, whose student one must consider Ni-en, believed
before the great revolution that the workers would have to support the
bourgeoisie in their struggle to free themselves from the rule of the Emperor. . . . Later the workers, under his leadership, obtained power; but his
successor, Ni-en, acted exactly like an Emperor. The backwardness of the
country Su [Soviet Union], of which Mi-en-leh had always spoken, continued
to manifest itself in this phenomenon. The great machinery was constructed
not by the citizens under people's rule, but by workers under the rule of an
Emperor. (12: 538)

CONSTRUCTION AND REGRESSION UNDER NI-EN

Under Ni-en's leadership industry without exploiters was being constructed
in Su and agriculture collectivized and furnished with machines. But the associations [Communist parties] outside Su decayed. It was no longer the
members who elected the secretaries, but the secretaries who elected the
members. The guidelines were issued by Su and the secretaries were paid by
Su. When mistakes were made, those who had criticized the mistakes were
punished; but those who had made the mistakes remained in office. Soon the
office holders were no longer the best members but merely the most servile.
. . . Those who issued the orders in Su no longer learned any facts, because
the secretaries no longer reported facts that might not have pleased them. In
view of these conditions the best members were in despair. Me-ti deplored
the decay of the grand method. Master Ko turned away from it. . . . In Su all

wisdom was directed toward the construction and chased out of politics. Outside Su all those who praised Ni-en's merits, even those which were undeniable, became suspect of corruption; inside Su all those who uncovered his mistakes, even those from which he himself suffered, became suspect of treason. (12: 539)

These are aphorisms in a literary experiment and one might argue that they were points of view Brecht was proposing for discussion and did not express his own position. He never published *Me-ti*, which indicates a reluctance to attack Stalin and the Soviet Union openly. The same ambivalences toward Stalin and the Soviet Union, however, are found in his *Work Journal*, where he considered Korsch's critiques with the utmost seriousness.[29] *Me-ti* represents Brecht's most comprehensive juxtaposition of Korsch's positions with "official" Marxian doctrines and shows that throughout the exile period he pondered questions of practical and theoretical Marxism. *Me-ti*, Brecht's letters, and his *Work Journal* show that he continued to reflect upon, and to contrast his own views with, the ideas of his teacher and friend Karl Korsch, the theorist who helped provide the foundation for Brecht's Marxist aesthetic.

Notes

Thanks to Steve Bronner and Betty Weber for stimulating discussions of topics in this paper and help with revisions.

1. The theme was first discussed in Wolfdietrich Rasch, "Bertolt Brechts marxistischer Lehrer" in *Merkur* 188 (1963): 94–99. Other contributions to the discussion include the material in *Alternative* 41 (1965); Klaus-Detlef Müller, *Die Funktion der Geschichte im Werk Bertolt Brechts* (Tübingen: Niemeyer, 1967; 2d ed. 1972); Ingeborg Muenz-Koenen, "Brecht in westdeutschen Publikationen," *Weimarer Beiträge* 15 (1969): 123–47; Reiner Steinweg, *Das Lehrstück* (Stuttgart: Metzler, 1972); Heinz Brüggemann, "Bertolt Brecht und Karl Korsch," *Über Karl Korsch* (Frankfurt: Suhrkamp, 1973), pp. 177–88, and *Literische Technik und soziale Revolution* (Reinbek: Rowohlt, 1973); Franco Buono, *Zur Prosa Brechts* (Frankfurt: Suhrkamp, 1973); and Werner Mittenzwei, "Nachwort" to the DDR version of *Me-ti* (Berlin: Henssel, 1975). *Alternative* 105 (1975) contains a Korsch-Brecht issue that summarizes the discussion of the Korsch-Brecht relationship.

2. See *Alternative* 91 (1973) and 93 (1973). Interpreters who downplay or denigrate Brecht's Marxism include Martin Esslin, *Brecht—The Man and His*

Work (Garden City, N.Y.: Anchor, 1961), and Eric Bentley, who tries to disassociate Brecht from Marxism and to associate him with Beckett; see "Brecht Was a Lover, Too," *The Village Voice*, May 3, 1976.

3. See Brecht, 20: 46 and 15: 129, where he states "when I read Marx's *Kapital*, I understood my plays" and describes Marx as "the only spectator for my plays."

4. For a detailed reconstruction of Korsch's political activity and theory see my introduction to *Karl Korsch: Revolutionary Theory*, ed. Douglas Kellner (Austin: University of Texas Press, 1977).

5. See Brecht, 20: 65, and his letter to Korsch, end of March 1945, "You know that you are a teacher for life, so take it easy," cited in *Alternative* 41: 45. Concerning Brecht's relation to Korsch, Hedda Korsch has written me:

> K.K. met B.B. in the early twenties, I think through the mediation of Felix Weil and the Frankfurt people who introduced him also to the Malik Verlag, George Grosz, etc. K. was greatly interested in the modern literary and artistic movements and followed them eagerly although his personal taste and direct enjoyment remained mostly with Goethe. An exception, you might say, were the works of B.B. We saw *The Threepenny Opera* at its first night or shortly after and were immediately and totally captivated by it. We met B.B. not there but at the same time. K. admired him and was also attracted by his original personality. B.B. attended K.'s private courses pretty regularly and joined in the discussions after courses in a cafe at the Alexanderplatz. He never agreed with K.'s criticisms of the Soviet developments. To discuss it all more in depth he organized meetings between himself and some friends with K.K. and some friends of his; those were held at B.B.'s apartment about 1930 and were discontinued when such meetings became dangerous for the participants. By then K.K. and B.B. were friends. K.K. never thought much of Pollock, not too much of Horkheimer as a philosopher, but liked and esteemed Walter Benjamin. We admired the works of Döblin who also attended Karl's courses and discussions.

6. See Karl Korsch, *Marxism and Philosophy* (London: NLB, 1970); "The Marxian Dialectic" and "On Materialist Dialectic," *Karl Korsch: Revolutionary Theory*; Karl Korsch, "Why I Am a Marxist," *Three Essays on Marxism* (New York: Monthly Review, 1972); and Karl Korsch, *Karl Marx* (London: Chapman and Hall, 1938), p. 24.

7. Korsch, "Why I Am a Marxist," pp. 64–65.

8. Korsch, *Karl Marx*, p. 86. Brecht also consulted with Korsch on theoretical and aesthetic issues throughout the exile period. See the Korsch-Brecht correspondence published in *Alternative* 41 (1965) and 105 (1975). Much of Brecht's "Marxian Studies" is a dialogue with Korsch: see the passages that summarize Korsch's works and set out theses developed in Korsch's seminars, e.g. 20: 68–72.

9. *Brecht on Theater*, ed. and trans. John Willet (New York: New Directions, 1964), p. 140.

10. E.g. *Brecht on Theater*, pp. 91–99, 136–47, 191–96.

11. Walter Benjamin, *Understanding Brecht* (London: NLB, 1973), p. 8.

12. *Brecht on Theater*, pp. 42, 86–87, 104, 134, 139, 198–205.

13. Korsch, *Marxism and Philosophy*, pp. 70–73; and Brecht, 18: 156–58, and 20: 156–58.

14. Korsch, *Marxism and Philosophy*, pp. 95–98; and Brecht 18: 156–58.

15. See Betty Nance Weber, "Marxismus, Brecht, Gesamtkunstwerk" in *Brecht Jahrbuch* (1976): 120–27, and Colin MacCabe, "The Politics of Separation," *Screen* 16, no. 4 (1975–76): 46–61.

16. *Brecht on Theater*, pp. 33–36.

17. See Karl Korsch, "What Is Socialization?" *New German Critique* 6 (1975): 60–81, and "Fundamentals of Socialization," *Karl Korsch: Revolutionary Theory*, pp. 124–34.

18. Brecht, 19: 119–34, 137–216. For discussions of Brecht and film see the two issues of *Screen*, 15, no. 2 (1975) and 16, no. 4 (1975–76), and the book by Wolfgang Gersch, *Film bei Brecht* (München: Hanser, 1975).

19. *Brecht on Theater*, pp. 33–36, 42. For Brecht's attack on Lukács and argument that the revolutionary artist should revolutionize form as well as content, see "Against Georg Lukács," *New Left Review* 84 (March-April 1974): 36–38.

20. *Brecht on Theater*, p. 41.

21. Hans Eisler, *Alternative* 78/79 (1971): 132.

22. See Brecht's *Arbeitsjournal* (Frankfurt: Suhrkamp, 1973), entry for 25 February 1939, where he calls *Galileo* a "technical regression" and praises the learning plays *Fatzer* and the *Bakery* as technical models. My interpretation of the learning plays is much indebted to Reiner Steinweg's scholarship and the issues of *Alternative* (78/79, 91, and 107) dedicated to Brecht's learning plays.

23. Brecht, "Die Grosse und die Kleine Pädogogik," *Alternative* 78/79 (1971): 126, and "Theorie der Pädogogien," 17: 1022–24.

24. Cf. "Gespräch über *Die Maßnahme*" and Reiner Steinweg, "Das Lehrstück" and "Die Lehrstücke als Versuchsreihe," *Alternative* 78/79 (1971).

25. Steinweg, "Das Lehrstück," pp. 102–3.

26. Brecht admired the left-communists Korsch and Rosa Luxemburg because of their activism and the workers' councils. In Lenin he respected the ability to translate revolutionary theory into practice. Stalin, as *Me-ti*, the *Work Journal*, and unpublished manuscripts and clippings in the Brecht archives attest, elicited an ambivalence that has prevented consensus among critics on the subject of Brecht and Stalin. There is little evidence of his attitude toward Trotsky. In the *Work Journal* during the period when Trotsky was heatedly debated within the international communist movement, Brecht offered no substantive discussion of the issues.

27. Many commentators have stressed the tension between Brecht's communism and his aesthetic practice; however, most fail to see the tension and the ambiguities within the former. Esslin's biased interpretations of attacks on Brecht by communists should not obscure the provocative material he presents. For

Brecht's debate with Lukács, see "Against Georg Lukács" (n. 19) and Helga Gallas, *Marxistische Literaturtheorie* (Neuwied: Luchterhand, 1971).

28. Regarding Brecht's acceptance of Korsch's position that the workers' councils were indispensable to the construction of socialism, see Brecht's theses "On the Model R [*Räte* = workers' councils] as a Moment of the Proletarian Dictatorship" in 20: 119 and Brecht's letter to Korsch in 1941 where he asks Korsch to write a historical account of the relationship of the councils to the party explaining the suppression of the councils system, *Alternative* 105 (1975): 252.

29. For a fuller discussion of these problems see Helmut Dahmer, "Brecht and Stalin," *Telos* 22 (1974–75): 96–105. Dahmer, however, neglects many passages in *Me-ti* and wrongly says that Korsch's views on the development of the Soviet Union are missing (p. 67).

Me-Ti

KLAUS-DETLEF MÜLLER

In a letter to Karl Korsch Brecht wrote:

> I want to continue writing the little book in the Chinese manner, some of
> which you already know, on proper rules of behavior. As I was looking
> through the material I came across the enclosed sentences. They are so very
> useful that I would like to ask you for a continuation. You know, the sen-
> tences can be fitted in, they can be taken out of context, they can be spo-
> radic. Couldn't you send me a handful? They can be completely in a sketch
> form, irresponsible in the scholarly sense—you understand. It would be ma-
> terial to work with.[1]

Unfortunately the enclosure that he mentions has not been preserved,
but Korsch noted on the margin of the letter: "Those are my aphorisms,
which I discussed, in part, together with Brecht and which I formulated."
We have no record that he answered Brecht's request for further material, and it is not very likely, but one can assume that Brecht sought
Korsch's intellectual partnership for his *Book of Twists and Turns, Me-ti*.
The project, which remained a sketch and collection of material, has a
consciously eclectic nature. The title points to the Chinese philosopher
Me-ti, whom his German translator and editor Alfred Forke has called a
"theoretician of social ethics." Me-ti was frequently understood in the
scholarly literature of the nineteenth century to be a socialist.[2] Brecht
owned Forke's edition and studied it carefully. However, Forke's classifi-
cation of Me-ti, which is doubtful, was not important for him, but rather
Me-ti's position that ethics is a part of political science. Me-ti's founding
of rules of behavior on sociopolitical considerations determines an important part of the work, although Brecht modernized the content. In addition Brecht took over Me-ti's style of presentation, the unsystematic
presentation of teachings that hang together thematically as sayings of
the master, introduced with the typical formula: "Master Me-tse said."
The title, *Book of Twists and Turns*, was not taken over by Brecht from
Me-ti but was formed in analogy to the *I-ging* (actually, *Book of Trans-*

formations), one of the five canonical books of the Confucians.[3] The concept *changes* or *change* has, to be sure, a different sense than in Chinese philosophy. It refers to the dialectic identity of opposites which demands a historical specification. Programmatic for this is the aphorism "On Changes": "Mi-en-leh taught: The introduction of democracy can lead to the introduction of dictatorship. The introduction of dictatorship can lead to democracy" (434). The false unequivocalness of a historical phenomenon is taken back into the higher truth of the historical process and "changed." The change as an intellectual principle cancels the finality of judgment by clarifying the tentative nature of logical determinations in the face of ambiguity and changeability of reality. In particular the "transformation" of the old concepts belongs in this context.[4] The *Book of Twists and Turns* is, therefore, a school of dialectics which becomes concrete as rules of behavior in the casuistic sense, as applied dialectics. The pseudoscholarly wording of the introduction (419) points in its transparent contradictions to the estrangement style of presentation, the "Chinese style." The reader is expressly requested to consider "less the stamp of genuineness than the content" in order to be able to "read the book with profit despite the eclectic traits" (419).

From an unprinted variant of the story "Destruction Which Is a Process of Learning" (457), we can see that the use of the Chinese style is also a trick for the propagation of truth: "In exile Bertolt Brecht wrote a 'Book of Experiences' from which the following story comes. It is written, in order to conceal the authorship, as if it came from an old Chinese historian."[5] "A Little Book with Rules of Behavior," "Book of Twists and Turns," "Book of Experiences"—these are the terms that Brecht uses to describe a collection of examples of materialistic dialectics which, at this point, is still unsystematic.

[2]

From this point it can also be understood why he sought the collaboration of Karl Korsch. Korsch was the only person to whom Brecht consistently conceded the honorable title of teacher, a title that he occasionally used for Margarete Steffin, for Sergei Tretiakov, and for Fritz Sternberg, among others. Korsch was Brecht's authority, especially in questions of dialectics. Brecht was formed in his study of Marxism and of dialectic materialism in a decisive way by Karl Korsch and always recognized without reservation the authority of his friend in all questions of theory. This fact has been demonstrated sufficiently, and it cannot be considered a legend.[6]

Some scholars still maintain that Brecht's relationship to Korsch is a legend,[7] but this is a defensive strategy that is intended to free Brecht from a supposed suspicion of heresy which the scholars feel has falsely been laid at his door. Such a strategy is unnecessary, for a pupil-teacher relationship between Brecht and Korsch does not mean that Brecht accepted all of Korsch's ideas. After all, his studies of Marxism did not restrict themselves to the writings of Korsch and to the classics. He knew, for example, especially the writings of Lenin and of Rosa Luxemburg. With all the care that such a distinction demands, it can perhaps be said that he saw in Lenin primarily the revolutionary politician; in Korsch, however, the theoretician of revolutionary dialectic materialism. Both positions were, in his opinion, quite compatible and his efforts were directed to the reconciliation of divergences that arose. One must note that Korsch was a follower of Lenin explicitly until 1927, almost to the appearance of the German edition of Lenin's *Materialism and Empiriocriticism*. Korsch understood his basic work *Marxism and Philosophy*, which appeared in 1923, to be a further development of Marxism under the changed conditions of class struggle, and he saw it as analogous to Lenin's efforts in the development of the Soviet state.[8]

It was the reorganization of the European communist parties under the hegemony of the Communist party of the Soviet Union, which Korsch first understood as a deviation from true Leninism,[9] which led to a basically changed approach. Korsch's criticism directed itself then against Lenin, too, as the intellectual father of the Leninistic practice, the basic fault of which he saw in the atrophy of revolutionary dialectics. He stated that Lenin's "Materialism and Empiriocriticism" had developed into a philosophical base for an ideology of Soviet Marxism, which he could not accept. This induced him to write a vehement "criticism of the primitive pre-dialectic and, indeed, pre-transcendental understanding of the relationship between consciousness and being," in which he saw the foundation for an "ideological dictatorship" which "is practiced in present-day Soviet Russia in the name of the so-called Marxism-Leninism over the entire intellectual life, not only of the ruling party organs, but also the entire working class, and, indeed, which one has attempted to extend in recent times beyond the borders of Soviet Russia to all communist parties of the West, and the whole world." As "dictatorship of the party or party leadership over the proletariat" it forms an "intellectual system of oppression."[10]

This criticism defines Korsch's political views at the moment when Brecht became his pupil. But Brecht never accepted it in this form. He took from Korsch what seemed to him to be important, his understanding of dialectic materialism as one of the relationships of theory and practice leading to a proletarian revolution, which does not remain static as a classical teaching but which must be made concrete and specific in each historical situation. From this understanding of dialectics, Brecht developed his dramaturgy of change through which theater becomes the medium for the development of revolutionary consciousness, the school of incisive thought and practical criticism. It is not surprising that Brecht thus came to contradict the understanding of socialist realism that was developed on the basis of the theory of mirroring, a theory that Korsch had attacked as naive. This contradiction was then discussed in the "expressionism debate." In his consideration of the foundation and practical use of Marxist aesthetics, Brecht was dependent on Korsch, and therefore could say: "You will remain my teacher for life."[11] At the same time, he tried to view the Soviet Union more pragmatically, and at this point he can clearly be differentiated from Korsch.

Now we must try to understand the basic and considered compatibility of these two positions. Since the Korsch legend is almost exclusively developed from the text "On My Teacher,"[12] which is indeed very critical, it is often overlooked that Brecht at this point explicitly introduces himself as a pupil of Korsch. In addition, the criticism, as all later testimony demonstrates, is not meant as a denial. What he accuses the teacher of is his exaggerated theoretical rigor, his placing his ideas and expectations above reality, his standpoint of everything or nothing, and his disappointed resignation when he does not see the theory substantiated by the course of events. This refers primarily to Korsch's relationship to the Soviet Union. In a letter to his teacher, Brecht writes in late 1942:

> I view you as my teacher. Your work and your personal friendship mean much for me, and it is only important that you have patience with me. We have differed for a long time in our appraisal of the Soviet Union, but I believe

that your attitude toward the Soviet Union is not the only use that one can make of your scholarly endeavors. I have for a long time been discussing all the points in question in my imagination with you before writing something.[13]

A year earlier he had regretted Korsch's position on the "first workers' state in history," which he considered to be the sole point of divergence in the face of basic agreement with the analyses of his friend. He explained their differing approach by saying that he was more concerned with the "practicability of analysis" than with the mere "capability of being verified."[14] He urged Korsch to understand the contradictions in the development of the Soviet Union dialectically as the result of a historical constellation. He also declared that he knew no one besides Korsch who could examine the historical reasons for the defeat of the *Räte* (Workers' Councils). He demanded a critical history of the Soviet Union on the basis of the dialectic method with which Korsch should relativize his objections. Korsch had postulated in his "Marxism and Philosophy" that the concept of materialistic history be used to refine the concept of materialistic history itself.[15] Now Brecht demands the use of the dialectic method on Korsch's understanding of the Soviet Union. The proper use of his scholarly endeavors demands a dialectic view of dialectics.

[3]

The attempt at such a use can be found in aesthetic form in *Me-ti*. The work must be viewed not only as a quarry for Brecht's theories but also for its structure. Since Brecht did not prepare the work for publication, we can only derive conclusions from the themes that are dealt with. The central themes are the "grand method" and the "grand order," that is, dialectics and socialism. In an entry in his *Work Journal* for 7 March 1941 Brecht, to be sure, had termed the "definition of socialism as a 'grand order'" an error: "It can rather much more practically be defined as a 'grand production.' Production must, of course, be taken in the broadest sense, and our battle must be directed toward the freeing of all bonds on the productivity of all people."[16] In essence, this later modification was already present in *Me-ti*, for all of the things said about the "grand order" relate in content to the freeing of the bonds on productivity.

The somehow estranging conceptuality of these central themes be-

comes a theme in the work itself, to the extent that one of the dialectic
principles used refers to the correction of concepts. This occurs, on the
one hand, directly through new definitions that clarify the social context
of the concepts,[17] and, on the other hand, through the use of an individual terminology that demystifies the words. In this sense "grand method"
and "grand order" are not Chinese fakery but recognizable paraphrases
for dialectics and socialism. Indirectly, terminological corrections occur
primarily in the reinterpretation of ethics as rules of behavior. Virtues
and vices are not understood abstractly as moral norms but discussed in
their function for a specific social order. In this process, vices are transformed into virtues and virtues into vices as the result of a dialectic view.

These changes make up one of the ideational centers of *Me-ti*, insofar
as it is a little book with rules of behavior. It is, therefore, even more important that Brecht here is proceeding not with axioms and definitions
but with casuistry. It is not a matter of the replacement or transformation
of bourgeois ethics with socialist ethics, but, at the most, a matter of the
significance of ethics for socialism. The aim is to clarify the dispensability
of virtues for the "grand order." "If the institutions are good, then man
does not need to be particularly good. To be sure, he then receives the
chance to be good" (520).[18] Me-ti holds to only one imperative: "Thou
shalt produce" (499). Ethics is therefore no longer the study of individual behavior in an individual situation but the analysis of situations as a
prerequisite to action and behavior. Ethics thus becomes, as it was with
the Chinese philosopher Me-tse, a part of political science.

At the same time, the sphere of that which can be regarded as behavior
expands: it is no longer a question of norms of individual action but of
the fundamental principles of political action in the elimination of this
limited understanding of norms of behavior and in the exposure of its
ideological character. The casuistic approach employed results in the
analysis of behavior becoming a form of historiography. This refers in *Me-
ti* to specific manifestations of fascism and, especially, to the development of socialism in the Soviet Union.[19]

If, therefore, on the one hand, a life according to the "grand method" is
recommended (500–501), if the individual is named as his historian
(551), and if it is suggested to him that he live in the third person (548),
then the Chinese cloak, on the other hand, allows one to present political
history as the behavior of historical personalities. That is necessary be-

cause an ideological controversy between the leaders of the Russian Revolution and their critics is taking place here, and it is measured by the criterion of political practice in the historical situation, that is, by the manner of behavior. In their estranging condensation to situation, principle, and behavior, politics and contemporary history are comparable with the changed understanding of ethics, whereby both remain directed to the "grand order" as a political goal and are definable through the "grand method." If we see *Me-ti* in this light, it is a work in which the themes are developed much in the manner of a musical composition.

[4]

In two ways *Me-ti* refers directly to Korsch: (1) The understanding of the "grand method" derives from Korsch's definition of dialectics as a revolutionary principle. In *Me-ti* both the statements about dialectics and the use of dialectics as a formal principle of thought emanate from this theory. The *Book of Twists and Turns* is at the same time a book about dialectics and a dialectical book. (2) Korsch appears as the philosopher Ko or Ka-osch, and, under this designation, as a critic of "Su" (the Soviet Union). His criticism is directed specifically to the process by which the state apparatus and the party apparatus become autonomous and thus hinder the realization of the "grand order" (537), the combination of the "clubs" (parties) outside of Su through Ni-en (Stalin), that is, the Bolshevization of the communist movement (539f.), and the restriction of freedom after the "grand transformation" (revolution) in Su.

In part his criticism corresponds to the norms of applied dialectics developed in *Me-ti*, according to which the development of the "grand order" should result in a continual withering away of the state. In part, however, Ko is put in the group of bourgeois intellectuals for whom the "transformation" and "grand order" are not goals but prerequisites of a realization of oneself which is basically still a bourgeois one. This is especially true in regard to the dialectical suspension of the concept of freedom. In any case, Ko is the opposite, in relation to Su, of Me-ti or Kin-jeh (Brecht): Ko even denies appearances when Su, at least in part, represents a state "as the masters have demanded it" (424f.). Just as in the text "On My Teacher," he appears as a disappointed person who turns away from things because they do not proceed according to his conception of them, who sets too much value on his personal freedom, who places the purity of principles over the practical necessities of the battle, and who becomes unjust because he becomes bitter. Even when he is right with regard to the individual question, he still draws the false conclusions from Stalinism: "Me-ti lamented the decline of the 'grand method,' Master Ko turned away from it" (539).

[5]

The direct criticism that culminates in this accusation of turning away from the "grand method," that is, the renunciation of revolutionary action because of individual disappointment, is only one side of Brecht's discussion with his teacher and friend. This criticism becomes general and basic when Brecht presents the history of Su (the Soviet Union) in *Me-ti*. That is done in the form of individual stories that recount the pre-revolutionary years, the early history of the revolution (447–49), the struggle between Stalin and Trotsky (503), and the Stalinist trials (522–23). Brecht uses these incidents, which are explicitly interpreted by Korsch as a betrayal of the revolution, to demonstrate the "grand method." He brings together, therefore, that which for Korsch cannot be united: the dialectical method and Leninism-Stalinism. In literary form he makes clear to his teacher and friend that another, better use of his scholarship can be made, and that his turning away from the "first workers' state in history" is a false conclusion. Apparently it was this possibility of using Korsch's insights against their author which allowed Brecht to hold to his teacher as long as he lived. Only when he did not confute him, but understood him better, could he demand of him the most precise exposition of Marxist theory, even though he had to contradict him on such an important point.[20] Nevertheless, Me-ti mourns the decline of the "grand method" under Ni-en, and Brecht himself had every reason to criticize a false development since his work would be repudiated by the dominant Soviet theory of literature which demanded a non-dialectic, in Korsch's sense, mirroring of nature.

The dialectic interpretation applies primarily to Mi-en-leh (Lenin), who had recognized that neither the people nor the *Räte* would have been in a position, under the circumstances, to carry out the revolution, but that the Party was in such a position: "The people and the *Räte* do not all know the same amount and they act according to what they know. The club knows as much as could be learned and acts without knowing everything according to the directions of a few" (430). Rosa Luxemburg's criticism is rejected: "Master Sa accused Master Mi-en-leh of pretending that the people rule, but in reality of ruling over the people" (430). This rejection occurs in the form of a parable about a champion and his trainer, who change the appearance of the relationship of master and slave by making clear the sense of the behavior (431). In the story the trainer gives orders to the champion but is in fact his slave. This literary procedure is at the same time historically prefigured, for Brecht cites a parable of Lenin's that Lenin had used to explain his actions, "Mi-en-leh's Parable of the Climbing of High Mountains" (425–27). Lenin here directs himself against critics who incorrectly surmise from his undogmatic behavior that he has become false to the revolution, and he confutes them with this parable. Brecht considered this parable to be "one of the great masterpieces of international literature," and he uses parabolic forms in *Me-ti* in order to clarify the dialectic content of historical occurrences. The parable simplifies the complicated historical relationships to easily observable models of their dialectic structure. Thus, the Russian Revolution appears in two stages: the expulsion of the emperor, which is organized by Mi-en-leh's club, and that of the smithy lords of Su by the plowsmiths who have allied themselves for this purpose with the small peasants, and who now provide the country with iron plows in order to fight hunger.[21]

That is, as becomes evident, a practicable estrangement which allows the author to grasp and clarify the contradictions in the construction of the "grand order." That Lenin begins with the distribution of land after the revolution and does not go on according to program directly to the collectivization of agriculture is justified as a correct decision insofar as it has made possible a learning process for the people concerned. The small peasants recognized through experience that they had to consolidate their land holdings in order to be able to plow them economically with iron plows. And the plowsmiths, since they were not building plows for profit, supported these consolidations by selling the plows only to those new, larger land holdings. The didactic content of these parables is brought together by sententious sayings. Here, in an excellent example of dialectic argumentation, which presents itself as a transformation, we hear that "Mi-en-leh's password was: You wanted the land because of the grain; well, give the land to us now because of the grain!" (450). The broader historical teaching is phrased: "Mi-en-leh laughed at all who believed one could, in a single day, through decrees, end a thousand-year state of necessity, of need, and he proceeded on his way" (449).

What Brecht demonstrates in this example is that Mi-en-leh is loyal to principles but does not lose sight of historical possibilities. Lenin's strong point, and in this he proves himself to be a master in the "grand method," is the ability to adjust his behavior according to the situation. While the "theoreticians of the 'grand order' in the countries outside of the Soviet Union" (512) measure him by his program, Mi-en-leh takes "the next possible step," if necessary with the full consciousness of its being a step in the wrong direction. Only a knowledge of the "grand method" allows us to understand the necessity of this behavior through which the revolutionary impatience of the pure theoretician, for example, the strict attention to principle of Master Sa (i.e., Rosa Luxemburg) or Korsch's attitude of "everything or nothing," is shown to be undialectic: "One may not imagine this order to be something which was imposed in a single day, something which is complete in all its parts, different in all its parts from the old order" (508). It is one of the foundations of the "grand method" which Master Hü-jeh (i.e., Hegel) had already recognized, that one can, with a specific thesis, "be right at one specific point in time and in a specific situation, but after some time and after the situation changes, can be wrong with this thesis" (494).[22]

The characterization of Mi-en-leh as a revolutionary, the pointing to the necessity of compromises in history, the orientation toward that which is possible, the criticism of the leftist radicalism of pure theoreticians, and so forth, corresponds in detail with Lenin's understanding of himself, as it is especially clear in his essay "'The Leftist Radicalism,' the Childhood Sickness of Communism." Correspondences in detail make clear that Brecht, in his portrayal of Lenin, referred specifically to this essay.[23]

While Lenin's political behavior does not demonstrate a decline of dialectics at all, but rather, on the contrary, its consistent situationally appropriate and practical practice, the criticism of the lack of freedom in the Soviet Union (Su) rests on a falsely understood, to a large extent still bourgeois, concept of freedom, which is dialectically superseded in *Me-ti*: "Me-ti attacked everyone who lamented this lack of freedom in Su, although they themselves still lived in countries which had not yet gotten rid of their economic masters" (438). Under this false premise, they want "to be free in organizational matters" because they "are free in economic matters": they do not understand "that the process of becoming free is an economic task and one which must be organized" (439), and that, under the changed conditions of production, the collectives become free and can be active. For the individual the sentence is true that it is "better to be un-free in a good country than free in a bad one" (540). Nevertheless, Brecht does recognize the danger of a bureaucracy becoming independent, which would be a hindrance to the goal of the "grand order," that is the withering away of the state. For this reason, Me-ti repeatedly attacks the bureaucrats who work to become indispensable instead of to become superfluous, and thus diminish the possible measure of freedom.[24]

[6]

This is the point at which the criticism of Stalin begins. I mentioned already the worst reproach, that is, the decline of the "grand method" (539) which expresses itself in the assimilation of the clubs outside of Su, the prohibition of every criticism, the hindrance of every "presentation which would have allowed a carefully planned action." But Brecht's criticism of Stalinism is not radical. Me-ti recognizes that wisdom "is chased out of politics," but at the same time that it is "directed to the creation of the state" (539f.), that the development of a socialist economic order progresses despite the decline of dialectics. While the philosopher Ko sees the development of a powerful state bureaucracy to be an unsurmountable hindrance for the realization of the "grand order" and finds in the wars for succession between Ni-en (Stalin) and To-tsi (Trotsky) the thesis confirmed "that the principles of Mi-en-leh were used up" (537), Me-ti considers the criterion of the practice to be important, which he shortens to the question of whether in Su the development of the "grand order" is furthered as a "grand production."

Me-ti finds an affirmative answer to this question despite all limitations

of Stalinism. With this emphasis on affirmation of practice, theory is of
secondary importance, for it is clear that "the principles which Ko himself suggested showed a clear weakness where Mi-en-leh's had their
strength," although, on the other hand, Ko did point out "the weaknesses
of the principles of Mi-en-leh very well" (537). The battle about principles leads, in the last resort, to a dead end, and there is, therefore, no
sensible alternative to Soviet Marxism, however imperfect it may be. It
would be senseless, therefore, to sacrifice a practice (albeit imperfect)
which, after all, does seek to attain the goal of the "grand order." Thus
Stalin becomes a necessary evil. Brecht defended him because the alternative to Stalinism in the given circumstances was not in Brecht's opinion
a better socialism but the counter-revolution. In a note on the Moscow
trials he tried to explain that "the existence of active plots against the
regime" had to be considered proven and that Stalin was following a
Leninist practice when he battled a "de facto counter-revolutionary
humanism" by treating his opponents as enemies of the Russian Revolution.[25] In his *Work Journal* Brecht noted that even the arrest of his closest friends (Tretiakov, Carola Neher, and others) could not cause him to
assume a consistently anti-Stalinist standpoint. "For the Marxists outside
the Soviet Union much the same attitude is created as that of Marx toward German Social Democracy. Critical in a positive sense."[26] This is
doubtless less than satisfying, but the experiences of German Marxists in
exile apparently formed a bitter school for the powerlessness of "good"
theory.

Thus, his pragmatic determination can be understood: "Me-ti defended
Ni-en" (495). In the great battle between Stalin and Trotsky about the
possibility of socialism in one country, practice speaks for Stalin: "To-tsi
declared the development of the order in one country impossible. Ni-en
began the development" (503).

Whereas *Me-ti* shows through the example of Mi-en-leh that contradictions are elements of a dialectical process, that compromises, tactics, and
flexibility with regard to principles are appropriate and even necessary
behavior in given situations, something similar is only postulated for Ni-
en: the contradictions in Su are considered to be the consequence of a
political situation that had become more difficult. Brecht wrote to
Korsch: "It seems very clear to me that the specific form of government
(that is, the Stalinist) had developed in closest connection with the econ-

omy (with the five-year plans, with the collectivization and industrialization of agriculture, and with defense). ... The dialectic situation, a contradictory situation, demands dialectic action in the same sense."[27] Brecht's treatment of occurrences in the early history of the Russian Revolution in a parabolic manner in order to use them as a demonstration of dialectic processes (a treatment which, without doubt, was useful also and this certainly cannot be ignored) becomes an apology for Stalinism.

As a matter of fact, Brecht was much more critical of Stalin in direct statements, for example, in his discussions with Walter Bejamin, than in *Me-ti*, where his desire to arbitrate prevails. To be sure, he rejects the cult of Stalinism here, too, but he holds it to be acceptable so long as it serves the development of the "grand production." As a dialectician, Me-ti would prefer to call Ni-en (Stalin) the "useful" rather than the "great." The mild condemnations of the Stalinist trials, to which close friends of Brecht like Carola Neher and Sergei Tretiakov fell victim, are tempered by an attempt to find a dialectic compromise.[28] The trials appear as the result of theoretical battles on Party policy in which the opponents of Ni-en had to surround themselves, of necessity, with "criminals." Here too, circumstances supposedly legitimized action.

This attempt at a justification of Stalinism is to be understood rather as a provocative hypothesis if we compare it to Brecht's other statements on this topic, a hypothesis that makes clear the danger of the cryptic parabolic form of *Me-ti*.[29] It is not mere chance that Brecht wanted sentences by Korsch which would be lacking in scholarly rigor (*verantwortungslos*). Still, *Me-ti* is to be taken seriously as a collection of examples of dialectics, for it makes clear how Brecht wanted the "grand method" to be understood. The actual uses of dialectics are not so important. They are many times *verantwortungslos*—lacking in rigor, irresponsible. But the manner in which dialectics is used is important. The individual objections that Korsch has to Soviet Marxism are certainly more precise than Brecht's rejoinders, which in a sense evade theory as the actual realm of the controversy. *Me-ti* is not a theoretical treatise and should not be cited as a source of views that Brecht held, as is done again and again. It is a literary, consciously entertaining manual of dialectic thought, and is probably an attempt to seduce Korsch to another view, the scholarly foundation of which is expressly left for the teacher himself.

In addition, *Me-ti* is a warning against a distorted understanding of the "grand method." The "grand method" for Brecht, the playwright, is a theory. It may not become autonomous, but must be changed if it conflicts with real practice. Brecht considers even the Marxist theoreticians to be "Tuis" if they insist on their theoretical views. In conversation with Benjamin, he hinted "that those who have appropriated the theoretical teachings of Marx and have treated them will always form a priest-like and intriguing faction. Marxism is simply too easily interpreted."[30] This reproach applies to Korsch as well, although he was the one who had fought the dogmatization of Marxism most strongly. That does not mean that Brecht had cut himself loose from his teacher: evidence from letters demonstrates that this is not the case. However, one must understand that Brecht's appraisal of the Soviet Union, which was different from that of Korsch, does not mean a rejection of the understanding of Marxism and of dialectics that Brecht gained from Korsch. *Me-ti*, which has as its subject this understanding of the "grand method" and its goal, the "grand order," is, at the same time, an attempt to arbitrate the contradictions in Su with the help of the "grand method." *Me-ti* refutes the theoretician Korsch and also suggests how his theory could be applied "properly."

From this vantage point the material gains the contours of a rounded work which has a distinctive profile, especially if compared to the notes in Brecht's writings on politics and society that deal with a similar theme. Where the notes are intended primarily to help Brecht himself understand questions, *Me-ti* is designed to arbitrate. The dispute with Korsch is surely not the only integrating view, but it seems to me a possible and a practicable access to an understanding of Brecht's concept of his work.

Translated by Hubert Heinen

Notes

1. Cited in *Alternative* 105 (1975): 247. The letter probably was written in 1937.
2. Alfred Forke, trans. and ed., *Mê Ti des Sozialethikers und seiner Schüler philosophische Werke* (Berlin: Vereinigung Wissenschaftlicher Verleger, 1922), see pp. 67–68, 73–74. A copy of this edition with numerous underlinings is in Brecht's library at the Brecht Archives.
3. *Me-ti Buch der Wendungen* (12: 417–585) is cited in the text parenthetically by page number.

Mê Ti was a rival of Confucius with opposing views, a fact which surely did not escape Brecht, who knew Chinese philosophy well. The combination of opposing forces underscores the eclectic character of the Chinese cloak.

4. BBA, 134: 12. The catalogue entry for this item includes "introduction of new concepts, transformation of old ones."

5. Archives of the Berliner Ensemble, 1334: 45 and 1444: 19.

6. Wolfdietrich Rasch, "Bertolt Brechts marxistischer Lehrer," *Merkur* 188, no. 10 (August 1963): 988–1003; Klaus-Detlef Müller, *Die Funktion der Geschichte im Werk Bertolt Brechts: Studien zum Verhältnis von Marxismus und Ästhetik*, 2d ed. (Tübingen: Niemeyer, 1972) and "Der Philosoph auf dem Theater: Ideologiekritik und 'Linksabweichung' in Bertolt Brechts 'Messingkauf,'" *Text + Kritik. Sonderband Bertolt Brecht I* (1972), pp. 45–71; Reiner Steinweg, *Das Lehrstück: Brechts Theorie einer politisch-ästhetischen Erziehung* (Stuttgart: Metzler, 1972), pp. 110 ff.; Heinz Brüggemann, *Literarische Technik und soziale Revolution: Versuche über das Verhältnis von Kunstproduktion, Marxismus und literarischer Tradition in den theoretischen Schriften Bertolt Brechts* (Reinbek: Rowohlt, 1973), pp. 117–38; Franco Buono, "Bemerkungen über Marxismus und Geschichte bei Bertolt Brecht," *Zur Prosa Brechts* (Frankfurt: Suhrkamp, 1973), pp. 92–120; Jan Knopf, *Bertolt Brecht: Ein kritischer Forschungsbericht* (Frankfurt: Athenäum, 1974), pp. 149–64; "Brecht/Korsch-Diskussion," *Alternative* 105 (1975).

7. The thesis concerning the legendary nature of Korsch's influence on Brecht was formulated by Ingeborg Münz-Koenen, "Brecht im Spiegel westdeutscher Publikationen," *Weimarer Beiträge* 15 (1969): 123–47, and Werner Mittenzwei, "Erprobung einer neuen Methode: Zur ästhetischen Position Bertolt Brechts," *Positionen: Beiträge zur marxistischen Literaturtheorie in der DDR* (Leipzig: Reclam, 1969), pp. 59–100. Recently, Mittenzwei has repeated it in his "Der Dialektiker Brecht oder Die Kunst Me-ti zu lesen," *Das Argument. Sonderband 11: Brechts Tui-Kritik* (Berlin: Argument, 1976), pp. 135–49.

8. Cf. Michael Buckmiller, "Marxismus als Realität: Zur Rekonstruktion der theoretischen und praktischen Entwicklung Karl Korschs," *Jahrbuch der Arbeiterbewegung* 1 (1973): 15–85. See especially pp. 42–44, and p. 49: "The contradiction of 'Marxism and philosophy,' which was totally ignored in the previous interpretations, consists of Korsch's identifying his own practical-political position, from which he formulates his highly theoretical essay, with the revolutionary practice of Lenin, at the same time developing the theoretical foundations of a scientific criticism of Leninism which become of primary importance for his later oppositional stance."

9. Ibid., p. 70.

10. Karl Korsch, *Marxismus und Philosophie* (Frankfurt: EVA, 1966), pp. 53, 67, 72.

11. Brecht, letter to Karl Korsch, Santa Monica, end of March 1945. Cited in *Alternative* 41 (1965): 45.

12. Brecht, 20: 65–66.

13. Cited in *Alternative* 105 (1975): 254.

14. Brecht, letter to Karl Korsch, Santa Monica, early November 1941. Cited in *Alternative* 105 (1975): 253.

15. Korsch, pp. 34–35.

16. Bertolt Brecht, *Arbeitsjournal 1938–1942* (Frankfurt: Suhrkamp, 1973), p. 247.

17. Cf. *Me-ti*: "Catalogue of concepts" (517–18, 534–35), "Statements of the housepainter" (442f.), "The grand method (concerning the concepts)" (533), "Utility of renaming" (556), etc.

18. See "Ki-en-leh's manner of expressing himself" (574–75), where Me-ti is characterized by his "classical studies concerning the unessential nature of virtues." Cf. especially *Me-ti*: "There should not need to exist a special morality [*Sittlichkeit*] in a country" (455–56), "Condemnation of ethical systems" (476–78), "Concerning countries which create special virtues" (518), "When do vices become famous?" (519), "Conditions which necessitate special virtues" (519).

19. See *Me-ti*: "Conversations concerning Su" (424–25), "Opinion of the philosopher Ko on the establishment of order in Su" (537), "Creation and decline of order under Ni-en" (539–40), "Freeing and freedom" (543).

20. Brecht, letter to Karl Korsch, Santa Monica, early November 1941. Cited in *Alternative* 105 (1975): 253.

21. Brecht quotes the German translation of Lenin's parable verbatim from *Die Internationale* 7, no. 6 (28 April 1924): 234. Brecht's comment on the parable is quoted from Hans Bunge, *Fragen Sie mehr über Brecht: Hanns Eisler im Gespräch* (Munich: Rogner and Bernhard, 1971), p. 95. Eisler stresses that Brecht was a Leninist. He especially appreciated Lenin's reading Marx "through the eyes of Hegel." The same can be said of Korsch. Cf. *Me-ti*, especially: "Concerning the lack of freedom under Mi-en-leh and Ni-en" (438–39), "To do one's job and let nature do its" (447–48), "Destroying which is a process of learning" (457–58), "The grand method" (493–95), "Mi-en-leh caught at arguing speciously" (512); "Concerning the state" (540–41), "Mi-en-leh's parable concerning the climbing of high mountains" (425–27), "Theory of To-tsi" (523–24).

22. Me-ti criticizes those philosophers who demonstrate and demand steadfast principles in the struggle against exploitation as having "understood nothing of the 'grand method,'" since "they disregard the circumstances completely" (428).

23. Klaus Völker maintains that Brecht "often cited verbatim" thoughts of Lenin out of his *Leftist Radicalism*: "Das alte Neue: Anmerkungen zu den aus dem Nachlaß herausgegebenen Me-ti und Tui-Texten," *Kürbiskern* 4 (1966): 157–66, here p. 158. That is, as far as I can tell, not correct as stated.

24. Cf. *Me-ti*: "Concerning the state" (540–41), "The police of Su" (547), "Experiences must be socialized" (547), "The poor official" (554), "The government as object of dialectics" (500), and others.

25. Brecht, 20: 111, 113.

26. Brecht, *Arbeitsjournal 1938–1942*, p. 36.

27. Letter of early November 1941. Cited in *Alternative* 105 (1975): 253.

28. Walter Benjamin, "Gespräche mit Brecht," *Versuche über Brecht* (Frankfurt: Suhrkamp, 1966), pp. 117–35, especially pp. 128–31. Cf. *Me-ti*: "The adulation of Ni-en" (491), "Recommendation by Me-ti concerning Ni-en's surname" (467), "Ni-en's reputation" (467), "The adulation of Ni-en (2)" (536), "Self-control of Ni-en" (538–39). See also "The trials of Ni-en" (522–23, 538).

29. Peter Bormanns uses *Me-ti* in the usual fashion, as a theoretical statement that can be treated as if it were a direct comment: "Brecht und der Stalinismus," *Brecht Jahrbuch* (1974): 53–76. That brings with it the danger of misinterpretations.

30. Benjamin, "Gespräche mit Brecht," p. 128.

The Life of Galileo and
the Theory of Revolution in Permanence

BETTY NANCE WEBER

In Brecht's opinion the dramatization of, for example, the Soviet Trials is resolved with the dramatization of Galileo. It is resolved technically. The self-
analysis of Bukharin who, at the moment of his analysis, rises far above his
personal situation—more so than anyone else in the courtroom.
—Noted during rehearsals in January 1956 by one of Brecht's collaborators.

When the Fascists gained control of the government and the people in
Germany during the 1930s, Bertolt Brecht was forced to accept exile as a
long-term, perhaps permanent situation for himself and his work. Given
the loss of his audiences, he was compelled to reexamine the dramatic
forms that served him well in the rough-and-tumble scenes of theater and
politics during the Weimar Republic. During the twenties he had developed two primary modes of theater: on the one hand, the entertaining,
provocative, satirical, even grotesque style of pieces such as *The Jungle
of the Cities*, *The Threepenny Opera*, or *The Rise and Fall of the City of
Mahagonny*—pieces that could be performed in large theaters for bourgeois audiences as exposés of the corruption, brutality, and contradictions of capitalism; on the other hand, the precise, argumentative,
dialectical style of learning plays such as *Flight over the Ocean*, *The
Baden Learning Play of Consent, The Yes-sayer and the No-sayer,* or *The
Exception and the Rule*—pieces that were directed toward small, politically interested, and progressive audiences. Could he continue these
modes of writing in exile?

Most critics have argued that Brecht's drastically altered situation precipitated a decisive shift in dramatic form. From the point of view of
many of these critics, this shift was welcome, as it culminated in the "universal," nontendentious, mature dramas: the epic "masterworks." More
recently other critics have viewed this very development negatively, as a
backsliding on Brecht's part from the exciting experimental theater of

the 1920s to uninteresting, traditional, even simplistic plays for old-fashioned stages. Such historical divisions and literary classifications—regardless of the political convictions of the critics—have hindered an appreciation for the strong continuity in Brecht's work, in form and subject. There is, in fact, a sequential development from the Weimar years into the exile years: his playful, satiric exposure of contradictions in the forces of capitalism evolved into mocking, angry derision of the Nazis; his terse, direct, often abstract learning plays evolved to colorfully theatrical, indirect epic dramas, with contemporary issues dispersed in a historical prism.

Although the first of these assertions, that there is continuity in form and intent from satire of capitalism to farcical treatment of fascism, comes as no great surprise, the second assertion, which links the learning plays and the masterworks, seems to fly in the face of received opinion. Exile supposedly prevented further development of the learning-play form. Both the loss of audience and the real or imagined danger of repercussions in the Soviet Communist party during the 1930s halted, critics have argued, dramatization of the most controversial conflicts among Marxists. Brecht could not risk a play such as *The Measures Taken* while in exile. Given, however, Brecht's enduring interest in the internecine struggles on questions of ideology and strategy, given, furthermore, the inherent dramatic quality of the effort in the Soviet Union to leap from feudalism to industrialism in a matter of decades, it is difficult to believe that Brecht would forgo shaping this development into theater. In fact, he did not: the recently published *Me-ti* prose anecdotes and evidence from notes and early versions of the masterworks indicate that Brecht in exile cloaked political issues—much as he had in learning plays such as *The Yes-sayer and the No-sayer* or *The Exception and the Rule*—in pseudo-historical or exotic garb, and that he indeed aspired to be the epic recorder of the revolutionary era.

In the four major exile plays that function as sequels to the learning plays, *The Life of Galileo*, *Mother Courage and Her Children*, *The Good Woman of Szechwan*, and *The Caucasian Chalk Circle*, Brecht chronicled Soviet history from 1917 to 1938. In so doing he dramatized the doubt, hope, success, failure, brilliance, stupidity, arrogance, humility, gentleness, and brutality of the grand upheavals between the February Revolution and the Moscow Trials. The consistency and determination with which Brecht sought to render an all-encompassing account of these years has been largely overlooked in Brecht criticism. Critics have noted topical, even politically blasphemous allusions, but ignored Brecht's systematic, rational pattern of relating history in reverse, i.e. from 1938 backward. The further Brecht probes into the past, progressing from history (*Galileo*) through the picaresque (*Mother Courage*) and fairy tale (*Szechwan*) to legend (*Chalk Circle*), the greater the distortions in official Soviet record and, therefore, the greater the need for Brecht to counter the falsification of history. For each piece he locates a historical/legendary situation in which there are inherent parallels to the aspects and events of twentieth-century history he would dramatize. The inherent parallels are used as scaffolding for the play; other elements of the sources are altered slightly to correspond with contemporary history; and, finally, fictitious material is added to complete the composition. This strategy of composition is already well developed in the first of these pieces, *Galileo* (1937–38).

In *Galileo* the playwright rearranges church history, the initial thrust of Protestantism, and the devastating consequences of counterreformation in the seventeenth century to parallel the history of the old Social Democratic Workers' party in Russia through waves of revolution and reaction in the twentieth century. In making such an analogy Brecht follows the well-established practice of measuring contemporary events against historical models. Since Marx and Engels, every episode of social upheaval has been meticulously compared with events of the French Revolution. One of the most celebrated books to employ this type of analogy appeared only a few months before Brecht began writing *Galileo*: Leon Trotsky's *The Revolution Betrayed* (1937). To use this shopworn frame of reference would have reduced a play to allegory and precluded any possibility that worldwide audiences might abstract from the fable, that they might distill the conflicts of the piece without prejudgment. A seventeenth-century setting allowed Brecht greater freedom in molding his material.

Identifying the tradition in which Brecht is writing discloses the prejudices or preferences on which much of the critical literature on *Galileo* is based. The accepted equations of Galileo with Brecht or compromised scientists in Germany or the United States lose force beside a juxtaposition of the fictitious character Galileo with the revolutionary figure who was perhaps the most colorful and the most disputed of all: Trotsky. Brecht's Galileo and the historical Trotsky share many character traits: a naive trust in intellect and reason, unqualified commitment to a new scientific discipline (Galileo, to the study of nature; Trotsky, to the study of society), arrogance, intellectual vanity, the capacity for unscrupulous treatment of associates or family when commitment or science demanded, the impatience of the very bright, a cultivated understanding for art and the pleasures of everyday living, a demagogic ability to sway youth, masked cowardice, the inability to conquer their enemies in deed coupled with the talent to rebut and defeat in word. Both preserved their arguments concerning the truth in writings, but failed to realize many of their goals in actions.

Brecht's strategy of composition in the play is to interlace moments of authentic seventeenth-century history with anachronisms and invented history to create a consistent set of parallels between two epochs. For those already familiar with Trotsky's then famous autobiography, *My Life* (German edition, 1930), and his analysis of the bureaucracy, *The Revolution Betrayed* (German edition, 1937), the Galileo analogy points to the genesis of the play. Trotsky had already likened his old friend Christian Rakowski (as a representative of all Trotskyites in Russia who had become comfortable in pampered positions and recanted in spite of their superior insights) to the seventeenth-century scientist. Just as Galileo's recantation could not change the revolution of the earth, the recantations in Moscow, produced by the carrot-and-stick policies of the Party, could not, Trotsky maintained, alter either the truth of his criticism of the bureaucracy or the Jacobinic character of the Party. On the contrary: the recantations proved, in Trotsky's view, the accuracy of his analysis; Trotskyites such as Rakowski had been corrupted by the privileges of position. Thus, in this brief analogy, Trotsky had described the major failing that later would be discussed as the major paradox in the character of Brecht's Galileo: the capacity to recognize and analyze the corrupting influence of privilege and yet fall victim to it. In his composition Brecht extended this analogy of Galileo on trial and Trotskyites on trial to the lives and theoretical work of the two figures.

The play depicts some twenty-five years of Galileo's life. In January 1610 he provided the foundations for scientific truth concerning the permanent revolution of the earth by proving Copernicus's theory and disproving the generally accepted Ptolemaic theory of earthly stasis. For the balance of his life Galileo maneuvered with the church hierarchy to gain recognition for his arguments. Ever insistent that he was a loyal child of the church, he became increasingly subservient and often unaccountably reticent in expressing his deepest convictions. With the death of the old pope, a new, scientifically trained man ascended the papal throne. This old acquaintance disappointed Galileo, put him on trial, convicted him, and finally humiliated him with enforced exile.

The parallels run like a red thread through the play. In January 1910—three centuries later to the month and year—Trotsky provided the scientific arguments concerning the permanent revolution of society in his Vienna "Truth," *Pravda*, and thus disproved the generally accepted theory that revolution must erupt in industrialized countries rather than agrarian lands. He further contended that Russia would spearhead revolution in the twentieth century. The middle segment of Galileo's life in the play (scenes 4–8) parallels Trotsky's struggle to gain recognition for his theories in the Bolshevik hierarchy, his submission to the Party and increasing subservience during the First World War, and the eight years of Lenin's leadership in the Soviet Union. Brecht altered the historical date of the old pope's death (i.e. the ascension of the new pope Barberini) from 1623 to 1624. The year 1924 saw Lenin's death and the ascension of Joseph Stalin, the man often referred to as the "red pope" or the Barbarian. Though he was trained in the science of Marxism, Stalin took control of the Party hierarchy, put the loyal child of the Party on trial, defeated him, and finally humiliated Trotsky with enforced exile. As in the seventeenth century when the Ptolemaic theory of the universe was upheld against the Copernican by way of force, the theory of "socialism in one land" was upheld by way of force in the twentieth century against the theory of permanent revolution.

An outline of the parallels between Brecht's *Galileo* and Russian history follows. For each scene, the summary from the play is presented first; the historical parallel follows in italic.

SCENE 1

Galileo reviews his experience of the last twenty to twenty-five years. He has taught in universities in "free" (vs. papal) states, where he may conduct whatever research he will, but he cannot make progress because of the pressures of time and finances. With the invention/discovery of the telescope (1608), he has at his disposal, for the first time, an instrument with which he can prove the theory he has long held to be true: the theory of the permanent revolution of the earth around the sun. With this breakthrough (1610) Galileo proclaims a "new era" (fictitious).

Trotsky (as well as many other revolutionaries) spent most of his time before 1917 in the "free" western countries (vs. tsarist Russia), where he could voice his view but had too little time. He had to write for journals with which he did not agree in order to make a living. With the founding of his Vienna Pravda *[Truth] in 1908, he at last had an instrument with which he could argue the theories he had long espoused: the theory of permanent revolution. Trotsky often expressed the view that a "new era" had dawned in human history.*

SCENE 2

Galileo uses the telescope to obtain additional funding from the city managers.

Trotsky used his Pravda *to obtain additional funding from the Bolshevik Central Committee.*

SCENE 3

1610: Galileo presents the evidence for substantiating the truth of his revolutionary theory. Cheap, inferior models of the telescope flood Padua.

1910: Trotsky presented his evidence in Pravda *for substantiating his revolutionary theory. Cheap, inferior issues of a second* Pravda *(edited by Stalin) flooded Petersburg.*

SCENE 4

Galileo fails to convince the Florentine court that his theory of the organization of the universe is valid. They ignore and ridicule his evidence (fiction).

Trotsky failed to convince the Party leadership, especially Lenin, that his theory of party organization was valid. They ignored and ridiculed his evidence.

(See detailed discussion of this scene below.)

SCENES 5A AND 5B

During the plague Galileo continues his work (an anachronistic element for the years 1610 to 1616). Officials make bumbling efforts to contain the disease (fiction).

During the Balkan Wars and World War I (which he referred to as the plague) Trotsky continued his work. Diplomats made bumbling efforts to contain the war.

(See detailed discussion of this scene below.)

SCENE 6

In 1616 (historically 1611) the court astronomer in Rome, Clavius, recognizes the validity of Galileo's discoveries and proofs and points to the danger for papal authority.

In 1916 court intellectuals in Petersburg recognized the validity of the arguments of the revolutionaries and pointed to their danger for tsarist authority.

SCENE 7

Galileo confronts Cardinal Bellarmine and Cardinal Barberini at a carnival in Rome. In the disputes concerning the revolutionary theory, the two cardinals are weaker intellectually but stronger politically than Galileo. Almost against his will, Galileo joins their merrymaking (fiction). The Copernican theory is placed on the index and Galileo is forbidden to support the theory in earnest. Details in this scene are extremely important. Bellarmine takes the mask of a dove (in an earlier version, a fox). Barberini takes the mask of a lamb (in an earlier version, a jackass). Galileo has no mask (fiction).

Trotsky confronted the longtime Bolsheviks Lenin and Stalin during the revolution in Petersburg. (There are astonishing parallels between the historical figures Bellarmine/Lenin and Barberini/Stalin.) In their disputes concerning revolutionary theory, the Bolsheviks were weaker intellectually but stronger politically than Trotsky. Almost against his will, Trotsky joined the Bolshevik party—at the expense of his theory of permanent revolution and his notions of democratic party organiza-

tion. *The masks Brecht chooses correspond in character to the positions taken by Lenin and Stalin during the revolution. Both were famous for their disguises. Trotsky refused to use a mask or to go underground after the February Revolution.*

SCENE 8

Galileo's discussion with the young monk who is of peasant origin indicates the devastating effect the scientific revolution will/must/could have on the poorest and least educated segment of the society, the peasants. In order to battle the church hierarchy, Galileo desperately needs the support of the segment that can least understand or sympathize with his theory.

The question of educating and winning the great mass of peasants has been crucial for every revolutionary effort in the history of Russia. In the early part of this century, revolutionaries such as Trotsky were creating visions of the future while the peasants still suffered feudal conditions. During the campaign against Trotsky and his followers, Stalinists accused him of failing to understand and of being harsh in his treatment of peasants.

SCENE 9

With the news (eight years later, 1624) that the old pope is bedridden and dying and that Barberini probably will become the next pope, Galileo abruptly discontinues his research on the floating objects (the historical Galileo did this work in 1611), turns his attention to the sunspots (also done historically in 1611), and declares a "new course" for his research (fiction). This scene was originally set in 1636.

This fictional change of power corresponds to the historical events surrounding Lenin's illness and death in 1923–24. While Trotsky outwardly supported Stalin's rise to power, he was privately wary. In 1923 he began, abruptly, to argue for a "new course" (develop criticism, support intellectual freedom, examine facts) which actually recalled goals he had long cherished. The first trials in Moscow were in 1936, the year in which Stalin attained the equivalent of papal powers in the Soviet Union.

SCENE 10

As in Galileo's famous *Dialogue Concerning the Two World Systems*, published in 1632, the position of the church is made to appear ridiculous and Galileo's theory triumphant. There is no spectacular procession recorded in 1632.

In the 1920s and 1930s people's uprisings in many parts of the world—especially in China—seemed to lend credence to Trotsky's theory of permanent revolution, thus making the Stalinist theory of socialism in one land untenable. Trotsky was expatriated in 1932.

SCENE 11

Both the concern Galileo shows for modernizing industry and agriculture and the degree to which old friends and supporters desert him are fictional. He is summoned to Rome for trial in 1633.

During the late 1920s Trotsky advocated importing technological expertise from the West and modernizing industry and agriculture. During the early thirties, many old supporters began to shun Trotskyism and seek favor with the Party. In 1932–33 preparations were being made for summoning to trial the Left Oppositionists who remained in Russia.

SCENE 12

Urban VIII (formerly Barberini) is presented as a pawn in the hands of the church apparatus, and especially the Inquisition. He is a product of the church hierarchy (fiction).

*During the 1930s the Left Opposition criticized the top Party hierarchy for assuming "papal infallibility." Trotsky described the "deified Stalin" as the personification, the product of the bureaucracy. "Like the Catholic Church, it [the commanding caste] has put forward the dogma of infallibility in the period of its decline, but it has raised it to a height of which the Roman pope never dreamed." (*The Revolution Betrayed. New York: Pioneer, 1945, p. 277.)*

SCENE 13

Galileo recants on 22 June 1633.

In The Revolution Betrayed *Trotsky compared the recantation (1933–34) of his old friend Christian Rakovsky to that of Galileo, an act that could not refute the truth of his previous work. In earlier years Trotsky himself had often "recanted" in the face of Party pressure: when he was threatened with expulsion from the Party in 1927, for example, he denied the assertion that a Soviet thermidor was in progress.*

SCENE 14

The conditions of Galileo's house arrest as depicted in the play—with constant surveillance and harassment, etc.—are much more restrictive than can be documented historically. During this time Galileo reviews his previous scientific work and consolidates it in the famous *Discorsi*.

*The conditions under which Trotsky lived in Alma-Ata and in Prinkipo (Turkey) were very difficult. He was constantly spied upon and harassed. During this time, however, he reviewed his previous work and wrote the monumental volumes for which he is now famous—*The Permanent Revolution *(1929),* History of the Russian Revolution *(1932), and* The Stalin School of Falsification *(1932).*

SCENE 15

Galileo's former pupil, Andrea, smuggles the manuscript of the *Discorsi* over the Italian border in 1637 (fiction). The initial draft of the *Discorsi* was completed in 1633. In 1636 a Dutch bookdealer received a copy. It was printed in 1638.

Trotsky's The Revolution Betrayed, *a review in summary of his criticism of Stalin and the bureaucracy, appeared in 1937. Trotsky also journeyed to Mexico in this year, and the Dewey Commission found him and his son Leo Sedov "not guilty" of the crimes they were accused of during the Moscow Trials.*

As this brief juxtaposition of major parallels between the play and Russian history in the twentieth century indicates, Brecht's strategy of composition is extremely complex. He does not construct traditional allegory in which each fictitious character stands in a one-to-one relationship with a given historical figure. He does incorporate in the Galileo figure and his associates in the play both the actions and the spirit of those—primarily figures from the Left Opposition—who sought to guard the dynamic and scientific qualities of the revolution against ossification and dogmatization. This is to say that Brecht's Galileo is larger than the person of Trotsky. On the other hand, however, the individual Galileo is smaller than Trotsky: by endowing both Galileo and his pupils with elements of Trotsky's character and life, Brecht can present a rich and varied perspective on Trotsky's activities in the panorama of twentieth-century history.

Viewed from this perspective—that Brecht was writing a play with the backdrop of Trotsky's significance in Russian history from the earliest squabbles and triumphs of the tsarist years to his final confinement, persecution, and defeat in exile—one can confront anew many questions about the play which have puzzled critics for forty years. How does one explain the anachronisms, the invented history, and the scenes without historical model, which Brecht always insisted were necessary. Three examples illustrate the importance of Trotsky's biography for the structure of the play: Andrea and Galileo's confrontation with the Florentine court (scene 4), the plague (scenes 5a and 5b), and Galileo's discussion with the young monk (scene 8). In these scenes parallels between the historical Galileo (the paragraphs in roman type) and Brecht's Galileo (in italic) are almost nonexistent. It is Trotsky's life and Russian history (set in boldface type) which provide the structural scaffolding for the play.

SCENE 4

[1]

No historical record.

In a chance encounter Andrea (representing Galileo's view) and the young Cosmo de Medici, the Grand Prince of Florence, meet and discuss the two models for world systems, the Ptolemaic and the Copernican. The impatient, impolite Andrea announces to Cosmo that the Ptolemaic system is incorrect and shows him the correct Copernican model. The young prince is infuriated and the two of them come to blows and tear the Ptolemaic model apart. This encounter is the prelude to the official discussion between Galileo and the court philosophers later in the scene. (Apparently set in the year 1610.)

In a chance encounter in a train station on the way to the Copenhagen meeting of the Social Democratic party (1910), Lenin and Trotsky met, discussed the two models for party organization, Leninistic centralism and Trotskyistic decentralism. Lenin was infuriated by Trotsky's criticism of centralism, a criticism that was to be published at the beginning of the upcoming congress, and the two of them practically came to blows. This meeting and dispute was the prelude for the official confrontation between the two opposing sides in Copenhagen. Because of it, party unity was destroyed and the split between the two factions became inevitable.

[2]

There is no recorded confrontation of the kind described in Brecht's play between Galileo and the Florentine court. Such a meeting was also very unlikely: Galileo had been invited to Florence in 1609 by the Grand Duke Cosimo II to demonstrate the telescope. The prince, who was an adult at the time, was Galileo's former pupil and had great respect for his old teacher. Relationships between the ducal family and Galileo were always warm and Galileo was given every protection and assistance possible against Rome. It was the professors in Padua who refused to look through the telescope.

After he moves to Florence, Galileo tries to convince the young Cosmo, a theologian, a philosopher, and representatives of the court of the truth of his arguments. Court ideologues accuse him of deception, of painting the stars on the telescope, and refuse to look through the instrument.

After the traumatic confrontation between Lenin and Trotsky at the international congress of socialists in Copenhagen, the Bolshevik wing of the Party took every opportunity to attack Trotsky and accused him of deception in his arguments in the Vienna *Pravda*. Stalin ridiculed Trotsky in the Petersburg *Pravda*. It was later demonstrated that neither Lenin nor Stalin had actually read Trotsky's works with any care and much of their criticism was based on hearsay and prejudice.

[3]

There was no outbreak of the plague in this part of Europe until 1630.

Soon after Galileo had settled in Florence, the first cases of the plague were reported. Officials, however, deny that it is the plague and dismiss these cases as isolated incidents that should cause no alarm.

In the years before the First World War, small-scale military confrontations in the Balkans were treated in the official diplomatic circles as isolated incidents. Most of the socialist parties also failed to interpret these warning signs as an indication that greater conflagration lay ahead.

SCENE 5A

No historical record.

Galileo refuses to leave his work in spite of the danger of the plague.

Trotsky continued his works and writings—including the internecine struggle in the Party—in the midst of the First World War (compare the 1915 Zimmerwald meeting).

SCENE 5B

[1]

No historical record.

Galileo ridicules the unscientific approaches to analyzing the causes of the plague.

Trotsky ridiculed the analysis according to which the First World War was a result of national defense. He discussed the war as a result of economic confrontations and considerations. He also argued that his was a scientific analysis of the war.

[2]

No historical record.

In the midst of chaos, while under surveillance, Galileo continues his research and demands books when there is hardly bread.

In the midst of war, while under surveillance, Trotsky continued work in libraries and visited art museums.

[3]

No historical record.

Details in the scene point to the conditions of war and political conflict: soldiers dressed for combat appear. Galileo remarks, "That is their whole concept of government. They cut us off like a sick branch of a fig tree, which can bring no more fruit" (3: 1275).

Trotsky often referred to the First World War as the plague.

[4]

No historical record.

Andrea is forced to leave Florence, escapes, is captured once, escapes again to return to his work with Galileo on the revolution of the planets.

Trotsky was forcibly transported from one land to another as the war nears—finally to the United States. He escaped, was captured once, and finally managed to return to revolutionary activities in Russia.

SCENE 8

[1]

No historical record.

This scene reemphasizes Galileo's ability to argue brilliantly and thus win youthful followers.

Trotsky was recognized—even by his worst enemies—as the most adept proponent of revolutionary action among the young.

[2]

No historical record.

The young monk confronts Galileo with the primitive conditions that still exist in the countryside and describes the devastating effects the revelation of revolutionary thinking would have on the peasants who had spent their lives in toil. There would be no solace for them if their faith and toil were to lose "meaning."

On the eve of the revolution, even as workers were demanding bread and peace, the peasants of Russia were still subjected to feudal conditions as primitive as those of the Middle Ages. Their faith in religion and hierarchy remained intact. Release from serfdom had not changed their situation.

[3]

No historical record.

Galileo refutes the reasoning of the young monk and insists that machinery will do them more good than theory. Even the greatest technical advances cannot, however, ultimately eliminate this need for teaching them to think. He calls for their "divine anger" (Zorn).

During the revolution the Bolsheviks made a concerted effort to win over the

countryside; they viewed this effort as vital for a socialist revolution. Trotsky was an avid supporter of supplying the peasants with better machinery (October 1917, Conference of Factory Committees) and thus improving the lot of the peasants. At the same time he insisted that supplying them with machinery would do no good unless they, too, were revolutionized. He often called for "people's anger" (*Zorn*).

[4]

No historical record.

Though Galileo's opponent is a monk, the young man has peasant origins and demonstrates the possibility of bridging a tremendous social gap in one lifetime.

The soldiers and workers who radically gave their allegiance to the Bolsheviks were largely of peasant origins. Although they resisted the notion of revolution over long periods, they ultimately led the peasants' uprisings in 1917.

This unveiling of the historical scaffolding for the Galileo drama should not be interpreted as an effort to expose Brecht's secret political life. Whether Brecht sympathized with Trotsky, Lenin, Stalin, or whomever has little to do with the primary issue of the play: the truth of the Copernican view of the universe and Galileo's guilt. Whether the scientific evidence would receive official recognition depended—according to Brecht's depiction—on the steadfastness of its most able advocate: Galileo. If he submits, all opposition could be systematically crushed. Galileo's subsequent remorse over his earlier misjudgment (scene 14) recalls Trotsky's scrutiny of the past from his exile in Prinkipo:

> GALILEO: I have become convinced that I was never in any real danger. For a few years, I was as strong as the authorities. (3: 1341)
>
> TROTSKY: I have no doubt that if I had come forward on the eve of the twelfth party congress [1923] in the spirit of a "bloc of Lenin and Trotsky" against the Stalin bureaucracy, I should have been victorious even if Lenin had taken no direct part in the struggle. (*My Life*, p. 481)

Both figures realize that instead of offering effective resistance at the opportune moment, they had, as Brecht expresses it, given their knowledge "to the powermongers, to use or not to use, to misuse, as it served their purposes. . . . The steadfastness of one man could have precipitated grand convulsions" (3: 1341). This view echoes another observation from

Trotsky's biography: "The fate of the revolution was being decided. . . . At the most critical moment it rested on a single battalion, on one company, on the courage of one commissary" (*My Life*, p. 397). The conviction that he had failed to respond properly at a critical moment in history, a moment that could not be retrieved, is the key issue on the question of Galileo's/Trotsky's guilt.

In the play, then, Brecht is focusing on a particular "crime" that had nothing to do with the public accusations at the trials. The issue of treason (of which the Dewey Commission exonerated Trotsky) was of little consequence in comparison with the moral issue. Both Galileo and Trotsky with their unique talents of persuasion at a unique moment of history failed to make a singular, very necessary contribution to the values in their fields. Like Galileo in the field of natural and physical sciences, Trotsky failed to write a Hippocratic oath for the field of Marxism as a science of society, an oath that might have altered the course of Soviet history after Lenin's death. Trotsky's were crimes of omission and recantation. The moment at which a Hippocratic oath for Marxism could have been proclaimed was passed.

Brecht's *Galileo* marked the beginning of a series of theatrical learning plays about the most significant stages in the effort to revolutionize feudal Russia. In *Galileo* Brecht had explored the questions of guilt and self-sacrifice, vital questions for the Left during the year in which he wrote the play. Moving from current events to recent history in *Mother Courage and Her Children*, he again treated the topic of party history: here during civil war. In *The Good Woman of Szechwan* he presented the difficulties of modernizing and industrializing in an underdeveloped land. Finally, in *The Caucasian Chalk Circle*, he probed party history and the saga of the grandiose revolutionary year 1917. Viewing revolutionary history from the perspective of the late 1930s made each earlier stage seem less complex, less difficult, with the battle lines more clearly delineated. This experience is reflected in the style and mood of the plays which progress from document to legend.

Brecht did not intend the historical scaffolding for the plays to transport history onto the stage as pure information. There was no need for such literature: a multitude of volumes ranging from document to reflection, mostly by Russians in exile, was being published in these years. Within the Soviet Union, the first volume of official history, *The History of the Civil War* by M. Gorky, S. Kirov, W. Molotov, K. Voroshilov, A. Shdanov, and J. Stalin (published in Russian in 1936; in German translation in 1937), inaugurated the tendency to monumentalize the events and the heroes of the revolution. What distinguishes Brecht's plays from these various historical sources, especially the reports written by active participants, is his lack of doctrinaire sobriety in favor of lively urbanity. Instead of railing at the long since victorious or vanquished, he takes leave of the old squabbles in jest. Despite the gravity of his own situation in exile, he caricatured the revolutionary figures—regardless of their political inclinations—without minimizing their strengths and their achievements. In opposition to the ever-increasing tendency to monumentalize history, Brecht practiced "demonumentalization." International stars of revolutionary history are depicted as provincial ruffians or clowns so that an audience may assume the critical, distanced stance of those who would learn, the characteristic stance for a learning play.

With the disclosure of direct links between those plays generally considered to be Brecht's least tendentious, least political pieces and the most controversial issues and events in the revolutionary history of the twentieth century, one of the oldest problems in Brecht's work surfaces once again: the difficulty of writing the truth in "dark times." Much of Brecht's open political comment—whether in dramatic form, *Señora Carrar*, for example, in pseudo-mask as in *Me-ti*, or in the diaries and journals—has too often been taken at face value. Brecht was acutely aware of the possible danger of blatant political remarks, even in private papers, falling into the wrong hands. Family and friends were vulnerable. In this situation, public statements should be viewed as necessary strategic maneuvers that had little to do with his scientific assessment of revolutionary history. Because of the real or imagined dangers of exile, Brecht incorporated his testament of political commitment in the least suspected hiding place, in the rollicking, exotic plays of the late thirties and early forties.

Selected Bibliography

A. BRECHT'S *Life of Galileo* AND HISTORY

Borchardt, Frank K. "Marx, Engels and Brecht's Galileo," *Brecht heute* 2 (1972): 149–72.

Fehn, Ann Clark. "Vision and Blindness in Brecht's *Leben des Galilei*," *Germanic Review* 53 (1978): 27–34.

Hecht, Werner, ed. *Materialien zu Brechts "Leben des Galilei."* Frankfurt: Suhrkamp, 1963.

Müller, Klaus-Detlef. *Die Funktion der Geschichte im Werk Bertolt Brechts: Studien zum Verhältnis von Marxismus und Ästhetik.* Tübingen: Niemeyer, 1967.

Nägele, Rainer. "Zur Struktur von Brechts *Leben des Galilei*," *Deutschunterricht* 23 (1971): 86–99.

Schumacher, Ernst. *Drama und Geschichte: Bertolt Brechts "Leben des Galilei" und andere Stücke.* Berlin: Henschel, 1965.

Stern, Guy. "The Plight of the Exile: A Hidden Theme in Brecht's *Galileo Galilei.*" *Brecht heute* 1 (1971): 110–16.

Szczesny, Gerhard. *Bertolt Brecht: "Leben des Galilei."* Frankfurt: Ullstein, 1966.

B. TROTSKY AND RUSSIAN HISTORY

Abosch, Heinz, ed. *Trotzki Chronik.* Munich, 1973.

Brahm, Heinz. *Trotzkis Kampf um die Nachfolge Lenins.* Cologne: Wissenschaft und Politik, 1964.

Carmichael, Joel. *Trotsky: An Appreciation of His Life.* London: Hodder and Stoughton, 1975.

Deutscher, Isaac. *The Prophet Armed. The Prophet Unarmed. The Prophet Outcast.* London: Oxford University Press, 1954, 1959, 1963.

Keep, John L. *The Russian Revolution.* London: Weidenfeld and Nicolson, 1976.

Treviranus, G. R. *Revolutions in Russia.* New York: Harper, 1944.

Serge, Victor and Natalia Sedova Trotsky. *The Life and Death of Leon Trotsky.* Translated by Arnold J. Pomerans. New York: Basic Books, 1975.

Trotsky, Leon. *My Life.* New York: Grosset and Dunlap, 1970; *Problems of Everyday Life and other Writings on Culture and Science.* New York: Monad, 1973; *The Revolution Betrayed.* New York: Pioneer, 1945.

C. GALILEO GALILEI

Galilei, Galileo. *Dialogue Concerning the Two Chief World Systems, Ptolemaic and Copernican.* Translated by Stillman Drake. Berkeley: University of California Press, 1953.

Drake, Stillman. *Galileo Studies: Personality, Tradition, and Revolution*. Ann Arbor: University of Michigan Press, 1970.

Ronan, Colin A. *Galileo*. New York: Putnam, 1974.

Santillana, Giorgio de. *The Crime of Galileo*. Chicago: University of Chicago Press, 1955.

Shapere, Dudley. *Galileo: A Philosophical Study*. Chicago: University of Chicago Press, 1974.

Shea, William. *Galileo's Intellectual Revolution*. London: Macmillan, 1972.

Part Two
production

Brecht and the Soviet Theater

EFIM ETKIND

KALLE: What do you have against philosophy?
ZIFFEL: Nothing, as long as it isn't practiced as a science.
Discussion among Exiles, fragment.

The greatest misfortune that could have befallen Brecht was to become a classic. Unfortunately, this has happened. Brecht has truly become a classic. Today one studies his relationship to everything in the world. In my opinion a classic is someone whom we feel compelled to connect to other classics with the help of an *and*. This means Brecht *and* Shakespeare, Brecht *and* Tolstoy, Brecht *and*, *and*, *and*. Not this, but another aspect of this Brechtian problem is of interest to me. Although it is also an *and*, it is perhaps less classical: what interests me is Brecht and the significance of his theater for the Soviet Union, for the contemporary Soviet citizen.

Since I mentioned earlier that it was unfortunate for Brecht to have become a classic—and Brecht would probably have agreed—I would like to add, however, that this is what enabled his work to survive in the Soviet Union. There is an unwritten law in the Soviet Union according to which the classics are not censored. Were Brecht not a classic and thus subject to censorship, then I would have had nothing to tell here, for not one Brecht play, not even *Coriolanus*, not even *The Threepenny Opera*, could have appeared in the Soviet Union. One need not mention the works that Soviet readers and publishers would have found completely impossible, such as the "Discussion among Exiles," from which the epigraph for this paper comes. This epigraph alone would have been a bombshell, even though a small one, since the possibility of pursuing philosophy in a scientific manner is highly valued in the Soviet Union. The recognition of Brecht in the Soviet Union was not purely academic, not merely the discovery of just another playwright, just another poet. It was truly a gigantic event when Brecht was rediscovered. This took place in the mid-1950s, not at the time of the first theatrical productions, but when Brecht's poetry and several of his plays were first republished. I say republished because there was a time in the 1920s when Brecht was well-known in Russia. This time, however, had long since passed. There was a gap of several decades. This breakthrough in the mid-fifties will certainly be treated as such when the history of Soviet social thought or Soviet literature is written. It was of great import.

The breakthrough occurred in two spheres, inspiring innovations first in literature and second in theater. It was as a poet and rejuvenator of language that Brecht was first discovered in the 1950s. Those who have no idea of what Soviet life in the 1940s and early 1950s was like cannot imagine why this was so. Up until Stalin's death and the Twentieth Party Congress in 1956, literature and art were, let us use the term, *classical*. All forms were frozen by convention. Modernism was not spoken of at all, except as something to be cursed. Actually the term *modernism* had always been a curse word. One could not mention free rhythm or other such things that were no longer considered modern discoveries in the West. Such things were unthinkable in the Soviet Union until the mid-fifties.

The first breakthrough in this direction was the translation and publication of Brecht's poetry, which became possible for many reasons. Brecht was an author of the German Democratic Republic, therefore he already had a visa, a passport into Soviet literary circles. Because he came to the Soviet Union from East Germany, he was something of a fellow citizen, and what he wrote was assumed to be politically acceptable. This was one very important aspect of Brecht's influence. The Brechtian tradition of the chansonnier, a tradition that has almost been forgotten in Germany, excepting perhaps one Brecht pupil, Wolf Biermann, in the 1950s caused a renaissance in the Soviet Union of the political, the intellectual song, as seen in the works of Okudzhava, Galich, Vysotskii, and Kim. And this renaissance followed the new translations of Brecht songs of the twenties and thirties, although the Russian counterparts were quite different. Another important aspect, besides the modern side of his poetry, with its free rhythm, is the new relationship between poetry and prose, poetry and drama. That was also something that the Soviet Union had forgotten, and it was important that here, too, innovation appeared.

The breakthrough of Brecht in the theater was of primary importance, which even my closest friends in the West have not always understood. For example, "the cult of personality" is often misunderstood. It is believed to be a cult of Stalin: that is completely false. The cult of Stalin was only one of the most obvious examples of the *"Führer* principle" that existed in the Soviet Union from 1930 to 1956. In every activity and in every area there could be only one man or one authority, and every other person was implicitly an opponent. It had nothing to do with the fact that this person might be well-respected and at the same time a talented artist or creative scientist.

The people in question usually had nothing to do with the fact that they were made authoritative figures of this or that field. The authority in psychology was Pavlov; consequently there was no room for a Freud— not because one had anything against Freud, but because Freud was a second authority. And because there was a Lysenko in botany, there could be no Vladilov. He was arrested and destroyed because he was a second authority. In prose fiction this authority was Gorky; in poetry unfortunately it was Mayakovsky—unfortunately, because his work was exploited after his suicide in 1930. Pasternak once wrote that Mayakovsky was destroyed a second time when he was made an official figure. In theater it was Stanislavsky, who was a very good director. But when he was made into a cult figure, this was a frightening thing. It was the tyranny of a good director, which is not much better than the tyranny of a bad one. Stanislavsky provided excellent theater in the worst years; but because it became the only theater, it displaced and suppressed any theater that was not based on empathy.

In 1956 Brecht was discussed in the Soviet Union as an anti-Stanislavsky figure, a circumstance that did not please Brecht at the time. He wrote many essays and notes on the problem of Stanislavsky, always trying to clarify the relationship of their dramaturgy and to explain that there was no personal conflict. That may be correct, but what is important for us is not Brecht's understanding of Stanislavsky. What is important is that Brecht represented a second theater. And if there is a second theater, there can be a third, a tenth one. This is the problem of having more than one authority. Brecht was a second party in theater. This is the reason we writers of the mid-fifties wrote with such insolence and lack of regard for aesthetic categories. When we wrote literary articles on the problem of empathy versus alienation, we were at the same time writing political articles. The *Führer* principle and the possibility of creating a second theater, indeed of creating a fiftieth theater, were at stake. This was the gigantic effect Brecht had on the Soviet theater in the 1950s and 1960s.

The strange thing about this phenomenon was that Brecht did not represent anything foreign to Soviet literature and the Soviet theater. Brecht was the return of our own 1920s. We are now accustomed to having to reimport our own riches every decade or so from the West, even those that we tried to destroy and forget. This is true in the case of Russian formalism of the 1920s, which was strangled in the Soviet Union and which is now being reimported from the West in the form of structuralism. In this regard it is very important to consider the influence of Meyerhold on Brecht, and not only of Meyerhold but also of Vakhtangov and his "Princess Turandot," of which Brecht thought very highly, and also of the worker theater of the Blue Shirts in the 1920s. Without this improvisational theater, one could scarcely imagine either Piscator or Brecht. All of this, which came out of the revolutionary twenties, where it originated quite naturally in Russia, was reintroduced with Brecht and no one dared point out these connections.

I would like to add one comical bit of evidence to support this thesis, the history of the word *Verfremdung* (estrangement). The word *Verfremdung*, in Russian *ostranenie*, means "to make foreign" from *strano*, foreign. *Ostranenie* is then equivalent to *Verfremdung*. This word came to Brecht through his friend Sergei Tretiakov, who was a member of Russian formalist and futurist circles. This word, however, had to be retranslated into Russian in translating Brecht's theoretical writings. What was to be done? Had we written *ostranenie*, Brecht simply would have been forbidden. "Aha, you want to reestablish those false formalist theories!" So we had to translate the word differently; we chose to translate it *ochuzhdenie*, which is precisely the same thing. *Ochuzhdenie* and *ostranenie* mean the same thing; the words are synonyms. Thus *ostranenie* became *Verfremdung*, which in turn became *ochuzhdenie*; and today when one reads Russian translations of Brecht, one will never find *ostranenie*, only the other word. The other word is not considered formalist, because it is a Brechtian word and comes from the DDR and thus belongs to a democratic poet of the 1930s and 1950s and that is legitimate. We had to do this in order to recover Brecht.

It was not only the formal aspects of his plays that were so important for us and introduced the possibility of plurality into the theatrical and aesthetical environment. There was also another aspect of great import, the themes Brecht treated. I will name only some of the basic themes that were of great importance for us. "Tie on the feed bag first, then worry about morality." This is an important theme especially for the Soviet Union, where the populace has been trained for a long time (even though Marxism was distorted to arrive at this) that morality is more important than nourishment. In fact, the latter is hardly important at all and can be done away with entirely if there are special difficulties with it. Thus, when these Brechtian words echoed so clearly from the stage, it was certainly not a mere play on words. I saw *The Threepenny Opera* later in various countries, in France, for example. In my opinion the French, the well-fed French (perhaps they are not all well-fed, but in that theater they were), did not worry very much about what this sentence meant. But my fellow Russians for whom we translated this play understood it exactly as the classic (or nonclassic) Brecht wished.

Another Brechtian theme that is important, not so much for the theater or for aesthetics but for human beings in their day-to-day lives, is one of the most important ideas of our century. A quite offensive idea, it is expressed in the title of the famous play *A Man is a Man*. Indeed, Brecht discovered it only after he had written the play. It was an idea that was not often given expression in the Soviet Union. A human being can always be replaced. No human being is irreplaceable. Today one is there; tomorrow another. And again, what is important is what one does. *A Man is a Man* probes the problem of the possibility of replacing one human being with another.

I will formulate still a third theme. It is the theme so well expressed in the *Discussions among Exiles*: "All grand ideas are shipwrecked by people." I believe it to be one of the most important Brechtian themes, and it has achieved a special significance even, or perhaps particularly, in the Soviet Union.

Finally, I would like to mention one further point, namely, the necessity of understanding everything, especially the necessity of understanding society, and even more especially, the background of the society. As expressed in *Galileo*, that idea played a very significant role for the Soviet Union. I do not know whether you can really imagine that there is a nation without any statistics and without any sociology and where one knows absolutely nothing about his own country. Not only do the simple people know nothing about it, even the authorities do not know, the same authorities of whom Kurt Tucholsky once said that they organized surveillance but not records. I do not know whether the authorities in the Soviet Union really have records. I was present several times in various theaters for the presentation of *Galileo* and I know what sort of impression this dialogue made. This dialogue is important, and I ask that you do not read it as one is accustomed to reading the words of Brecht in the West.

> GALILEO: Truth is a child of the times, not of authority. . . . Why do we claim to know so much now, when we can, at last, clear away a little bit of our ignorance! I had the inconceivable good fortune to get hold of a new instrument with which one can observe a small corner of the universe a bit, not much, more closely. Use it, gentlemen.
> PHILOSOPHER: Your Highness, ladies and gentlemen, I just ask myself where that will take us. [These words were followed by thunderous applause in the Russian theater.]
> GALILEO: In my opinion we may not, as scientists, ask where the truth will lead us. [Again applause.]
> PHILOSOPHER (extremely agitated): Mr. Galileo, truth can lead us to all sorts of things! (3: 1269–70)

In the Soviet Union these sentiments have more than a superficial meaning. Every sentence of the dialogue, even every sentence in *Galileo*, is uniquely and pointedly relevant, and has remained as relevant for the Soviet Union now as it was in the 1950s and 1960s.

In closing I will allow myself the liberty of expressing a few lyrical words. As I translated Brecht into Russian, I never dreamed that I would later, let us say, ten years later, feel these poems to be my own poems. I almost feel as if Brecht, in those poems I have translated, copied and gave expression to what I feel today and to what I myself would have written. And I would like to recall for you these two short texts. The first is from the short poem "And in Your Country":

> Whoever harms no one
> Lands, in our country, beneath the wheels
> But the fortunes
> Are gained only by rascality.
>
> In order to get a lunch
> One needs the bravery

With which otherwise empires are founded.
Without looking death in the eye
No one helps a miserable person.

Whoever says an untruth is pampered
But whoever says the truth
Needs a bodyguard
But finds none. (9: 720–21)

And finally one more short text:

I've always found the name we were given false: emigrants.
That means people who move away. But we
Did not move away, independently
Choosing another country. Neither did we
Go to a country in order to remain there, perhaps forever.
Rather we fled. We are exiles, banished.
And the country which took us in should not be a home,
    but rather a place of exile.

                                    .   .   .

. . . Each of us
Who walks through the crowd with tattered shoes
Bears witness of the shame which defiles our country now.
But none of us
Will stay here.
The last word
Has not been spoken. (9: 718)

Translated by Nancy Zeller

Major Brecht Productions in the Soviet Union since 1957

HENRY GLADE

Unquestionably, Brechtian theater was one of the more important influences in the revivification of the Soviet theater during the 1960s. Brecht attracted attention because his works and his approach to staging were a refreshing change from the museumlike atmosphere of Soviet theaters in the 1950s. Acceptance of Brecht's play per se on the Soviet stage, however, was another matter altogether because of the almost unbridgeable gulf created by the basic differences in cultural and theatrical tradition. The gulf eventually was spanned after a long period of trial and error, and the process constitutes one of the most fascinating chapters in the annals of Soviet if not world theater. It is also an instructive story, for the evolution of viable models for a Soviet Brecht production may serve as a paradigm, or at least as a worthwhile lesson, on the subject of staging Brecht in any country.

The history of the reception of Brecht on postwar Soviet stages can be divided roughly into three phases. The first one, dating from the Berliner Ensemble's visit to Moscow and Leningrad in the fall of 1957, extends to late 1964. During this period Soviet directors (primarily in Moscow, Leningrad, and the former Baltic states) sought to come to terms with Brecht's theater. The second phase is dominated by Yuri Lyubimov's Brecht productions of *Szechwan* (December 1964) and *Galileo* (1966) at Moscow's Taganka Theatre. In 1967–68, new productions at the theatrical centers of the Russian Soviet republics were almost nonexistent, but there was an ever-increasing number of stagings in the non-Russian Soviet republics. The third phase coincided with the 1975–76 DDR festival in the Soviet Union and is marked by an even more radical shift of focus to the theaters of the non-Russian republics. Significantly, the one major production to date in this cycle has been Robert Sturua's Georgian *Chalk Circle* at Tbilisi's Rustaveli Theatre.

The reception of Brecht's plays in the Soviet Union reflects the cultural and political developments in the Soviet Union during the past twenty years. The Berliner Ensemble's visit to Moscow and Leningrad in 1957 coincided with a turning point in Soviet theater. In the years between 1955 and 1960 the more creative and talented directors were engaged in a struggle to overthrow the hegemony of the Moscow Art Theatre—the unquestioned, stultifying theatrical authority since the thirties. The Ensemble's visit came at an opportune time and not only made a great theatrical impact but also provided a weapon for the reformers. They realized that they could use Brecht's works as a Trojan horse in which to smuggle Meyerholdian ideas back into the Soviet theater to broaden the aesthetic range of the concept of realism by reintroducing formalistic elements (*uslovnost* in the Meyerholdian sense). This did not, however, mean the acceptance of Brecht's theater per se. Reading between the lines of some fifty critical essays dealing with the Berliner Ensemble's visit, one senses receptivity to new ideas and new models. But this receptivity is marked by a qualified enthusiasm—qualified because much of Brecht runs counter to the theatrical traditions, desires, and needs of the Russian Soviet theater.

Much of the resistance to Brecht is based on his alienation effect, as is understandable if one considers the Russian cultural and theatrical tradition. Usually the Russian theater offers its audience a highly charged emotional, if not spiritual, experience. For Brecht, however, emotion had negative associations on two levels: historically, with the frenetic hysterics and supercharged emotionalism of Nazism; and theatrically, with the declamatory style of acting prevalent during the Weimar Republic.

The differences between Brechtian theater and the Russian theatrical traditions created enormous problems for Soviet directors when they started to stage Brecht's plays. In addition, there were the usual difficulties: should directors strive to imitate the Berliner Ensemble style or create an adaptation of Brecht? And if they should choose the latter course, how far could they go without doing violence to the dominant spirit of Brecht's works?

The first notable Soviet Brecht production was mounted by Voldemar Panso, a very European type of director who had strong links with the German theatrical tradition. His staging of *Puntila* opened at the King-isepp Theatre in Tallin in 1958. Panso has the distinction of being the first director to realize the potential of a synthetic approach to Brecht—an approach that combined Brecht's text and Finnish-Estonian folklore, or, more specifically, in the words of the eminent Moscow theater critic Boris Zingerman, it combined "reality and theatricality, authentic psychological delineation and caricature, genre and buffoonery." [1]

The real test for Brecht on the Soviet stage came with Mikhail Straukh's direction of *Mother Courage* at the Mayakovsky Theatre (Moscow) in November 1960. In his first directorial assignment Straukh sovietized Brecht in a manner that was consistent with his background as a longtime Stanislavskian actor and a pupil and friend of Meyerhold and Eisenstein. Thus, Meyerholdian-Eisensteinian revolutionary pathos and Stanislavskian "inner realism" inform his directorial thrust. In the process, Straukh's production of *Mother Courage* shifted the emphasis from the historical-parabolical level to the topical, focusing on a people's broad struggle in their heroic resistance to war.

This publicistic, even propagandistic staging finally convinced a heretofore predominantly anti-Brecht cultural bureaucracy that this playwright belonged, after all, to the socialist-realist camp, as I learned from private conversations in Moscow. This staging, however, raised a number of questions for theater critics, the most fundamental of which was this: could Straukh's staging be justified if it completely ignored the epic level? It had already become apparent in 1957 that the estrangement effect irritated audiences and critics alike. Thus, Helene Weigel's distinguished acting as Mother Courage was much admired, but her use of estrangement perturbed theater goers and critics. This clash of national temperaments and of differing expectations had surfaced during the discussions between Soviet critics and Helene Weigel, Manfred Wekwerth, and the actors of the Berliner Ensemble at the Dom Akterov (13 May 1957). Alexander Anikst, an eminent Shakespearean scholar and one of the foremost Soviet critics of Western literature, forcefully stated the Soviet position:

> Earlier we ourselves went through a period in the Soviet theater in which intellect predominated. Frankly speaking, our audiences became tired of it. They desired a theater of passion, of intensity, of feeling. In this respect your theater does not seem to achieve the maximum in the reaction of the Soviet audiences, precisely because they demand an emotional theater. [2]

And an "emotional theater" is clearly what Straukh gave the Russian audience with his *Mother Courage*. At first critics praised him for his bold

Soviet approach to Brecht, but by 1965 most Soviet Brecht specialists had come to the conclusion that this production, which went counter to almost all of Brecht's principles, was flawed.[3]

If Straukh's thoroughly sovietized *Mother Courage* represented one pole, then the other was the imitation of Berliner Ensemble performances. Initially, Soviet Brecht specialists and critics praised the Berliner Ensemble type of staging, because they considered it "authentic" Brecht, but audiences were not entranced by authenticity. A good case in point is V. Dudin's staging of *The Caucasian Chalk Circle* at the Mayakovsky Theatre in 1964. Here, the epic plane was in the foreground, but stylized devices served to fragment rather than to reinforce the impact of the work. As Zingerman observed, stylization should have only one purpose: to reveal the main idea of the play. Stylization is called for when it has metaphoric significance.[4] This, Dudin's staging failed to accomplish.

The presence of metaphoric significance, the contrapuntal combination of the dramatic and epic planes form the very basis of Brecht's dramaturgy. They also make for good theater, as was demonstrated in the highly successful 1964 staging of *The Threepenny Opera* at Kaarel Ird's Vanemuine Theatre in Tartu. Tartu is a university town in Estonia, and Ird attributes the success of his austere production to his "non-philistine audience." In Leningrad, on the other hand, the reception of the same production was lukewarm and critics complained about its "dull and cold" quality.[5]

Almost all Leningrad as well as Moscow critics preferred the more bourgeois stagings of *The Threepenny Opera* in their own cities. In Moscow the director Semyon Tumanov mounted a production in 1963 at the Stanislavsky Theatre which justifiably has been dubbed a Stanislavskian operetta. The lone but formidable voice of dissent was Zingerman, who thought that "in Moscow of the sixties one cannot play *The Three-penny Opera* with the grim and bitter passion of Berlin of the late twenties. New times dictate new rhythms and moods." Furthermore, Zingerman felt that the production kept the Vakhtangov tradition "with its gravitation to colorful, riotous, optimistic theatre." Whatever one's judgment of the need for such an adaptation, there is no question that the "culinary" aspect of the play made it ipso facto a big hit in the Soviet Union as well as in Eastern Europe. Where else (at that time at least) could the audience revel in ersatz naughtiness and the lively, haunting music of Kurt Weill? In all fairness, it needs to be stated that the young, talented director could hardly be faulted for such a lighthearted, superficial interpretation. Here, as in other Soviet theaters, even if the directors are willing, they must win the cooperation of actors trained in and accustomed to the Stanislavsky system. In his statement at the Moscow Conference on Brecht in 1965, Tumanov elaborated on this problem: the actors forced him to cut monologues, to change seemingly unrealistic dialogue—in short, they resisted him all the way.

Nothing, however, can rival the collisions, conflicts, and unmitigated aggravation that the Polish director Erwin Axer experienced when he was called upon by Georgi Tovstonogov, artistic director of the Leningrad Gorky Theatre, to direct *Arturo Ui* in 1964. (Axer, of the Leon Schiller school, had already distinguished himself with an outstanding production of this play in Warsaw.) His statement to the actors of the Gorky Theatre early in rehearsal that "with your concept of realism one cannot play Brecht" is often cited. Less often one hears the actors' side of the story: "We are different people with different habits, different temperaments." E. A. Lebedev, an outstanding actor of the company, who had excelled in roles in Gorky's plays and stage adaptations of Dostoevsky's works, felt particular anguish in adjusting to the Brechtian role of Arturo Ui: "I have been brought up with the concept of 'perezhivanie' (experiencing the role), why change the principles I believe in?" Finally Axer gave in and accepted a Dostoevskian Arturo Ui. Sergei Yurski as Givola, however, adapted to the "alien" style much more rapidly and, incidentally, stole the show.[6]

While Erwin Axer was even unsuccessful in persuading the Leningrad actors to play *Arturo Ui* in cabaret style, Sergei Yutkevich (together with Mark Zakharov) mounted just such a production at the Moscow University Theater in 1964. I consider this production to be a landmark in the development of Soviet staging, although the emphasis upon action-at-any-cost and a generous sprinkling of nonsensical stage business was somewhat distracting. Still, for once the actors felt completely at ease performing in a highly stylized manner. There was an abundance of farce and buffoonery in a cabaret-style setting with a marvelous orchestra in full view of the audience. Clips from newsreels were projected on a screen to parody the action on stage.

The subtext daringly exposed a touchy subject: the cult of personality, commonly used then as a code for Stalin's legacy of fear and suppression.[7]

Thus, Arturo Ui made his entrance to military music, inspiring fear from the start. A dangerous impostor, Ui successfully camouflaged his ruthless ambitions behind a screen of bourgeois respectability. However, his motives were quite ordinary and not those of a superhero. The most strikingly innovative additions to the text were the interludes with five dancers. Four played the roles of killers who were grouped together and the fifth was a victim who tried to elude them by constantly moving.

The Soviet directors' search for a viable sovietized Brecht came to an end late in 1964 when Yuri Lyubimov's production of *Szechwan* established a model for Soviet Brecht stagings. There has been much comment, both in the Soviet Union and in the West, on Lyubimov's work.[8] I will therefore restrict my considerations here to his sovietization of Brecht's plays.

Lyubimov recast *Szechwan* into a Vakhtangovian mold, and this synthetic approach, which fuses Stanislavsky and Meyerhold, creates a unique irony and is no doubt the closest Soviet directors can get to the Brechtian estrangement effect. From the beginning Lyubimov showed a predilection for dramatic themes that deal with the conflict between the individual and society. This helped give his theater its special reputation. Thus, the evils of Soviet bureaucracy were indirectly pilloried in *Szechwan*. For example, the three gods conduct their inquiry with the arrogance, indifference, and condescension of typical Soviet bureaucrats. The songs were treated as more than lyrical digressions and retained their contrapuntal, metaphorical significance. Lyubimov, however, made concessions to the affective nature of Soviet audiences and introduced guitar players whose songs were quite mellifluous.

In one of Lyubimov's rare moments of self-analysis—occasioned by the tenth anniversary of his theater in 1974—he singled out three approaches that have characterized the repertoire of the Taganka Theater. One of them, perhaps the most important, is the contemporization of the classics: Molière, Shakespeare, Ostrovsky, Gorky, Chernychevsky—and Lyubimov includes Brecht in this category.[9]

Though *Szechwan* bore the imprint of contemporization, it is only with *Galileo* that Lyubimov took the significant step of freely contemporizing a Brecht play. From a strictly aesthetic view the *Galileo* staging can be faulted for Lyubimov's indiscriminate use of widely divergent styles and devices. Obviously he was above all else concerned with the

forceful presentation of some of the burning issues of the post-Stalinist
era. In fact, the play is a tailor-made vehicle for Lyubimov's and, in a
broader sense, the intellectual's overriding concern: the relationship of
the creative individual's freedom to the power of the authorities. Lyubimov's interpretation of the play had an electrifying impact on those who
saw it. Audiences reacted with thunderous applause to such passages as:
"Truth is the child of the times, not of authority. . . . I have had the un-
imaginably good fortune of getting hold of a new instrument. . . . Use it"
(3: 1269–70). The members of the audience became tense, listened
alertly and/or snickered at lines such as: "Unfortunate is the country
which needs heroes" (3: 1329). "Only that amount of truth is promul-
gated which we promulgate" (3: 1297). The reference to the smuggling
out of the manuscript caused a real commotion in 1966 when I first saw
the Taganka production (around the time of the Sinyavsky/Daniel arrests). It was deleted in later performances.

Lyubimov's most drastic contemporization, however, was in the end-
ing of the play. There, after the weak but sly Galileo droned a self-accusa-
tion, an alternate reading was added: Galileo suddenly straightened up,
started in again, and spoke with a youthful and powerful voice. He turned
to the audience as if to say: It is all up to you to see to it that the liberal
forces here and now win out over any attempts of the Stalinists to reas-
sert themselves. The last word, however, belonged to the Young Pioneers
who scurried across the stage spinning the globes they carry, proclaim-
ing: "*And still it moves.*" [10]

After the heyday years of 1960–67, interest in staging Brecht gradually
declined. Directors no longer considered it challenging or daring to put
on Brecht. More importantly, the Soviet theater by that time had consciously or unconsciously absorbed all the Brechtian ideas and devices it
cared to. Symptomatic of the altered status of Brecht's theater in the Soviet Union was the reception accorded the Berliner Ensemble on its second visit to Moscow and Leningrad in the fall of 1968. In contrast to
1957, the Berliner Ensemble was received by a more sophisticated audience which was not overly impressed with Brechtian stage innovations, such as those in *Coriolanus.* After all, Russians had seen equally
stirring experimentations in their own theaters in the intervening years.
Only Gisela May's evening with Brecht songs was enthusiastically
received.

The third phase of the reception of Brecht on the Soviet stages coincided with the DDR festival in the Soviet Union in 1975–76. The festival provided a powerful impetus for a new cycle of Brecht productions in the USSR. The previously noted trend of a shift of interest from the theaters in Moscow, Leningrad, and the former Baltic States to those in the non-Russian republics was drastically accelerated. To be sure, Moscow was accorded the honor of officially opening the DDR festival in November 1975 with the performance of *Galileo* by the Moscow Art Theatre. Director Vladimir Bogomolov used a new translation of the play by Yevgeny Ilmas and Yuri Riashchentsev; with its heavy Schillerean overtones it was a perfect vehicle for the glittering operatic staging by the Moscow Art Theatre, which typically put great emphasis on the historical correctness of sets and costumes. The distinguished actor and former director of the Soviet Army Theater, Alesei Popov, played Galileo, and his performance won acclaim from the DDR festival jury. Although he did manage to capture the true Brechtian spirit at times, more often than not he was overwhelmed by the excessively romantic pathos of the production.[11] A fresh and exciting new start could have been made if Lyubimov's *Turandot* (ready for performance four years earlier) had been cleared by the censors.

This is not the place to give an account of new Brecht productions throughout the USSR.[12] In short, it can be said that in this new phase a few twists and turns were added to the prevailing styles, but nothing more. There is one exception: Robert Sturua's production of *The Caucasian Chalk Circle* which opened in the fall of 1975 at the Rustaveli Theater in Tbilisi, Georgia. In an astonishingly short time this production was recognized as the most significant Soviet Brecht staging in more than a decade. On tour in Moscow in the fall of 1976 the performances elicited unstinted praise from Moscow critics, and in the spring of 1977 in Saarbrücken, Düsseldorf, and Hamburg, as well as in the summer at the annual festival in Guanajuato,[13] the Georgian troupe scored another success—all the more remarkable in view of the language barrier and the lengthy performance (three-and-a-half hours).

Robert Sturua deleted the prologue and started his *Chalk Circle* with the singer's introduction of a ballet, a tumultuous group dance, set against the sparse, abstract and stylized backdrop. Sturua added Georgian accents to his production, yet kept the parabolic character of Brecht's play intact.[14] The success of the production was due to Sturua's superb skills in synthesizing Georgian and modern Western elements with those of Brecht's theater: "Constantly ceremony is blended with the grotesque, the circus with realism, farce with lyric, a cock-and-bull tale with social discourse—all this with a humor, a liberty of invention, a true wit and tenderness quite exceptional here [in Moscow]."[15] Both composer and choreographer provided excellent support for Sturua's synthetic approach. Gia Kentsheli's score was a heady mixture of ancient church and pop music, folk music, tango and waltz with a bit of jazz and atonal melodies. Yuri Zaretski, the choreographer, in turn, combined Georgian folkloristic motives with rock-and-roll dancing.

It is important to realize that the director accomplished these things in the face of tremendous opposition. Georgian theater critics and audiences accept only one theatrical school and style: the illusory, mimetic theater, especially of the heroic-romantic and melodramatic type. To counter this monolithic tradition, Sturua "smuggled in" Brecht by adapting the play to Georgian tastes without forsaking the essence of Brecht's theater. He did this by making the *Chalk Circle* a festival production, permeated with carnival boisterousness and replete with fast-paced, colorful scenes. There were, of course, a number of questionable adaptations; for example, the Grand Duke in hiding masquerades as a woman in a conscious reference to Kerensky's flight in disguise. The Grand Duke flirts and swings his hips in a womanly walk to the great merriment of the audience. Despite such defects, Sturua's production is of epochal significance and "marks the beginning of a new state in the history of the Georgian theatre."[16]

In summary, it can be said that Soviet Brecht productions (with the exception of the Vanemuine Theater in Tartu) have been successful in direct proportion to the degree that they have been purged of Teutonic elements. Or to put it into positive terms, they have been successful in direct proportion to the degree of their effective contemporization, or, in Brecht's term, historicization. Unquestionably, the Lyubimov and Sturua productions created the most viable Brecht models to date. Lyubimov accomplished this by his successful blending of Brechtian and Russian/ Soviet elements into a synthetic whole. Even more important is his creation, largely through the medium of Brecht's work, of a poetic-political theater, through which he became a catalyst for one of the most exciting new trends in post-Stalinist theater. The lyrical component speaks to a deep-seated need of the Russian audiences, and Lyubimov's super-charged, poignant topicality has a special meaning in a society where the theater functions in considerable measure as a safe political forum. At times Lyubimov's political stabs are daringly provocative. He can get away with it by staging the classics, which are less stringently censored, and by using the camouflage of a subtext for which Brecht's laconic style is a natural ally. As Martin Esslin shrewdly observed in another context, Brecht's style "suits the conditions of a theatre in which criticism by implication rather than explicit statement has become a necessity."[17] It is too early to assess the full impact of Sturua's *Chalk Circle*. But one hopes that Sturua's concept of "total" theater can serve as a model for the 1970s and perhaps inspire other theater directors in the non-Russian Soviet republics to fashion their Brecht productions in accordance with indigenous traditions and tastes.

The lessons to be learned from the Soviet Russian experience are obvious. To be effective, Brecht's plays have to be treated as classical texts, rigorously subjected to a contemporizing process, in the manner demonstrated for Shakespeare by Jan Kott. In an incisive essay, Andrzej Wirth has already set down some fundamental principles for adapting Brecht for our contemporary world. He rightly declares that Brecht's work should be treated as a classic and be subjected to the same treatment that he himself used in dealing with the classics. Contemporization, or historicization, then, is the key word for a Brecht production, especially in a country like the Soviet Union where theatrical tradition and habits are antipodal to Brecht. To be sure, such a far-reaching adaptation requires a director at once creative, daring, and attuned to the spirit of the times: the best Soviet Brecht directors are also the most independent, creative, and daringly innovative ones. In the words of Nikolai Okhlopkov: "Brecht belongs to the avant-garde of the builders of the new world. The fruits of his art will be harvested primarily by those who do not copy him. His art demands independence and individuality of the others."[18]

Notes

1. *Soviet Life* (January 1971). All quotes from Zingerman not otherwise identified are from this source.

2. Cited from the taped proceedings of a roundtable discussion.

3. See, among others, Boris Zingerman, "Stenogramma zasedanija soveta po dramatičeskim teatram of tvorcestve B. Brexts," M. (10 March 1965): 5 (MS).

4. Ibid., p. 13.

5. See, for example, Mark Ljubomudrov, "Uroki brextovskix spektaklej," Rezhissura v puti, M. (1966): 148 (MS).

6. Mark Rexel's, "Erwin Axer i ego spektakl' 'Kar'era Arturo Ui' B. Brexta na cene Len. Gos. BDT im. A. I. Gor'kogo," (MS).

7. For substantiation of this view, see Mezhuev, "Stenogramma obsuzhdenija spektaklja 'Kare'ra Arturo Ui' postavlennogo studenticeskim teatrom MGU," M. (26 January 1965): 28–31 (MS).

8. Most recently, Ljudimilla Bazhenova analyzed Lyubimov's approach to Brecht from the vantage point of the mid-seventies, *Teatr* 4 (1976): 17–21. For a Western treatment of this topic, see Henry Glade, *The Drama Review* 12 (1967): 137–42.

9. "Algebra garmonii," *Avrora* 10 (1974): 62. A German version of this article appeared in Joachim Fiebach, *Sowjetische Regisseure über ihr Theater* (Berlin: Henssel, 1976), pp. 216–29.

10. Of interest in this connection is Lyubimov's statement in an interview by Margaret Croyden: "There is a poem in Pasternak. It goes something like this: 'I strain to make the far-off echo yield a cue to the events that may come in my day.' This quotation, from the 'Hamlet' poem in Pasternak would apply to the classic plays that I am doing." *New York Times*, 31 October 1976.

11. It should be noted that this staging was sharply criticized by participants of a theater conference at Moscow State University, December 1975, for "its insufficient grasp of Brecht's aesthetics," see A. A. Fedorov, "Zametki o teatral'noj konferencii na filologičeskom fakul'tete," *Vestnik moskovskogo universiteta: Filologija* 3 (1976): 91.

12. For a report on this, see Vladimir Scexovcev, "Klassik, Brecht und Gegenwart," *Sowjetliteratur* 6 (1976): 186–87; V. Klujev, "Odno iz zven'ev. Festival' dram. iskusstva GDR v SSSR," *Teatr. Zhizn'* 5 (1976): 6–8; Henry Glade, "DDR-Dramatik in der Sowjetunion," *Die literarische Tat*, 7 November 1975, pp. 26–27.

13. See the enthusiastic appraisal by Michal Coveney, "Festival in Guanajuato," *Plays and Players* 24 (July 1977), 38–39. For remarks about the Edinburgh Festival in August 1979, see Christian Ferber, "Echte Kaukasier am Kreidekreis," *Die Welt*, 27 August 1979.

14. Lev Kopelev provides some telling details: "The singer (narrator), Arkadi Tscheidse, characterized by Brecht as a Georgian, appears on the Georgian stage as an explicitly western and timeless (and anonymous) figure. . . .The sets and costumes (by Georgi Messchischwili) are just as indefinite in time and place, in part abstract." *Theater heute*, 4 April 1976, p. 40.

15. Nicole Zand, *Le Monde*, 8 April 1976.

16. My analysis is based in large part on the authoritative assessment of the production by the eminent Georgian Germanist Nodar Kakabadze, "'The Cauca-

sian Chalk Circle.' 'Don't Ogle So Romantically' (Brecht), or the Rustaveli Theatre's Staging of Bert Brecht's 'The Caucasian Chalk Circle,'" *Tsiskari* (in Georgian) 11 (1976): 122–33, cited p. 133.

17. Review of Michael Hamburger, "Art as Second Nature: Occasional Pieces 1950–74," *Times Literary Supplement*, 25 June 1976.

18. Jan Kott, *Shakespeare, Our Contemporary*, trans. Boleslav Taborski (Garden City, N.Y.: Doubleday, 1964). Andrzej Wirth, "Brecht in Polen," *Akzente* 12 (1965): 394–403. Nikolai Okhlopkov quoted in John Willett, *Das Theater Bertolt Brechts* (Hamburg: Rowohlt, 1964), p. 236.

Ironic Tension and Production Techniques:
The Measures Taken

IAN MCLACHLAN

How are we to establish the relevance of a revolutionary play for a non-revolutionary audience? This is the basic question that a theater group involved in the production of a Brecht play in most parts of North America must attempt to answer. It is an obvious question, of course, but one that seems increasingly to be avoided in the apolitical contexts of commercial theater where Brecht is daily in danger of becoming a classic like any other.

The question is probably most acutely posed by Brecht's learning plays and, in particular, by *The Measures Taken*. The gap between the play and the audience—if indeed the play may be thought of as assuming an audience at all—seems unbridgeable. Surely, it will only antagonize, widening the distance between us, its exponents, and those with whom we seek to communicate.

Given the difficulties, it is tempting to take refuge in one of two possible excuses. Either we can go back to the early Marxist critics of the play who saw in it the imposition of theory upon an inadequately conceived practice:

> The author of *Die Massnahme* [*The Measures Taken*], Bert Brecht, must be told that knowledge of the theories of Marxism-Leninism is not enough, that the genius and wide reading of a writer cannot take the place of revolutionary experience and detailed day-to-day work in the movement.[1]

Or, alternatively, we may construct a model for the play, based on Steinweg's assiduous archaeology, which effectively renders it impossible, freezing its actuality in an unrealized history.[2] Then we can confine it to the theater schools not as a learning experience for young people but as the academic statement of an extreme from which the later Brecht withdrew.

But does not the meaning of the play—its refusal to lie down and die beneath our scholarly strictures—in fact exist in the space between those two assumptions? I suggest that the importance of the play results from the way in which it locates itself precisely at the point where theory and practice overlap yet refuse to become identical. It is thus central to our predicament as intellectuals in a world that will not respond adequately to our provocations. Its meaning derives, in a very real way, from the problems we encounter in trying to communicate our understanding of its meaning within a continually changing set of social circumstances.

As I say that, it is apparent how wholly I am at odds with Steinweg's elaborate reconstruction of what he takes to be the two fundamental rules that underpinned Brecht's theories of the didactic play. The *Basisregel* (basic-rule), he argues, rests on the assumption that the play can be meaningful only for its participants.[3] Thus, Brecht insisted that, though spectators might be tolerated, only the chorus and the actors could benefit fully from the learning process that the performance must constitute. At the same time, to prevent the participants from falling into the error of empathy, the performance also had to comply with the *Realisationsregel* (performance-rule) in its requirement that the play must be a demonstration of typical behavioral patterns rather than the definition of a decisive series of events in an individual life.[4]

The effect of both of these rules is to establish the play as an abstraction beyond the demands of changing theatrical or political contexts. They do this not arbitrarily or because of any internal inconsistency in their supporting arguments—on the contrary, those arguments seem to be sustained with impeccable consistency—but because they are founded on two presuppositions about literature which are dangerously misleading. The first is that an artist's intentions in a given work of art may be substantiated sufficiently on a conscious level for the meaning of that work to be defined adequately in terms of those intentions. And the second is that the forms of a work of art be described with such a degree of precision that the dynamics of its meaning may be determined ideally once and for all so as to enable us to categorize future interpretations of it as correct or incorrect.

These assumptions are clearly contrary to the whole nature of the theatrical experience as a focus of social change. If they were true, one might as well give up the precarious business of establishing the forms within which social and political realities might react upon each other in such a way as to promote the possibility of further change. But beyond that, and more specific to my topic, they are assumptions that contradict the essential dynamics of a play like *The Measures Taken*, so simple and solid and unchanging on the surface and yet so full of conflict and emerging ironic tension beneath that surface.

When our theater group set out to discover the relevance of the play to a small-town audience in Canada, it was that ironic tension that seemed to offer itself to us as a medium. The word *irony*, however, is insecure. By it I do not mean the kind of irony we find in Joyce or Pound, where Stephen Dedalus or Hugh Selwyn Mauberley become personae that enable the writer to detach himself from his personality in much the same way as a snake sloughs off its old skin. On the contrary, what I am implying is the kind of irony that enables the writer to probe beneath the assured surface of his accepted values; irony as exploration rather than evasion, a working out of the contradictions that define the potentials of personality rather than its limitations.

Let me try to describe that in terms of our production in Peterborough, Ontario. The most pressing problem in establishing the relevance of the play to a North American audience was to overcome a sense of the alienness of theme and language. There was a danger of the play being written off simply as "propaganda," and we were conscious that this had already happened with recent productions in Europe. It was clear that somehow we would have to contextualize the play in such a way that a bridge would be constructed between its past and our present. After considerable discussion we decided to focus on the play through the medium of an event that has achieved a symbolic and largely unquestioned significance in the history of the Left in North America—the hearings of the House Un-American Activities Committee. Our production began with a reconstruction based on the transcript of Brecht's own hearing presented in a documentary style.[5] The audience was drawn in; it was able to identify with the underdog and to make facile fun of the apes attempting to cross-examine the zoologist.

But at the point where Stripling, the counsel for the committee, began to quote from *The Measures Taken* with the intention of unmasking Brecht, the actors moved from a naturalistic to an epic style of acting, assuming the roles of the characters in the play. Thus, Parnell Thomas, the chairman of the committee, became the (one-man) Control Chorus,

Stripling became one of the agitators, and Brecht's lawyer took the part of the agitator who in turn took the part of the Young Comrade. Brecht himself, played by a worker from the local General Electric factory, moved from a state of alienated isolation to one of control, directing the play.

To establish another level of actuality, slides were projected on two screens with a wide range of alternating emphatic and ironic effects. During "The Blotting Out," for instance, we used, among others, many images from our own preparations—discussions, the making of the masks that were to be worn in that scene, rehearsals, and so on—and during the episode between the Young Comrade and the Rice Trader we projected slides of Mao Tsetung meeting Nixon or Trudeau.

At the end of *The Measures Taken*, the audience was returned again to the final minutes of the hearing, with its point of view changed. A wedge had been driven into its liberalism. Its sentimental identification with the victim of intolerance had been exposed to the pressure of a more radical series of political and moral dichotomies.

What we were looking for, I would insist, was not just a new, essentially arbitrary way of doing the play. On the contrary, we found ourselves increasingly involved in exploring and extending its methods and implications.

On the technical level, the movement of our actors from the hearing to the play added a further dimension to the role playing, the masks, the recession of identity in the play itself. This was particularly relevant to the crucial and continuing critical debate with regard to the question of empathy with or estrangement from the Young Comrade. It is evident that any adequate interpretation of the play cannot resolve the central theme into any single, clearcut opposition. It is not simply about the conflict between rigid and sterile ideology and heroic individualism, but neither can it any more accurately be said just to portray the conflict between an all-seeing and all-caring party and the overreactions of one of its misguided members. The explicit intellectual direction of the play as voiced by the Control Chorus may be centered primarily on the second of these two possible statements, but the emotional impetus of the play is closer to the first. Neither is true on its own because each, though it contradicts, also complements the other. That is what I mean by the irony of the play and why I would suggest that a monolithic ideological performance is as likely to distort it as a sentimental tragic one. Both potentials are present and in a state of painful tension that focuses most strongly at the point when the Young Comrade rips off his mask. There is no doubt that, whatever the Control Chorus must say, this is a moment of great emotional impact, fearful yet euphoric, and any production that seeks to lessen that force is bound to diminish the play. But the meaning of the play obviously cannot be left at that. It is not, after all—or at least, not only—a play about existential liberation, and the authenticity of the individual act has to be set in the countervailing context of the secular liturgy of sacrifice and self-sacrifice which succeeds it.

These are the tensions that keep the play alive and out of the museum. They center our imaginations with great intensity on the oppositions that may emerge between theory and practice and on the agony that is potentially present in the gap between. If that conflict is the theme of the play, it is also its style, and once we formulate it in those terms it is apparent why it is necessary to think of *The Measures Taken* as projecting forward to the recurrent antitheses at the core of *Szechwan* or *Galileo*, instead of allowing it to be dismissed as an excursion up the blind alleys of formalism or dogmatism.

It was to define and clarify this central conflict that we provided the further contexts we felt necessary for the audience to be able to respond in terms of its own experience. What it saw was a theatrical performance that portrayed two kinds of trial, two individuals in a moment of trial. One, the Young Comrade, acted in a spirit of self-sacrifice; the other, Brecht, in a spirit of survival. As a result of the dichotomy between these alternate responses, a whole series of tensions that are concentrated in the play were exposed—between the emotional and political necessities, between identification and estrangement, between liturgy and dialectic—and the roots of those tensions in Brecht's own personality were established. The point of the ironic interaction was to leave the audience not with a blurred confusion of subjective impulses but rather with a sense of arguments and conflicts that must be pursued both inside and outside the theater.

Notes

1. In *Die Rote Fahne*, cited by Martin Esslin, *Brecht: The Man and His Work* (Garden City, N.Y.: Anchor, 1971), p. 163.

2. Reiner Steinweg, *Das Lehrstück, Brechts Theorie einer politisch-ästhetischen Erziehung* (Stuttgart: Metzler, 1972).

3. Ibid., p. 87.

4. Ibid., p. 152.

5. *Hearings Regarding the Communist Infiltration of the Motion Picture Industry* (Washington: HUAC, 1947), pp. 491–504. The transcript is also included in Eric Bentley, *Thirty Years of Treason* (New York: Viking, 1971), pp. 207–24.

Political Climate and Experimental Staging: *The Decline of the Egoist Johann Fatzer*

WOLFGANG STORCH

The world premiere of the *Fatzer* fragment took place at the Schaubühne am Halleschen Ufer in Berlin on 11 March 1976. It was directed by Frank P. Steckel, and I participated in the production as dramaturge. In early December 1975 rehearsals for Elsa Lasker-Schüler's *In Wuppertal* had to be postponed for two months and a replacement had to be found: two pieces, the *Fatzer* fragment and Heiner Müller's *Philoktet*, were considered. In preparation for the discussion of the plays, Steckel and I distilled a version of *Fatzer* for the stage from the some 250 pages of Brecht's typescript. Steckel restricted the selection to Brecht's dialogues, excluding portions that had only been sketched. Our version was accepted for production at the Schaubühne on 15 December, and rehearsals began immediately. We felt that the preparatory phase, which may extend over several years at the Schaubühne, could be accelerated for Brecht, especially since his works from around 1930 were familiar after the productions of *The Mother* and *The Exception and the Rule*. The fragmentary character of *Fatzer* seemed to demand that we rehearse immediately, without first poring over texts for a long time.

What had we expected? The material defied Brecht's efforts to mold it into drama in the frame of his political intentions. That was important to us against the background of the ongoing debate concerning the function of the Communist party, and of the discussion about Brecht in particular, because interest in his work has been divided between the early plays and the learning plays. The *Fatzer* fragment, however, encompasses both phases. The reception of the production did not reflect our concerns. Our staging provoked little discussion either of politics or of Brecht. Reviewers concentrated on philology, which was not our concern. In short, according to Peter Iden, "The revitalization necessary for Brecht to work is not furthered by this evening" (*Die Zeit*, 12 March 1976).

During the late 1920s, Brecht was one of the writers attempting to come to terms with the years 1917–19, with the failure of the revolution, in order to clarify for themselves the development of a state under the Weimar Constitution and His Imperial Majesty's Field Marshal Hindenburg. As the economy became more and more overheated, one question predominated: "What is ahead?"

In this climate Brecht used history-play dramaturgy for *Fatzer*: in the biography of one man, experiences are linked which are to be examined in contemporary context. Brecht began work on *Fatzer* in autumn 1927. A year later, again in autumn, he attempted to work the hastily written dialogues and sketched-out scenes into a play. Unable to mold the material as a historical play, he turned in 1929 to the dramaturgy of the learning plays. Reflections about the decisions made ten years earlier were no longer sufficient in the face of economic collapse. The forces against reaction and apathy had to be mobilized.

In the historical play, Fatzer is conceived as someone who advocates change, an aspect that fascinated us in our work on the stage version. Here was a person who will not and cannot let loose, a person who sees an opening, and, if his path is blocked, resorts to terror. When another character, Büsching, complains, rages, or does not know where to turn, Fatzer clearly comprehends the situation and thus has Büsching in the palm of his hand. Fatzer is pushed forward by the blindness of the others. Although he needs the group in order to survive, he can survive only by leaving the others behind. The others, Koch, Kaumann, Büsching, are not individuals but objects for Fatzer.

These alterations in the play reflect the growing crisis of power struggle in the international Communist party in the 1920s. Whom does the Party support, when and why? Is power knowledge or vice versa? The reorganization of the Fatzer material into a learning play transforms Fatzer into an enemy figure. A chorus and an antichorus appear to judge him because he thinks only of himself. Ideology is produced; it seeks its victim. The chorus empowers Koch, now called Keuner, to liquidate Fatzer. Koch, the *enforcer*, takes over leadership against the deviationist.

The kinds of conflicts Brecht observed in the Party were paralleled in his professional life. The problem of always being the best in the collective, only using the collective, was Brecht's problem, too. These are character traits that German history has promoted. The point is that Fatzer is not an anarchist but an egoist. The positive capacity for claiming autonomy, as it is carried to an extreme, becomes a negative force for dictating the actions of others. Thus, only Fatzer survives, and he is the only one who finds himself, because the others are weaker and he puts them under pressure.

If Fatzer is always more knowledgeable than the others, how can the Party uphold its traditional stance on the wisdom of the collective above the individual? The play demonstrates that a party which proceeds as the chorus does will perish, as the Party did in those years. How can a party that gives teachings heed teachings, or even take note of them? A party with a hierarchical structure which attempts to gain strength by assimilating the army of the unemployed, but fails to extend power to the collective, has lost the struggle. In the sentencing and liquidation of Fatzer, the very core of Fatzer's character is celebrated with somber excess: the fear of anarchy.

Rehearsals on the production with seven actors on the periphery of major undertakings of the Schaubühne proceeded without interruptions, without a pause to catch one's breath, from mid-December until early March. Wolf Redl, who had been working with the director Steckel for over twelve years, played the lead role. He is an actor who returns a physical and artistic ponderousness to the art of acting, a very German kind of obstructionism, but also a paternal nurturing quality questioning the world and submerging self. Günther Lampe played Koch. He is radically different from Redl, constantly in search of new experiences and new landscapes, a wanderer seeking sheltered security. These are two actors who both work very privately, but in different ways, and who do not externalize private experience. They were confronted with a text that, more than almost any other of Brecht's, seems to expose the author, precisely in its vehement denial of the private and demand for a histrionic portrayal, a masklike quality.

The perfection of "Schaubühne style," as it had developed over five years, culminating in the extremely successful production of Gorky's *Summer Guests*, was an antihistrionic tendency. Thus, a return to experimentation with a rough, unfinished Brecht text promised to be useful. But it did not work. For those who had savored the incisive reading by Steckel in December and had not followed the rehearsals, the result was startling. Brecht had been treated as if he were his own opposite, one who limits himself, an Ibsen.

The performance derived its thrust from the acting of Otto Mächtlinger as Büsching and Klaus Theo Gärtner as Kaumann. These are roles that Brecht barely fleshed out. His sketches enabled the actors to develop distinct characters, just as Angela Winkler (Therese), Ilse Ritter (Fanny), and Gerd David (the soldier) could. They simply did not have enough text, enough material. The fragmentary quality, which was supposed to spark the actors' work, was completely extinguished during the rehearsals. Regrettably, the fragment was now welcome only because it prevented an unwelcome probing into unanswered questions. The actors presented a museum-piece, an exercise in theatrical philology, rather than exploring the fragment with their audience.

As such a museum-piece, the performance was generally well received, and yet we were disappointed in that we had failed to make the play relevant for the Federal Republic today. A positive aspect of political activity during the last eight years in the Federal Republic has been the work of individual groups, such as women's groups, political basis groups, or even those that founded day-care centers. Such group work is difficult in the Federal Republic.

It is precisely the difficulties groups have experienced in the last eight years which could serve as a focus for future productions. Brecht does present a group—not a collective, but rather a forum for Fatzer. New work on the fragment could expose the structures that determine both Fatzer and the action against him. Fatzer and Koch function as a Janus-head. The reaction against Fatzer is structured the same way as Fatzer's provocation. The extreme egoism of Fatzer also parallels the position of the chorus. His egoism results from a fear of anarchy, which drives him to negation of self in confrontation with order. What saves him, temporarily, is the struggle with his friends, whom he finally destroys.

In this particular example, the figures in the drama neither realize democracy nor achieve an awareness of self which would make a collective possible. By demonstrating the behavioral characteristics of Brecht's figures, the macho stance, the "phallocracy" which destroy relationships within the group and hinder progress, one can show how things are treated instrumentally rather than productively. A new production could present a thinking that is directed toward a totality versus a fear of ruin promoted by authoritarianism and typically masculine forms of behavior.

Editor's note: *This discussion of the dramaturgical intentions and accomplishments at the Schaubühne can be understood more fully if one compares it to the program notes compiled by Wolfgang Storch for the premiere. These are excerpted below.*

THE DOWNFALL OF THE "EGOIST" FATZER
[NOTE BY BERTOLT BRECHT]

In Mülheim on the Ruhr during the First World War, a time stripped of all morality, an incident took place involving four men, which ended with the complete downfall of all four, but which revealed the bloody traces of a new kind of morality in the midst of murder, adultery and degeneracy. In the third year of the war, four men, the crew of a tank, disappeared during a tank attack near Verdun and were listed as dead. In early 1918 they settled in Mülheim and kept out of sight; one of them had a room in a basement. Living from then on under the constant threat of being captured and shot as deserters, they had a difficult time making a living, especially since there were four of them. Nevertheless, they decided not to separate under any conditions, since their only hope was that a general revolt of the people would end the senseless war and legitimize their desertion. As a foursome they hoped to participate in the revolt they were waiting for. For two weeks they looked night after night for a possibility of getting rations, and only towards the end of the second week did the most alert of them, "Johann Fatzer," make the acquaintance of a train soldier who promised as a good comrade to provide them with rations from a commissary train. It was Fatzer who had advised them to desert and who had led them home by way of French prisoner-of-war camps, or at least close to home (their home towns were Liegnitz, Passau and Berlin). On the following night the foursome, led by Fatzer, was supposed to appear at the freight yard. But, although they had discussed everything thoroughly, this undertaking, on which everything depended, fell through because Fatzer did not arrive on time. Called to account, he made excuses, and when they pressed him, he refused to respond and remarked that he did not owe them any answer since he was a free man. He promised, however, to come the next evening, the last possible opportunity, because the train was to leave the following day. But Fatzer was not there on that evening either. (BBA, 108: 8)

BACKGROUND TO THE PLAY BY WOLFGANG STORCH

Brecht wrote to Helene Weigel from Augsburg in late July or early August 1927: "I'm working on Fatzer, very slowly, but it's coming along. . . . If I don't really get stuck in Fatzer, I'll be there for your last rehearsals." A year later, September or October 1928, he wrote to Helene Weigel from Kochel: "It's boring here to the point of despair, and so much work!! This Fatzer is a tough nut. I'm still tinkering around with the frame." In a press notice in 1929, Erwin Piscator stated that he was interested in the play. In 1930 a news item stated that Brecht was working on two plays, *Nothing Comes from Nothing* and *Johannes Fatzer*. In the first issue of the *Versuche* in 1930, Brecht published three scenes under the title *Fatzer, 3*—the third group of scenes—and a poem "Come, Fatzer."

Fatzer is a continuation of the early plays. *A Man is a Man* premiered in 1926. Brecht apparently broke off work on *Fatzer* in the early summer of 1930, while he was writing *The Measures Taken*. During these years he was occupied with plays that have a thematic affinity to *Fatzer*. He collaborated with Erwin Piscator on the dramatization of *Schweik*. It premiered on 23 January 1928. Ten years after the October Revolution, he discussed the possibilities of adaptation of *Drums in the Night* with Piscator. In the spring of 1929 he revised and staged *Pioneers in Ingolstadt* by Marieluise Fleisser, which premiered 30 March 1929.

There was general concern with World War I and its aftermath, the November Revolution and the Munich Republic of Workers Councils: memoirs and novels by Ernst Glaeser, Oskar Maria Graf, Max Hoelz, Ernst Jünger, Erich Maria Remarque, Ludwig Renn, Adam Scharrer, Ludwig Turek, Arnold Zweig, and others were published in these years. Brecht's other plays and projects from these years include: *The Threepenny Opera*, *Happy End*, *Rise and Fall of the City of Mahagonny*, and the fragments, *Daniel Drew*, *Joe Fleischhacker*, *Nothing Comes from Nothing*, and *The Bakery*. The early learning plays, *The Flight of the Lindberghs* and *The Baden Learning Play of Consent*, premiered in July 1929.

While working on *The Life of Galileo* in 1939, Brecht declared: "One should first examine the two fragments, *Fatzer* and *The Bakery*. Both these fragments exhibit the highest standard in technique" (*Work Journal*, p. 41). The *Fatzer* material encompasses well over five hundred pages. That Brecht did not finish his work on it is due to the fact that he abandoned his original dramaturgy and tried to apply the dramaturgy of the learning plays.

When Brecht was trying to come to terms with Hans Garbe, the "wage shark," and was developing a concept for *Büsching*, he referred to *Fatzer* in his *Work Journal*:

> Garbe told us the story of his life in three sessions, and now I have the notes in front of me. It would be a type of history play, i.e., it would not proceed from any basic idea. The Fatzer verse would be a possibility; I have taken volume 1 of the *Versuche* along. (*Work Journal*, p. 958)

And a day later: "What I have in mind, formally, is: a fragment in big, rough blocks" (*Work Journal*, p. 960). The reference to the "Fatzer verse" is noteworthy: it appears as the suitable means for making direct speech rhythmic and thus preserves its spontaneous character. But why use fragment dramaturgy?

> Taken from the material, a line: this worker undertakes to examine, while he is producing, everything that changes for him and around him when he, no longer the object of history, becomes its subject—under the condition that this is not a purely personal process, since, after all, it concerns his class. (*Work Journal*, p. 959)

The dramaturgy was obviously aiming for those moments when the subject tests his strength and brings about change. A dramaturgy free of a "basic idea," free of moralism, intended to trace the actions of a subject against prevailing norms— this was probably the basis for the initial work on *Fatzer*.

In 1929 Brecht experimented with the dramaturgy of the learning plays: "I, the writer, do not have to finish anything; it is enough that I learned. I merely do the experiment and it is my method in doing this which the spectator can examine" (BBA, 520: 7). The unity of "learning" and "doing the experiment" is not provided: the examination has been completed so far as he is concerned and the case is relegated to the category of morality. Fatzer becomes a parasite. A chorus and an antichorus appear to establish Fatzer's "deviations." Now one reads:

> Their odyssey begins with their misconception, caused by the individualist Fatzer, that they could stop the war as individuals. Thus, when they abandon the masses in order to live, they have already lost their lives; they never find their way back to the masses. (BBA, 827: 10)

The chorus chooses Koch and appoints him "administrator of liquidation." The new dramaturgy diminishes the alleged trust in the subject.

The plot was at first set in the spring of 1917; then it shifted to the turn of the year 1917/1918. Brecht, however, also considered setting it in the postwar period during the occupation of the Ruhr.

There is, to be sure, another consideration that prevented Brecht from completing the work: what he called the "fear center of the play" (BBA, 821: 30), Fatzer's seduction of Therese Kaumann with the ensuing consequences for the men. With this focus he had a "sex play" (BBA, 816: 17). The woman's emancipation is demanded, but is not realized.

The first version from 1927 is contained in the notebooks 818 and 821–823 [BBA]. Of fourteen planned scenes, eleven are written out, though mostly only in a rough draft. Our adaptation is based on this material. The attempted revision of 1929 can be studied in notebooks 820, 826, 827, and 323, but above all in portfolios 109–12 and 520 [BBA]. We have used the material from the revision to the extent that it did not violate the original gestus of the play by a superimposed moral.

Translated by Mark Ritter

Part Three
alteration *of* aesthetic values

Wuolijoki's and Brecht's Politization
of the *Volksstück*

MARGARETA N. DESCHNER

The work done thus far on Brecht's collaboration with the Estonian-born Finnish playwright Hella Wuolijoki on *Master Puntila and his Servant Matti* has been concerned mainly with establishing the extent of Wuolijoki's share in the German version.[1] Though the following remarks build upon research into the development of the text,[2] this paper is concerned primarily with posing the other side of the question: what happened to Wuolijoki, the author, and to her Puntila play under Brecht's influence? The investigation is of interest in the specific case of Wuolijoki but beyond that contributes to the larger study of the Brechtian influence at work on an already established author.

A summary of the aspects of Wuolijoki's life and work that illumine her collaboration, feuds, and yet lasting friendship with Brecht seems an appropriate point of departure. She was born in 1886 as Hella Murrik in Estonia, where Germans were hated as the oppressing "Baltic barons" and Russians were resented for their pan-Slavism. Hella demonstrated her qualities as a born fighter and schemer when, still a high school student, she led the struggle for the use of the Estonian language in the school system. Later, she managed to outwit the St. Petersburg bureaucracy and gain unprecedented permission to study in Finland. The General Strike of 1905 drew her into active participation in a variety of Finnish socialist causes and shifted her primary commitment from a militant cultural nationalism toward an idealistic Marxist cosmopolitanism. Her marriage to Suol Wuolijoki, a leading Social Democratic member of the parliament, thrust her into the midst of the bitter confrontation between nationalist "Whites" and socially radical "Reds" toward the end of Finland's struggle for independence in 1917. Through her marriage into the old Wuolijoki family from the province of Häme (Tavastland), she also found a new landscape, peasantry, and language to replace her beloved Viljandinmaa in Estonia. The prosperous, stubborn, and self-respecting Häme peasants provided her later with many of her internationally known dramatic characters, including Puntila. Her vision of Puntila influenced Brecht even as he was reshaping the landowner according to his own image of a master.

Wuolijoki's first period of political activity had brought her into intimate contact with leading Russian revolutionaries and "prison intellectuals." In the twenties Wuolijoki became known as a dramatist, but also as a remarkably successful businesswoman. The thirties established her as the leading Finnish playwright. Her reputation rested on plays about resourceful Finnish peasants who, in spite of a harsh history, had never experienced serfdom and who never believed in anyone but themselves. Wuolijoki could accept the necessity of weakening her social criticism in her plays since she finally had gained access to Finnish stages, but perhaps also because her life had constantly been torn between people, ideas, and loyalties that she attempted in vain to reconcile.

Wuolijoki's great moment came, however, in February 1939 when she suddenly found herself playing "an important role as secret go-between in the Soviet-Finnish peace negotiations." Those traits of hers which must have fascinated and frustrated Brecht so deeply can be seen in Max Jakobson's account of the clandestine meetings between Wuolijoki and her old Bolshevik friend Alexandra Kollontay, the Soviet ambassador to Sweden.

> Their way of conducting business was, by the standards of professional diplomacy, horrifyingly unconventional and haphazard: they kept no records; they freely spiced their reports with personal comments; they drew upon their vivid imagination to embellish, and improve upon, their official instructions; in short, they acted like two matchmakers determined to lead, or, if need be, mislead, a reluctant and suspicious couple into matrimony. But in the end they succeeded where orthodox diplomacy had failed: they got Finnish-Soviet peace negotiations started.[3]

According to Wuolijoki's daughter, it is quite likely that this heady political success only confirmed Wuolijoki's romantic-idealistic notions of Marxism and her own role as a mediator in Finland. During the "Continuation War" between Finland and Russia (1941–45) she was imprisoned and accused of harboring a Russian spy. After the armistice she was a director of the Finnish National Radio and an SKDL (ultra-leftist party) member of parliament. She died in 1954.[4]

Her collaboration with Brecht began during the summer of 1940 while he spent his Finnish exile as a guest on her estate, Marlebäck. They decided to do a joint revision of her work on the Puntila material and enter it in a Finnish drama competition (a goal that was not reached). Wuolijoki, in dictating a German translation of her play and film script to Margarete Steffin, already included some revisions based on her discussions with Brecht. He then revised this text in approximately four weeks. Later, in exile in America, Brecht continued to revise his copy of the text, and he directed its world premiere in Zurich in 1948. In the playbill he was listed as the author and she as the source for material. Wuolijoki meanwhile published her lightly revised Finnish translation of the common text in 1946 under the title *Iso-Heikkilän isäntä ja hänen renkinsä Kalle* [*The landowner Iso-Heikkilä and his servant Kalle*], with both writers, as contractually agreed, listed as coauthors.[5] A comparison of Wuolijoki's original works on the Puntila theme with the "post-Brechtian" version, *Iso-Heikkilä*, reveals the weakening of strong characters. Both authors were interested in developing a new *Volksstück*, and in this endeavor Wuolijoki's contribution to *Puntila* was more substantial than Brecht recognized.

From Actual Event to Short Story

The Puntila material is based on an event that occurred in the twenties: Wuolijoki's birthday celebration and her uncle Roope's remarkable nocturnal escapade in breaking down the garage door and driving seventeen kilometers into the Finnish summer night to swindle "legal alcohol" from the village druggist. Upon his return, Wuolijoki introduced her uncle to her English banker guests as a "Finnish Bacchus."[6] Sometime during the thirties she wrote a short story (still unpublished) entitled "A Finnish Bacchus" with Uncle Roope, renamed Johannes Punttila, provoked by a formidable Aunt Hanna. Auctorial additions also include political discussion as the tipsy Punttila fraternizes in the kitchen with the servants, expounding his good will toward Communists, Socialists, and Conservatives, and even lamenting past political divisions. These allusions to the Finnish political situation of the thirties are still a part of Brecht's play.

Finland had been a grand duchy under Russia from 1809 until the declaration of Finnish independence in 1917. The War of Independence quickly developed into a bitter civil war between the more nationalistic White Guards and the Red Guards who wished to continue the kind of revolution that was then under way in Russia. Although the Whites had won and established Finland as an independent nation, bitter feeling persisted and was a dominant factor in political life in the thirties. Punttila, in his cups, attempts to transcend it.

This Punttila, in the short story, is unambiguously jolly, witty, drunken. He is not yet a stingy, slave-driving capitalist, but an ex-peasant who by his own labor has added a wealthy estate to the sawmill he received through marriage. He glories in the memory of his youthful strength when he could wrestle down a bull, sow his fields, fool around with the kitchen maids to his heart's content, in short be a peasant among peasants. In his new estate, Punttila feels somehow "fallen," a henpecked landowner whose lifestyle is dictated by several women and whose peasant impulses have become unrespectable. Only Wuolijoki's mouthpiece understands him and asks, "Can't you let him be himself, at least when he's drunk?"

From "Pre-Brecht" to "Post-Brecht" Plays

Sometime in the thirties, Wuolijoki expanded this material into a three-act play, *Sahanpuruprinsessa* (sawdust princess), and into a film script. These versions, inspired by Wuolijoki's widely known intention to create a new Finnish *Volksstück*, focus upon peasant milieu versus "fine" urban world, upon strong characters (especially strong women), and upon abundant humor and social satire. Five important alterations in characters demonstrate the major differences between the pre- and post-Brechtian material.

PUNTILA

The polarization in the character of Puntila is, in the *Sawdust Princess*, still that between peasant and landowner and is basically a nonideological contrast. Puntila's night journey is told only in flashbacks with the aid of a gas-station attendant who helped him court his brides-to-be. The brides, all five of them, are engaged as "legally" as his liquor is obtained, and the engagements are solemnized, each with a curtain ring and a gulp of schnapps. So Puntila the peasant gets what he wants, and on his return vents his feelings about universal brotherhood, disdain for money, and reconciled political differences, all in keeping with "The Finnish Bacchus."

Puntila as a sober landowner is no hard-boiled capitalist. Even his friends, the village dignitaries, are no conceited representatives of the bourgeoisie as later in *Iso-Heikkilä*. The natural sense of community and good humor of a Finnish rural village are still intact. The friends side with the country brides who wish to revenge themselves for Puntila's nightly escapades. All want to teach him that rich landowners cannot play around with self-respecting country women, nor simply retreat behind the alibi "I was drunk," when caught in mischief. In short, they force Puntila to accept responsibility for his actions.

Iso-Heikkilä (as Puntila is called in Wuolijoki's Finnish revision of the jointly authored Puntila draft) is a split character: a large-hearted liberal when drunk, dreaming of reconciliation between the classes, and when sober a tough and selfish capitalist oppressor. Under Brecht's tutelage Wuolijoki has made him a figure like Shen Te / Shui Ta, and his very existence poses the question: who can afford goodness in a capitalist society, and how? The intoxicated Iso-Heikkilä, however happy and charming, is not a man recovering his original humanity but a sentimental weakling with a guilty conscience. One observation suffices as proof: when drunk he refuses to sign a contract—the sober capitalist attends to money matters.

AUNT HANNA

Strong women antagonists are familiar figures in Wuolijoki's plays of the twenties and thirties, such as *Juurakon Hulda* or the *Niskavuori* cycle. In the *Sawdust Princess* Aunt Hanna is clearly such a woman: a sour spinster and self-appointed moral guardian, but also a very shrewd woman who is quite capable of outwitting the men. She is eliminated in Brecht's revision (and in *Iso-Heikkilä*).

THE BRIDES

Wuolijoki's brides in the *Sawdust Princess* are vital characters: the omniscient Telephone-Manta, a class-conscious member of the Workers Union who threatens to call the staff of *Kansan Voima*, a communist-oriented newspaper, about the scandalous treatment of working women; Smuggler-Emma, who knows her indispensable role as the village boot-legger; the modest Cow-Liisu, whose ambition to get to dairy school be-lies her modesty; Josefiina, an established landowner "with a masculine voice," who is ready to attack Puntila physically; and finally the gypsylike fortune-telling "Woman of Grusia" with her broken Finnish.

This "labor union of Puntila's brides," chanting class-conscious slogans: "All Puntila's brides, unite!" (p. 49), "The bosses exploit proletarian women!" (p. 57), demands 50,000 marks per bride for breach of promise but settles for 500 when Kalle has the wit to tell them that Puntila is a Mormon who can legally add all five to his harem.

The colorful, self-confident brides of Puntila in the *Sawdust Princess* are transformed by Wuolijoki, reluctantly following Brecht's revisions, into pitiful, humiliated brides in *Iso-Heikkilä*, brides who go home from the promised engagement festivities with nothing but tears and sore feet. According to Brecht's *Work Journal*, Wuolijoki was shocked at Brecht's treatment of these deceived brides. Wuolijoki wanted them emphasized; Brecht insisted on the "beauty" of the fact that they were "almost forgot-ten." [7] He seems to have made little serious effort to enter into her comic vision.

Brecht's main interest at the time was writing *The Good Woman of Szechwan* with its theme of redefining goodness in a prerevolutionary society. Wuolijoki's material was interesting to him to the extent that it offered an opportunity for comic treatment of this theme. He did not need, aside from the strong proletarian Kalle (to complete the paradigm of master and servant), any self-confident characters; he needed ex-ploited supporting ones. A set of unionized brides midway through would destroy the new direction and cohesion of the play, which builds to Kalle's strike at the close.

EEVA

In the *Sawdust Princess* Eeva is a strong levelheaded character whose commonsense values have survived schooling and travel abroad. She leads her nitwit diplomat suitor around by the nose and discards him with ease when his usefulness in catching Kalle is over. (In the film script version Eeva is, in fact, the boss of the estate, especially when her father is drunk.)

About the change in the role of Eeva, Wuolijoki comments in her foreword to *Iso-Heikkilä*: "Iso-Heikkilä's daughter changed in Brecht's hands as well. In my version, Eeva was the same forceful woman that all my female characters are. Under Brecht's influence Eeva became a natural modest young girl—and I saw to it that she remained as much as possible a typical Häme girl" (p. 8). Nevertheless, the squeamish young lady in *Iso-Heikkilä*'s sauna scene is a far cry from any Finnish country girl. She is partially saved, as a character with spunk, through the well-executed scene at the end, where Kalle, upon demand, examines her potential as a future proletarian wife. In this bit of playacting she rises to her part with imagination. Then Wuolijoki accepts Brecht's conception of such a woman's role. One slap on Eeva's rear by Kalle deflates her humor and cuts her back to size.

THE CHAUFFEUR KALLE (MATTI)

In Kalle of the *Sawdust Princess*, Wuolijoki created a new character through whom to voice her own ideas. Though disguised as a proletarian, Kalle is in reality a rather sophisticated intellectual, Doctor Vuorinen, who, while fleeing from "fine" society, meets Puntila in a hotel, falls in love with Eeva's picture, and becomes Puntila's chauffeur in order to win Eeva. Wuolijoki presents Kalle as a cultural liberal, similar to the people in her own salon, which had become a gathering place for culturally and politically aware Helsinki intellectuals. Kalle speaks the same iconoclastic, humorous, sassy language as Wuolijoki and provides ideological and political comments critical of the right.[8] He makes fun of the "inferior corporal who sits on the German throne." In his inflammatory speeches to the brides' union, he claims that Puntila might want lots of sons for "Suur Suomi" (Greater Finland), a term with which ultra-rightists demanded that the Soviet Union return the territory of Carelia to Finland. When Eeva pretends to reject Kalle and Puntila tries to explain that he cannot really give his daughter in marriage to a chauffeur, the "proletarian" snaps, "You are quite right, Mr. Puntila. It is the job that makes the man. I am just a jobless cultural liberal, my head full of modern ideas" (p. 96). As a forceful figure, Kalle overshadows Puntila most of the time. His wit saves his master from the brides' union and it wins him Eeva. More importantly, his chauffeur's uniform gives him a chance to speak his mind.

Wuolijoki felt a need to apologize for this original Kalle in her foreword to *Iso-Heikkilä* "since the sharp-tongued chauffeur in my original play was only an engineer in disguise. . . . In this play he is a proletarian, created by Brecht, though as abrasive in speech as my chauffeur" (p. 8). In fact, whole sections of Kalle's speeches that Wuolijoki wrote were skillfully used by Brecht, since they totally befit the critical proletarian role of the new Kalle/Matti. Her chauffeur Kalle, changed from "cultural liberal" to critical proletarian, allows the essential focus of the play, under Brecht's influence, to become the tension between master and servant.

The *Volksstück* Genre

In these processes of alteration and revision, Wuolijoki's recreated genre of Finnish *Volksstück* temporarily came to approximate a Brechtian *Volksstück*. Jost Hermand has aptly commented on the change that the traditional *Volksstück* underwent in Brecht's hands. His *Puntila* is not the customary mishmash of hilarious and sentimental materials, supposedly taken from the people and dished back to it or to any intellectually undemanding audience. Hermand treats "the synthesis of intellectual incisiveness and folksy directness" as the key to Puntila's international success.[9] This characterization of Brecht's achievement could be applied as well to Wuolijoki's plays of the thirties, which radically upgraded the Finnish *Volksstück*. These plays are indeed entertaining, but they also have an edge, often a political edge. Though she called her original play about Puntila a "farce," she wrote in 1946: "That farce contained all kinds of irony and satire about our conditions. . . . The play had so much dangerous laughter that, for political reasons, it could not be performed in our theaters."[10] The two authors of the new *Volksstück* had more in common than their short-spanned collaboration could demonstrate. However, it seems that Wuolijoki, for Brecht's purposes, had not demonstrated the ideological stamina to use this renewed vehicle for dialectical theater.

Brecht was a determined Marxist, paying for his convictions by exile; Wuolijoki was still, at this time, a business genius with troubled Marxist convictions and a playwright whose plays could be played only when she muted their social criticism. Brecht made an overwhelming personal impression on Wuolijoki, and she was persuaded by him that her play had missed the mark. She was eager to convert her "farce" into a more serious play. Brecht wanted to put the ideological contrast between master and servant in the foreground, and with this clear focus, which Wuolijoki accepted, Puntila had to be changed into the representative of the master class and Kalle into a real proletarian. The other characters essentially were reduced to a structural framework.

Wuolijoki's *Volksstück* is a colorful slice of life that derives much of its quality from its sharp characters, especially women, but also from its sharp contemporary criticism, both societal and political. Wuolijoki's and Brecht's *Volksstück* baits the audience through laughter and demands ideological decisions.

During their protracted dramaturgical battles,[11] Brecht could not comprehend how such a "talented and charming story teller" could not see that her "naturalistic and psychologically" oriented drama was an unsuitable medium for her rich material. Wuolijoki, though she accepted Brecht's challenge and perhaps therefore very quickly his dialectical theater, did not willingly accept its consequences. She was losing the muscle of her strong characters before fully comprehending the necessity of sacrificing them. The early German translation based partly on her work and partly on Brecht's suggestions clearly shows the consequences. It has lost the strength of the *Sawdust Princess* without quite gaining the Brechtian consistency of purpose or making successful use of the Brechtian *Gestus*. If this version is all that Brecht ever read of the original Wuolijoki, his critical reactions are easier to understand.[12]

In her postwar plays, however, Wuolijoki again creates strong women, who are effective because they never let their emotions, however strong, get the upper hand of their reason. They have a striking power, dramatically and socially. Brecht's women, though dramatically very effective, are of a different cast. Even when they are endowed with both feeling and intellect they can usually follow only one at a time. Mother Courage and Shen Te are appropriate examples.

Brecht appropriated the Puntila material and was quite ready to take full artistic credit for the collaborative effort with Wuolijoki. When he heard that the critic Olavi Paavolainen had called their common *Puntila* version the classical Finnish comedy, he wrote with relish in his *Work Journal*: "I am now convinced that the *Edda* was written by a Jew and 'Isaiah,' by a Babylonian."[13]

Surely Brecht could have written a comedy of Finland, just as he created Chicago and Szechwan out of his fantasy. This Finnish comedy, however, is firmly rooted in the experience and creative power of Hella Wuolijoki. When she recognized that her play had been drastically challenged by Brecht, she was willing to learn and to compromise in *Iso-Heikkilä*, and in her foreword she attributed to Brecht his due and more. It is unfortunate that the time for collaboration was so short. Both authors were interested in developing a new, socially critical *Volksstück*, and Wuolijoki's contribution was more substantial than Brecht later remembered.

Notes

1. See Appendix A.

2. See Appendix B.

3. *The Diplomacy of the Winter War: An Account of the Russo-Finnish War, 1939–1940* (Cambridge: Harvard University Press, 1961), p. 209.

4. The primary source of this biographical sketch, Wuolijoki's four-volume autobiography, written in part during her imprisonment, is an important account of political, social, and cultural developments in Estonia and Finland. It is also a significant literary achievement and demonstrates an epic gift at least as impressive as her dramatic talent.

5. Hella Wuolijoki ja Bertolt Brecht, *Iso-Heikkilän isäntä ja hänen renkinsä Kalle* (Helsinki: Tammi, 1946). Because her *Iso-Heikkilä* appeared first, it has acquired the somewhat misleading label of "Ur-Puntila," although in fact Wuolijoki's later Finnish translation and reworking of the German manuscript jointly produced in the fall of 1940 is the immediate basis for Brecht's *Puntila*.

6. Vappu Tuomioja, "Puntilan isännän elävä esikuva" [The living model of the landowner Puntila], *Helsingin Kansallisteatterin ohjelmalehtinen* (1975/76), p. 2. For a sketch of Wuolijoki's life and works as they relate to "A Finnish Bacchus" and for a translation of the short story into German, see my "Hella Wuolijokis Punttila-Geschichte: Ein Vor-Brechtisches Dokument" and "Hella Wuolijoki: A Finnish Bacchus," *Brecht-Jahrbuch* (1978): 87–95 and 96–106.

7. Bertolt Brecht, *Arbeitsjournal 1938–55*, ed. Werner Hecht (Frankfurt: Suhrkamp, 1973), pp. 177–78.

8. The full name of this character, Kalle Aaltonen, with which this pseudo-chauffeur gains entry to Kurkela, comes from a Finnish popular song about "Kalle Aaltonen from the lands and the seas," a happy-go-lucky adventurer, in whose skin this Kalle feels at ease.

9. Jost Hermand, "Herr Puntila und sein Knecht Matti. Brechts Volksstück," *Brecht Heute—Brecht Today: Jahrbuch der Internationalen Brecht-Gesellschaft* 1 (1971): 117–36, especially pp. 122–23.

10. *Iso-Heikkilä*, foreword, p. 5.

11. Brecht, *Arbeitsjournal*, pp. 164, 177; Wuolijoki, *Iso-Heikkilä*, foreword, p. 6; Vappu Tuomioja, "Ettei totuus onohtuisi," *Suomen Kuvalehti* 49, nos. 15/16 (1965): 48, 70–71.

12. One might ask, parenthetically, whether Brecht really had time to pay proper attention to Wuolijoki's material. His share of the work on the collaborative effort was done in less than four weeks. For him the original *Puntila* (or *Iso-Heikkilä*) was almost like a finger exercise undertaken while he devoted his main effort to *The Good Woman of Szechwan*.

13. Brecht, *Arbeitsjournal*, p. 193.

Appendix A: The Contract between Wuolijoki and Brecht

The notice "modeled on the tales of and a play sketch by Hella Wuolijoki," is a recent addition to the text of *Puntila* editions. The original contract in German between the two authors was first reproduced in Friedrich Ege, "Brecht ist nur Mitverfasser des 'Herrn Puntila': Der nicht eingehaltene Vertrag und eine finnische Erstaufführung," *Theater Mosaik* 3, no. 4 (1965): 10. In English it reads:

CONTRACT

The play *Master Puntila and his Servant Matti* was written in a collaborative effort by Hella Wuolijoki and Bertolt Brecht. Both authors will share all royalties equally. The right of making contracts of all types for the play as well as making changes in the piece belongs to Hella Wuolijoki for the Scandinavian countries (including Finland) and to Bertolt Brecht for all other countries. However, Hella Wuolijoki controls the German rights as long as Bertolt Brecht cannot make contracts in Germany. The authors will use a pseudonym until the names of the authors can be made known. Both authors can include the piece in editions of their collected works in countries for which they have the rights, but each must name the collaborator.

Helsinki, 15 May 1941   (Hella Wuolijoki)
                                                          (bertolt brecht)

The Zurich premiere in 1948 listed Brecht as author and referred simply to his use of tales by Hella Wuolijoki. Research since 1965 has explored how the words "tales and a play sketch" came to be added to the published versions. (See references to Ege, Semrau, and Neureuter in Appendix B.) In the past decade Wuolijoki scholars as well as the Finnish press and Finnish theater people have urged recognition of Wuolijoki's coauthorship, while Brecht scholars in general have tended to stress

Brecht's independent re-creation of the material in his later versions of the play.

Hella Wuolijoki's daughter has published an account in Finnish of Brecht's reluctance to acknowledge the contractual state of affairs, parts of which are pertinent here.

> In the summer of 1949 I visited Switzerland, and to my surprise I heard that the Zurich Theatre had been performing Brecht's play on a Finnish theme bearing the title *Puntila* for a year. Only Brecht was named as author. However, on the inside of the theater program one could find in small print that the play had been written "modeled on the tales of the Finnish author Hella Wuolijoki."
>
> I returned to Finland and told my mother, who knew nothing of this. Neither had she received her percentage of royalties as per contract.
>
> My mother's reaction was unexpected. She thought it was terribly embarrassing that the Brecht she admired so much had behaved in this way. She was ashamed on Brecht's behalf, and did not want to take any measures.
>
> In October, however, she had to take a trip to Prague, and she also visited Berlin, where Brecht had moved from Zurich a few months previously. I do not know how Brecht explained the matter, but my mother was again powerfully taken by Brecht—they had again conversed the whole night through. Everything was settled. And from that time on she started to receive her contractual share from Suhrkamp Verlag.
>
> But when Hella Wuolijoki died the agreement was perhaps again partially forgotten. And since my mother had not made a big fuss over it I didn't want to either.
>
> However, when I was in London once I read in the newspaper that the BBC had presented *Puntila* on the radio, naturally again only as Brecht's work. Partly in fun, I sent a notarized copy of the contract to the BBC. I received an apology from them. When the play was performed a second time, Hella Wuolijoki's name was also mentioned and I received the contractual royalty. . . . Her share in this play is much, much greater than simply the idea.

The excerpt above is translated from Vappu Tuomioja, "Ettei totuus unohtuisi" [Lest the truth be forgotten], *Suomen Kuvalehti* 49, no. 15/16 (1965): 48, 70–71).

Appendix B: The Versions of the Puntila Material

The pioneering work in German was published by Friedrich Ege, "Zur Ur-Fassung von 'Herr Puntila und sein Knecht Matti': Brechts Zusammenarbeit mit der Dramatikerin Hella Wuolijoki," *Theater Mosaik* 2, no. 6 (1964): 3-7; "Brecht ist nur Mitverfasser des 'Herrn Puntila': Der nicht eingehaltene Vertrag und eine finnische Erstaufführung," *Theater Mosaik* 3, no. 4 (1965): 9-13; "Von der 'Sägemehlprinzessin' zum 'Puntila': Das erste Puntila-Stück—vor Brecht—uraufgeführt," *Theater Mosaik* 3, no. 7/8 (1965): 5-9. Richard Semrau's *Staatsexamen* thesis (Humbolt University, Berlin, 1959), "Das Volksstück Bert Brechts 'Herr Puntila und sein Knecht Matti' und die finnische Bearbeitung des Themas von Hella Wuolijoki" bears the notice "use disallowed" with a reference to intended publication; however, this manuscript has been available to some critics. A detailed account of the theme in the hands of Brecht and Wuolijoki, with bibliographical references, is given by Hans Peter Neureuter, "'Herr Puntila und sein Knecht Matti': Bericht zur Entstehungsgeschichte," *Mitteilungen aus der deutschen Bibliothek* (Helsinki) 9 (1975): 7-42. See also Neureuter's careful "Zur Brecht-Chronik, April 1940 bis Mai 1941," *Mitteilungen aus der deutschen Bibliothek* (Helsinki) 7 (1973): 11-35.

Apart from the above, this article is based upon the Finnish plays and autobiographical writings of Hella Wuolijoki and the following unpublished manuscripts kindly made available to me with the permission and assistance of Vappu Tuomioja, Hella Wuolijoki's daughter: (1) "A Finnish Bac[c]hus," undated, 11-page short story, Finnish National Archives (apparently more than one version exists); (2) *Sahanpuruprinsessa, 3 näytöksinen huvinäytelmä, kirjoittanut*, Ville-Akusti Lehtinen (one of Wuolijoki's pseudonyms), undated but probably before summer 1936, 100-page typescript of a three-act play, Finnish National Archives; (3) an alternative third act for *Sahanpuruprinsessa* in typescript, undated, pp. 65-105, Finnish National Archives; (4) *Elokuvakäsikirjoituksia: Sahanpuruprinsessa* (a film script of the three-act play), undated, though Neureuter has reason to date it as in progress March 1939, 133-page typescript, Finnish National Archives; (5) "Diktat, H. Wuolijoki [to] M. Steffin, Niederschrift," a German translation dictated by Hella Wuolijoki to Brecht's secretary, 152-page typescript, personal files of Vappu Tuomioja; (6) a carbon copy of Brecht's untitled typescript of his German version of the Puntila play, following Wuolijoki's dictated version, undated, but with numerous handwritten corrections by both Wuolijoki and Brecht indicating early fall 1940, 131 pages plus some unnumbered pages and some passages pasted in. This manuscript, Wuolijoki's copy of the text to which the contract refers, is in the personal files of Vappu

Tuomioja, and, apparently, is closer to the original form of the text than Brecht's copy now in the Brecht Archives, which shows evidence of deletions and further editing. (7) "*Sahanpuruprinsessa*, Huvinnäytelmä, kirj. Hella Wuolijoki, Radiolle sov. Saulo Haarla," radio adaptation by Saulo Haarla, first transmitted 13 September 1965, 70-page typescript, Archives of the Finnish National Radio, Urajävi.

Brecht and *Cahiers du Cinéma*

George Lellis

For more than twenty years the French film magazine *Cahiers du Ciné-ma* has been a major international force in film theory and aesthetics. The magazine is most famous for having developed the controversial *au-teur* theory of film criticism, whereby Hollywood directors such as Alfred Hitchcock or Howard Hawks were praised for their visual styles and thematic consistency. From the ranks of its critics emerged many of the directors of the so-called French New Wave, such as François Truffaut, Jean-Luc Godard, and Claude Chabrol, who made their first features around 1960. The magazine today, by contrast, follows a Marxist-Leninist line that is almost the direct antithesis of the viewpoints espoused in it during the 1950s. Superficially, this turnabout in position may be seen as a direct result of the events of May 1968, in which the call for political change from students and workers in France was accompanied by a call for cultural revolution as well. As the staff of *Cahiers* changed (in part because many of its former key figures were out making films rather than writing criticism), it moved sharply to the left, influenced by the political events of the time.

The process is hardly so simple, and a careful reading of *Cahiers* re-veals a second major (if less obviously important) date in the develop-ment of the magazine: December 1960, when the review published a special number devoted to writings on film by Brecht and about Brecht and film. Brecht has been a pivotal figure in the change in *Cahiers du Cinéma* from Platonist, Catholic, idealist writing about film to a Marxist, materialist approach. The incorporation of Brecht's ideas into the maga-zine has been a gradual but steady process that may be divided into two steps: first, the development, signaled in December 1960, of an increas-ing interest in Brechtian theory, not on a political level but on a stylistic one; second, the adoption after 1968 of Brecht's politics as well as his stylistics, the use of Brechtian principles to develop a systematically Marxist approach to film. Describing this transition calls for a tripartite discussion. The first part deals with the period before 1968. The second, a short transitional section, gives background to the influence of Roland Barthes and the intervention of structuralist thought in the magazine around 1968. The third part treats post-1968 writing. Although December 1960 and May 1968 mark two major turning points, there is a gradual progression toward the Marxist viewpoint, a continuity rather than a sudden about-face.

Cahiers before 1968

The issues of *Cahiers du Cinéma* of the 1950s and early 1960s are characterized by a philosophical involvement with both Platonism and phenomenology, a theoretical involvement with formalism and geometry, and a stylistic involvement with mise-en-scène and gesture in the cinema. All of these concerns are interrelated, and all can be undermined or modified by Brechtian thought.

The most articulate and direct advocate of Platonism in the early *Cahiers* is Eric Rohmer, who also writes under the name Maurice Schérer. Rohmer writes in 1951, for example, "The first end of art is to reproduce, not the object, without doubt, but its beauty; what one calls realism is only a more scrupulous search for this beauty." In other words, Rohmer believes in an ideal beauty that he can, at least conceptually, separate from its material manifestations. In another essay Rohmer compares the film medium to music, noting the aesthetic similarities. Elsewhere he praises the films of Alfred Hitchcock for their use of pure, underlying forms that are an integral part of their expression and that allow even mediocre scripts to become meaningful.[1]

The influence of phenomenology in *Cahiers* results in an attitude toward film that sees the medium as one of subjective perception rather than objective recording of reality. A 1952 *Cahiers* essay called "Neorealism and Phenomenology" by Amédée Ayfre, a Catholic priest, asserts about the earliest films of Lumière: "The single fact that he [Lumière] placed his camera in a particular spot, that he started or stopped photographing at a particular moment, that he inscribed the world in black and white on a flat surface was enough to admit an infidelity to the real."[2] This attitude is relatively compatible with Brecht's notion that realism does not show objective reality but embodies subtly the ideology that produces it. Where Ayfre (and many of the critics who follow him in the early *Cahiers*)[3] would maintain that film always presents a subjective rather than an objective reality, the later Marxist critics would substitute ideological for subjective and scientific for objective. Though Ayfre's conclusions, drawn from the same starting point, would differ from Brecht's, their similar premises here suggest a subtle affinity.

Platonism in the *Cahiers* leads to a tendency to describe films in purely formal, geometric terms. One of Jean-Luc Godard's most famous essays in his review of Alexandre Astruc's film *Une vie* (1958), in which Godard compares Astruc's work to a geometrical locus, a succession of horizontal and vertical lines and movements, seen as points on a graph. Similarly, critics in the *Cahiers* defend countless other films, from Hitchcock's *Vertigo* (1958) to Jacques Tati's *Playtime* (1968), on the basis of their formal achievements.[4] One of the primary considerations of the later Brechtian criticism in the journal has been that the form of a given play or film has political implications. On this level, therefore, both the old and new *Cahiers* share a preoccupation with issues of form.

Out of the phenomenological roots of the *Cahiers* comes an interpretation of film as an art of physical relationships among actors. Jean Domarchi writes in 1963, for example, in defense of the American cinema over the European art film, that "cinema is above all physical adventure more than interior adventure. Moral conflicts have sense only if they develop by means of physical oppositions." This is a notion very similar to Brecht's preference, expressed in his "Threepenny Lawsuit" observations, for commercial mass-audience films over bourgeois art: "What the film really demands is external action and not introspective psychology."[5]

One extreme group of *Cahiers* critics, known as the MacMahonists (who later start a separate publication, *Présence du Cinéma*), develops a theory of film criticism around the gestures of the actor and their accompanying mise-en-scène as elements to be considered equal to scenario, script, ideas, or themes. Although the MacMahonists are now thought to be in the extreme political right wing of *Cahiers* criticism, their emphasis on an approach to film structured on the physical gestures of the actor is a relevant parallel to Brecht's preoccupation with the social gest as a building block of drama.

One of the idols of the MacMahonist critics is Joseph Losey, whose films are praised for their physical elegance and the expressiveness of their mise-en-scène. One of Losey's significant achievements in the theater was his staging of Brecht's *Galileo* in the United States in the 1940s. Losey may have stimulated interest in Brecht among the *Cahiers* writers. The special Brecht number of the magazine appeared in September 1960, only three months after a special Losey number. (This Losey number marks the height of the MacMahonists' influence on the magazine.) The *Cahiers* Brecht issue features an article by Losey on Brecht, mainly about their collaboration on *Galileo*. Near the end of the essay, Losey outlines some theoretical concepts that he sees as important for a consideration of Brecht in the cinema. Losey minimizes both Brecht's political interests and his theoretical concerns and all but reduces the dramatist to a practitioner of technique. He writes, as the main thrust of his argument, "I had interpreted it as significant for Brecht not that truth is absolute but that it is precise, that there is a good manner of having access to it: justice of observation, economy of means of expression." [6]

Such an approach to Brecht was quite comfortable for the formalist critics at *Cahiers*. Indeed, one of the most significant citations of Brecht from this period occurs in Fereydoun Hoyveda's review of Losey's film *Eva* (1962), a melodrama based on a novel by James Hadley Chase. Citing Losey's article on Brecht, Hoyveda asserts about *Eva*, "for the first time in cinema, meaning is found entirely in form." Losey's use of precise technique on every level—not only dialogue, decor, and acting, but also camera movement, lighting, and construction—results for Hoyveda in "an impeccable distancing which refuses all possibility of identification to the spectator and leaves him, to participate in the work, only the free exercise of his intelligence beyond ease or constraint." [7] In other words, although Hoyveda praises *Eva* as an alternative to conventional Aristotelian drama, he reduces the estrangement effect to a certain stylistic coldness that appeals to intellectual rather than emotional responses.

Formalism in the *Cahiers du Cinéma* reaches something of an apogee just before 1967 in the publication of a series of theoretical articles by Noël Burch, which have since appeared in book form in English under the title *Theory of Film Practice*. Burch's writings explore the relationship between form and content in film, advocating films in which there is a "truly consistent relationship between the spatial and temporal articulations of a film and its narrative content, formal structure determining narrative structure as well as vice-versa." In his analysis of films like Renoir's *Nana*, Antonioni's *Chronicle of a Love Affair*, or Marcel Hanoun's *Une simple histoire*, Burch moves away from the Platonism of the old *Cahiers* toward studying the forms of a film only as materially present in it, in what might be called a closed system. In his introduction to the English edition of the book, Burch writes: "Although no special emphasis is placed upon the fact in this book, my entire approach was, even then, implicitly predicated on the conviction that the illusionist approach to filmmaking—comparable to what Brecht condemned in the theater as 'identification'—contains a fundamental principle of alienation that degrades both film-maker and spectator."[8]

The most interesting link between the old and new *Cahiers*, however, is the figure of Jacques Rivette, who begins with the positions held by the rest of the *Cahiers* critics. His early writings from around 1955 note Roberto Rossellini's ability to "see through beings and things to the souls and ideas they convey," praise Alexandre Astruc as a formalist, argue in favor of the American film on the grounds that its traditionally violent subjects allow the director to express himself through his mise-en-scène.[9] Rivette is, like the MacMahonists, a frequent defender of the films of Otto Preminger.

Rivette's formalism is, however, also linked to an interest in the theater of Denis Diderot, and one of Rivette's cherished projects as a filmmaker, which was realized in 1964, was to make a film version of Diderot's *La religieuse*. As Roland Barthes has pointed out, the affinities between Brecht and Diderot are remarkable. Both envisioned a didactic, morally potent theater; both thought of the theatrical presentation as a series of geometric tableaux; both advocated the use of typed characters; both argued for acting based on intellectual comprehension rather than emotionalism. Indeed, in discussing his first film, *Paris Belongs to Us* (1960), Rivette has observed, "I'd like to follow the example of Brecht: *Paris nous appartient* would be *Drums in the Night*; and the trilogy I am planning set in the eighteenth century, more or less an adaptation of *Edward II*."[10]

After 1968 there are signs in Rivette of politization. In a *Cahiers* roundtable discussion of editing, which is Rivette's last appearance in the magazine, he describes Eisensteinian montage as a way of achieving "critical thought" in a film, a way of avoiding mere passive observation of the world. It is a position comparable to Brecht's rejection of realism in favor of a form of spectacle that acknowledges itself as a discourse and calls attention to the dialectical process of its construction. Rivette continues by attacking the montage of Pudovkin as a bourgeois, capitalist perversion of Eisenstein: "This compromise and caricature of the 'art of montage' was transferred to a large part of the consumer cinema." Similarly, Jean-Louis Comolli, in reviewing Rivette's 1968 film *L'amour fou* in *Cahiers du Cinéma*, praises it as an alternative to traditional filmic representation.[11] Rivette's recent work as a filmmaker has been criticized (most notably by Jean-Luc Godard) for being part of the commercial French filmmaking establishment, and he has offered little further evidence of Marxist leanings as either a filmmaker or theoretician. Nonetheless, the progression in his thinking during the period in which *Cahiers* undergoes its main changes parallels these changes.

The single most important discussant of Brecht during this period is Louis Marcorelles, whose main theoretical position on Brecht in the cinema is directed toward the actor. As early as 1956, he sees in the Brechtian theater an alternative role for the performer and praises that approach for being far more lucid than the Stanislavsky method as employed by Elia Kazan or the Actors' Studio. By 1960 Marcorelles sees a Brechtian cinema as providing a chance for the actor to become cocreator in the film work, and reacts against the dominance of a director-oriented "pure cinema" in the other factions of *Cahiers*. Elsewhere, Marcorelles writes admiringly of Brecht's work, but comments also on what he sees as its lack of applicability to the film medium. In keeping with the bias of the *Cahiers* critics toward the forms rather than the politics of Brechtian theater, Marcorelles discusses Ingmar Bergman's *The Virgin Spring* (1960) as a film that applies the techniques of epic theater to a Christian, Protestant subject. As the 1960s progress, Marcorelles contributes less often to the *Cahiers du Cinéma* and becomes a champion of the *cinéma vérité* movement, which he sees as the true alternative to the traditional techniques of cinematic representation.[12]

Other criticism related to Brechtian thought appears sporadically in the magazine throughout the early to mid-sixties. Not only are the films of Jean-Luc Godard, which openly acknowledge their debts to Brechtian thought, discussed in the context of their distancing techniques and lack of conventional identification, but the early work of Claude Chabrol is admired for many of the same reasons. Other works, ranging from those of Francesco Rosi to Billy Wilder's *Irma la Douce* (1963) are discussed in similar contexts. Theoretical essays by Michel Mardore and Jean-Louis Comolli from the mid-sixties call for an awareness of the implicit political nature of all cinema and for films that provide not escape or mere emotional involvement but a cool, dispassionate evaluation of the world and its problems.[13]

Thus, in the pre-1968 era, there are an increasing number of precursory indications of politization in the *Cahiers*. Many of the former attitudes can be transposed to a Brechtian framework with only minor (but significant) displacements of emphasis and assumption. Elements common to both the old and the new *Cahiers* are a rationalism of approach (found both in Platonic and Marxist thought), an emphasis on problems of form, a vision of film as a medium best suited to the presentation of external actions and gestures, and at least an occasional rejection of conventional identification. To be sure, there are other movements to be found in *Cahiers* during the fifties and sixties, and the magazine at this time is devoted to the presentation of a plurality of points of view, but the above elements of the *Cahiers* approach are the ones that develop directly into the post-1968, politicized journal. They are the ones that relate directly to Brecht and the ones that foreshadow the work yet to come.

Roland Barthes and the Structuralist Intervention

One significant aspect of the *Cahiers* of the fifties and early sixties is the development of film criticism not so much as an adjunct of literary or theatrical criticism but as a unique practice with theory and methods of its own. (The special Brecht number is one of the rare exceptions to this rule.) In the late sixties, however, a film criticism very much influenced by developments in French literary thought, especially the school of structuralist and semiological thought led by Roland Barthes, can be found in the *Cahiers*. A short digression into Barthes's background, his relation to Brecht, and his eventual, largely indirect influence on *Cahiers* is therefore in order.

The introduction of Brecht into French culture in the fifties and the subsequent acceptance in France of his work was due largely to the efforts of Roland Barthes and Bernard Dort, who founded the review *Théâtre Populaire*. Although the first postwar productions of Brecht in French were considered significant failures (for both their misunderstanding of Brecht and their lack of popular success), the first performances of the Berliner Ensemble in Paris in 1954 were defended by Barthes and Dort in a special number of their magazine. In part due to these critics' efforts, the Berliner Ensemble received nearly unanimous praise when it returned to Paris the next year, and Brecht's death in 1956 was mourned by the French press as the loss of a great dramatist.[14]

Thus, Barthes and Dort may be viewed as Brecht's primary advocates in France. Dort contributed a major article to the 1960 Brecht issue of *Cahiers* in which he notes prophetically, "A Brechtian influence is brewing at *Cahiers*."[15] Barthes is even more relevant to the post-1968 *Cahiers du Cinéma*, since he is also a prime mover in the development of semiology, based in the linguistic study of signs and symbols, as a tool of literary criticism and analysis. His followers, such as Christian Metz, contributed to the semiological criticism of film. Even before 1968 a special issue of the *Cahiers* entitled "Film and Novel: Problems of Narrative" appeared (December 1966), containing articles of semiological research. While the work of Metz and others in this school is rejected by some of the *Cahiers* writers in the 1970s, it nonetheless creates a precedent for what is seen as the scientific analysis of film.

Barthes has consistently linked his interest in semiotics to his interest in Brecht. In the 1950s, he stated:

> For what Brechtian dramaturgy postulates is that today, at least, the responsibility of the dramatic art is not so much to express reality as to signify it. Hence there must be a certain distance between signified and signifier: revolutionary art must admit a certain arbitrary nature of signs, it must acknowledge a certain 'formalism,' in the sense that it must treat form according to an appropriate method, which is the semiological method.[16]

In the 1960s Barthes was associated with Philippe Sollers, head of the literary magazine *Tel Quel*, published by Editions du Seuil, the house responsible also for the semiological review *Communications*. Among the followers of Sollers are Jean-Louis Comolli and Jean Narboni, who are particularly prominent in the post-1968 *Cahiers*.[17] Thus, a network of influences and affiliations derives from Barthes.

The adoption of a Marxist-Brechtian approach in the *Cahiers* coincides with the founding in 1968 of *Cinéthique*, a magazine also linked to Editions du Seuil, Philippe Sollers, and the materialist philosophy connected with them. The fundamental tenet of *Cinéthique* writers is similar to that of Brecht in his lawsuit over *The Threepenny Opera*: since films are produced as commodities within a capitalist ideology, even would-be revolutionary films reflect the dominant capitalist ideology in their forms and structures. Whether the appearance of *Cinéthique* causes the shift of position is arguable, but the issues of *Cahiers* do begin to attack it for not drawing the correct consequences from its Marxist premises. Implicit in such attacks is an acceptance of the same fundamental assumptions. The eventual position in the *Cahiers* is somewhat less extreme than that in *Cinéthique* (not all narrative cinema, for example, is rejected as bourgeois). The magazine does, however, in the years following 1968, develop a position whereby the economic determinants of both the film medium in general and particular films are the prime starting place for discussion.

Cahiers after 1968

The first comprehensive statement of position in the new *Cahiers* is articulated in an article entitled "Cinema/Ideology/Criticism" (October 1969). Jean-Louis Comolli and Jean Narboni argue in a Brechtian manner against cinematic realism and representation as tools that serve the dominant capitalist ideology:

> One knows that the cinema, "quite naturally" because the camera and film are made for this end (and the ideology imposes this end), "reproduces" reality. But this "reality," so susceptible to being reproduced, reflected by instruments and techniques which are otherwise a part of it, one indeed sees as completely ideological. In this sense the theory of "transparency" (cinematographic classicism) is eminently reactionary: it is not the world in its "concrete reality" which is "seized" by (or, rather, imbues) a non-intervening instrument, but the vague, unformulated, non-theoretical, thoughtless world of the dominant ideology.[18]

An alternative is offered by the Dziga Vertov Group, the filmmaking collective formed by Jean-Luc Godard after May 1968, which released its

major work, *Tout va bien*, in 1972. Using *Cahiers du Cinéma* as an organ
for its theories, the Group announced that its goal is "to make political
films politically." That is, the political nature of a film is not just a question
of subject matter but also of form. How a film is made is as important as
what it is about. In a *Cahiers* statement on the Group, "epic" rather than
"dramatic" forms in Brecht's terms (with reference to his theoretical text
on *The Rise and Fall of the City of Mahagonny*) are called for to combat
the passivity of the audience, to force the viewer to take a stand.[19]

At a conference in Avignon (1972), *Cahiers* editors reorganized the
editorial policy. The four major topics for articles in the *Cahiers* were to
be: (1) the place of the spectator in the cinema, particularly in the light
of recent psychoanalytic theory; (2) the relationship of the film to the
real, e.g., representation, realism, the functions of montage; (3) narrative
structures, studied in the context of semiology; (4) the use of characters
and the fundamental questions of identification and distancing.[20] The second and fourth preoccupations are directly related to Brechtian theory
and may be found in the rejection by *Cahiers'* editors of both realistic
representation and audience passivity. The questions of psychoanalysis,
linked mainly to the post-Freudian and linguistic theories of Jacques
Lacan, are also concerned with the passivity of the spectator (and as such
represent an elaborate extension of Brechtian theory).

Given these parameters of interest, writings in subsequent *Cahiers*
continue to stress both theoretical and practical issues. In the writings of
Pascal Bonitzer and Jean-Louis Comolli, for example, one finds a systematic use of Marxist thought to refute conventional film theory and history
and offer alternatives. Bonitzer's writings seek to demystify the terms in
which film is usually discussed. He attacks the notion that there is any
pure denotation in film, questions the notion of the shot as the fundamental unit of film, critiques the commonly held conception of "off-screen"
space, and attacks André Bazin (one of the guiding influences of the early
Cahiers). Comolli, on the other hand, addresses conventional film historians, whom he accuses of pretending to write a scientific history of techniques, rather than a social and economic history of an inherently
ideological medium.[21] The implicit argument is that the dominant, capitalist ideology has influenced the way in which film history and theory
have previously been conceived. Conventional theories and histories of
cinema have been used as justification for films that make use of repre-
sentational techniques to encourage audience identification.

On the level of practical criticism, much space has been devoted in the recent *Cahiers* to *film progressiste*, that is, the commercial leftist cinema in which political discourse is rendered ineffective through the use of techniques determined by and supportive of capitalism. The films of Costa-Gavras, for example, like *Z* (1969), *The Confession* (1970), or *State of Siege* (1973), are sharply criticized. The audience of *Z* identifies with the "good guys" against the "bad guys" without being asked what makes one different from the other. *State of Siege*, in like manner, supports pacifism and human values without providing discussion of the relationships of property which cause the torture and violence attacked in the film. A study of recent naturalistic films with political content—such as Costa-Gavras' *Special Section* (1975) or Yves Boisset's *Dupont Lajoie* (1975)—discusses naturalism as a technique used by the social majority to stereotype minorities. In so doing, the majority avoids becoming cognizant of its role. The hero is always a "rounded" human being; the villain, a character stereotyped in such a way that the fascist in the audience will not identify with him.[22]

Similarly, in an article by a collective, Marin Karmitz's *Blow for Blow* (1972) is compared with *Tout va bien* and criticized. *Blow for Blow* is a self-styled Maoist film which treats the same subject as *Tout va bien* (a workers' strike), but in a realistic manner. Where Karmitz uses the techniques of empiricism, the collective argues, Godard employs those of dialectical materialism:

> In other words, to reflect a thing fully in its totality, to reflect its essence and internal laws, it is necessary to conduct an intellectual operation in submitting the given riches of sensory perception to an elaboration: one must leap from sensory knowledge to rational knowledge. This is what radically distinguishes dialectical materialism from empiricism. This is what Karmitz and his companions have forgotten and have not done.[23]

Blow for Blow, therefore, is anti-Marxist because, by merely making a factual presentation of the events of a strike, it stays on the level of sensory knowledge. Naturalism and representation are criticized even when put to superficially leftist ends.

Two conceptual notions are particularly noteworthy elaborations of Brechtian thought. One is the idea of *lecture*, the "reading" of a film; the second, *deconstruction*, an undermining of traditional techniques. The notion of *lecture*, which focuses on audience response, is in part borrowed from semiotic analysis,[24] and though it is first used in *Cahiers* in the mid-sixties, only after 1968 does it become a standard concept in the magazine. Jean-Louis Comolli describes it in 1967 as "the patient spelling out, shot by shot, task by task, of its [the image's] 'constituents.' . . . Beginning with such a marking—an operation of a scientific rather than critical nature—of the *facts of the image*, a second, more global, critical reading can be constructed." In other words, one must first understand the forms by which the film is constructed by an active process, then evaluate what those forms mean. *Lecture* is similar to the process of formal analysis advocated by Noël Burch, but after 1968 the term is used with the suggestion that a correct "reading" of a film is a political one. This approach is particularly evident in discussions of older films, such as the 1970 analyses of *Young Mr. Lincoln* (in which the John Ford film is related to the social and cultural codes that produced it) and Jean Renoir's *La vie est à nous*. One may see this notion of "reading" as a positive articulation of what Brecht meant in his critique of audience passivity with respect to the conventional film. The politically advanced film becomes, therefore, one that encourages a "reading."[25]

To Pascal Kané, who writes in 1975 about the estrangement effect with regard to historical films, the desired "strangeness" is what produces the need for a "reading." Indeed, Kané defines distancing as the production of a "space for reading." There is here, however, the potential for confusion. On the one hand, if one merely makes history "strange," one risks creating a new form of filmic fascination. Yet the distancing can also produce what Kané terms a sense of "false mastery" of the subject, dissolving the strangeness. For Kané, the social gest, when used properly, makes the viewer conscious of the way in which it produces meaning or sense: "The gesture will not illustrate, but, on the contrary, render unusual the process represented."[26] In other words, the social gest is not to be another form of representation, but an explicitly acknowledged process of discourse, intended to be "read" actively by the viewer.

The second notion, *deconstruction*, is aimed at the production of films that will encourage a political reading on the part of the audience. It is reflected, on one level, in the desire of the Dziga Vertov Group to "make political films politically." Films are demanded in which "the mise-en-scène is subordinate to a working in the film for political practice which fights specifically on the level of filmmaking itself against a profit-motivated ideology."[27] Thus, the aim is to find alternative styles and methods in film that will produce political thought, which implies a rejection of the techniques of the conventional narrative film that is produced to make money.

In supporting the films of Jean-Marie Straub, such as *Othon* (1969), *History Lessons* (his 1972 adaptation of Brecht's *The Affairs of Mr. Julius Caesar*, for which *Cahiers* published a complete script and découpage), and *Moses and Aaron* (1975), *Cahiers* critics recognize the films as realizations of their theories. Entirely characteristic is their defense of *Othon*, a film attacked by most French critics. Straub treats the Corneille text sovereignly and the actors speak French with foreign accents. Straub sets the action in modern Rome (with actors in togas) and incorporates on-location noise from automobiles. He often pays more attention to the aural qualities of the actors' deliveries than to the words themselves. All of this has been viewed as a desecration of Corneille. Against such criticisms, Jean Narboni argues that Straub employs a materialist style in attacking bourgeois representation through small displacements in traditional methods. The approach at once undermines representation by acknowledging theatricality, while also creating a work that does not just record a theatrical performance but is involved in an integral transformation of it. "Thus, to show a representation, Straub shows this representation in the process of making itself."[28] Narboni argues, in effect, that *Othon* is constructed entirely against cinematic and theatrical illusionism. Such a *deconstruction* is philosophically materialist because it is a manipulation of signifiers which makes no effort to presuppose any essential nature of the work of art. Implicit is the conviction that if bourgeois art reinforces capitalist society, undermining its forms automatically becomes politically subversive.

Summary

While the full range of thought in *Cahiers du Cinéma* in the post-1968 period cannot be covered in this study, it is clear that the philosophy of the journal becomes increasingly Brechtian in its attack on traditional representation in the cinema (and the inherent idealism and empiricism it embodies) as well as the passivity that this approach produces. The goals of the magazine have become: (1) to understand the operations of the bourgeois cinema through careful reading of both old and new films and through the reappraisal of film history and theory; and (2) to advocate films that attack capitalism on the levels of both form and content, that provide substantive alternatives to the bourgeois cinema.

These goals are very different from those of the early *Cahiers du Cinéma*. The alteration in the political tenor of the magazine was not a sudden, discontinuous process but the result of a steady, progressive undermining of the early assumptions. While external events (such as May 1968 or the founding of *Cinéthique*) suggest other influences, the seeds of change in *Cahiers* were sowed into a ground that was well prepared. If the early *Cahiers* reflects interest in Brecht more for aesthetics than for politics, the later *Cahiers* demonstrates how one can lead to the other.

Notes

1. Maurice Schérer, "Vanité que la peinture," *Cahiers du Cinéma*, no. 3 (June 1951): 24. Eric Rohmer, "Le celluloid et le marbre, IV: Beau comme la musique," *Cahiers du Cinéma*, no. 52 (November 1955): 23–29; Maurice Schérer, "A qui la faute?" *Cahiers du Cinéma*, no. 76 (October 1954): 6–10. Early issues of *Cahiers* were given volume numbers, but this practice has been discontinued in recent years. For the sake of consistency, therefore, all footnotes give only the number of the individual issue and its date. Unless indicated, all quotations are translated by the author.

2. Amédée Ayfre, "Néo-réalisme et phénoménologie," *Cahiers du Cinéma*, no. 17 (November 1952): 6.

3. Consider the following, written almost ten years later: "To make a film is thus to show certain things, and *at the same time*, and by the same operation, to show them with a certain bias; these two acts being rigorously indivisible." Jacques Rivette, "De l'abjection," *Cahiers du Cinéma*, no. 120 (June 1961): 55.

4. Jean-Luc Godard, "Review of Astruc's *Une vie*," in Peter Graham, ed., *The New Wave* (Garden City, N.Y.: Doubleday, 1968), pp. 81–83 (Also in *Cahiers du Cinéma*, no. 89 [November 1958]); Eric Rohmer, "L'hélice et l'idée," *Cahiers du Cinéma*, no. 93 (March 1959): 48–50; Paul-Louis Martin, "D'un Tati l'autre," *Cahiers du Cinéma*, no. 199 (March 1968): 27–28.

5. Jean Domarchi, "L'homme des cavernes," *Cahiers du Cinéma*, no. 149 (November 1963): 65–66; Bertolt Brecht, *Brecht on Theatre: The Development of an Aesthetic*, ed. and trans. John Willet (New York: Hill and Wang, 1964), p. 50.

6. Joseph Losey, "L'œil du maître," *Cahiers du Cinéma*, no. 114 (December 1960): 29.

7. Fereydoun Hoyveda, "L'eau et le miroir," *Cahiers du Cinéma*, no. 137 (November 1962): 36.

8. Noël Burch, *Theory of Film Practice* (New York: Praeger, 1973), pp. 15, xix.

9. Jacques Rivette, "Lettre sur Rossellini," *Cahiers du Cinéma*, no. 46 (April

1955): 19; "La recherche de l'absolu," *Cahiers du Cinéma*, no. 52 (November 1955): 46; "Notes sur une révolution," *Cahiers du Cinéma*, no. 54 (Christmas 1955): 17–21.

10. Roland Barthes, "Diderot, Brecht, Eisenstein," *Screen* 15 (Summer 1974): 33–39; Jacques Rivette, quoted in Peter Graham, ed., *The New Wave*, pp. 125–26.

11. Jean Narboni, Sylvie Pierre, Jacques Rivette, "Montage," *Cahiers du Cinéma*, no. 210 (March 1969): 29; Jean-Louis Comolli, "Le détour par le direct," *Cahiers du Cinéma*, no. 211 (April 1969): 44.

12. Louis Marcorelles, "Elia Kazan et l'Actors' Studio," *Cahiers du Cinéma*, no. 66 (Christmas 1956): 42–44; Louis Marcorelles, "D'un art moderne," *Cahiers du Cinéma*, no. 114 (December 1960): 44–53; Louis Marcorelles, "Au pied du mur," *Cahiers du Cinéma*, no. 116 (February 1961): 51–53; Louis Marcorelles, with Nicole Rouzet-Albagli, *Living Cinema*, trans. Isabel Quigly (London: Allen and Unwin, 1973), p. 123.

13. André S. Labarthe, "Le plus pur regard," *Cahiers du Cinéma*, no. 108 (June 1960): 47–50; Jean-André Fieschi, "Si nos brechtiens . . ." *Cahiers du Cinéma*, no. 143 (May 1963): 57–62; Jacques Joly, "Un nouveau réalisme," *Cahiers du Cinéma*, no. 131 (May 1962): 12; Michel Mardore, "La douce-amère," *Cahiers du Cinéma*, no. 149 (November 1963): 63–65; Michel Mardore, "Age of Gold (Buñuel), Age of Iron (Rossellini)," *Cahiers du Cinéma in English*, no. 3 (1966): 47–50 (also in *Cahiers du Cinéma*, no. 175 [February 1966]); Jean-Louis Comolli, "Contrariwise," *Cahiers du Cinéma in English*, no. 3 (1966): 57–58 (also in *Cahiers du Cinéma*, no. 168 [July 1965]).

14. Bernard Dort, "Brecht en France," *Les Temps Modernes* 15 (1960): 1858–59.

15. Bernard Dort, "Pour une critique brechtienne du cinéma," *Cahiers du Cinéma*, no. 114 (December 1960): 33.

16. Roland Barthes, *Critical Essays*, trans. Richard Howard (Evanston, Ill.: Northwestern University Press, 1972), pp. 74–75.

17. Thomas Elsaesser, "French Film Culture and Critical Theory: *Cinéthique*," *Monogram*, no. 2 (Summer 1971): 32.

18. Jean-Louis Comolli and Jean Narboni, "Cinéma/idéologie/critique," *Cahiers du Cinéma*, no. 216 (October 1969): 12.

19. "La 'groupe Dziga Vertov,'" *Cahiers du Cinéma*, no. 240 (July/August 1972): 4–9.

20. Jacques Aumont, "Group 3: Les acquis théoriques—premier bilan du groupe," *Cahiers du Cinéma*, no. 244 (February/March 1973): 42–43.

21. Pascal Bonitzer, "'Réalité' de la dénotation," *Cahiers du Cinéma*, no. 229 (May 1971): 39–41; "Fétichisme de la technique: La notion de plan," *Cahiers du Cinéma*, no. 233 (November 1971): 4–10; "Hors-champ (un espace en défaut)," *Cahiers du Cinéma*, no. 234–35 (December 1971–January 1972): 15–26; Pascal Bonitzer and Serge Daney, "L'écran du fantasme," *Cahiers du Cinéma*, no. 236–37 (March–April 1972): 31–40. Jean-Louis Comolli, "Technique et idéologie: Caméra, perspectif, profondeur de champ," *Cahiers du Cinéma*, no. 229 (May 1971): 4–21; no. 230 (July 1971): 51–57; no. 231 (August–September 1971):

42–49; no. 233 (November 1971): 39–45; no. 234–35 (December 1971 and January–February 1972): 94–100; no. 241 (September–October 1972): 20–24.

22. Jean Narboni, "Le Pirée pour un homme," *Cahiers du Cinéma*, no. 210 (March 1969): 54–55; Pascal Bonitzer and Serge Toubiana, "*Etat de siege*," *Cahiers du Cinéma*, no. 245–46 (April–May–June 1973): 49–54; Serge Daney, Pascal Kané, Jean-Pierre Oudart and Serge Toubiana, "Une certaine tendance du cinéma français," *Cahiers du Cinéma*, no. 257 (May–June 1975): 5–13.

23. Groupe Lou Sin d'intervention idéologique, "Les luttes de classe en France; Deux films: *Coup pour coup, Tout va bien*," *Cahiers du Cinéma*, no. 238–39 (May–June 1972): 8.

24. Roland Barthes, "Rhétorique de l'image," *Communications*, no. 4 (1964): 48.

25. Jean-Louis Comolli, "Le point sur l'image," *Cahiers du Cinéma*, no. 194 (October 1967): 29–30; "John Ford's *Young Mr. Lincoln*," *Screen* 13 (Autumn 1972): 5–44 (also in *Cahiers du Cinéma*, no. 223 [August 1970]); Pascal Bonitzer, Jean-Louis Comolli, Serge Daney, Jean Narboni, and Jean-Pierre Oudart, "*La vie est à nous*, film militant," *Cahiers du Cinéma*, no. 218 (March 1970): 45–51.

26. Pascal Kané, "Cinéma et Histoire: L'effet d'étrangeté," *Cahiers du Cinéma*, no. 254–55 (December 1974–January 1975): 77–83.

27. "La 'groupe Dziga Vertov,'" p. 5.

28. Jean Narboni, "La vicariance du pouvoir," *Cahiers du Cinéma*, no. 224 (October 1970): 43–47.

Part Four
uses of poetry

The Brechtian Influence and DDR Poetry of Political Criticism

RICHARD J. RUNDELL

PORTRAIT OF B.B.

Knows much,
doubts often,
enjoys everything.

Was seldom kind,
often fair,
always objective.

His consolation
is the laws of nature.
He can learn.

Heinz Kahlau

Although Brecht's influence is universally acknowledged, the extent and nature of his influence on the poets of the German Democratic Republic has not been examined fully. Apart from a small number of recent articles dealing with Brecht's impact on Günter Kunert, Volker Braun, and Wolf Biermann, the significance of Brecht's poetry as a stimulus and a model for the East German poets has received only passing mention.[1] Since Brecht is the DDR's best-known poet, it is natural to view much of the poetry written in the DDR in terms of its relationship to him.

Poetry in the DDR is no less many-faceted in its themes, techniques, styles, and messages than is West German poetry, despite the marked differences between these elements in the poetry of the two states.[2] Certain forms, such as concrete poetry, have been little used in the DDR, whereas some more traditional poetic modes, now thought out-of-date in the West, are still very popular in the East.[3] Until Biermann's predicament in the mid-sixties was widely publicized in the West, little Western attention was paid to most DDR poetry, in spite of its great popularity there as a literary genre, perhaps even greater than prose and drama (one spoke of a poetry boom in the sixties). DDR poetry was generally thought to be restricted to Stalinist panegyrics by Johannes R. Becher and Kuba (Kurt Barthel), or agit-prop songs by Erich Weinert, with a negligible body of "good" poetry in the background. A large number of interesting poems by competent poets were thus more or less ignored, with the notable exceptions of Peter Huchel and Johannes Bobrowski, and, somewhat later, Günter Kunert. Biermann's songs were perceived initially as a separate genre, of political rather than literary significance. Huchel and Bobrowski seem to have been warmly received in the West because their poetry was thought to be apolitical, thus aesthetically more deserving of serious attention than ideological hackwork. This kind of thinking has fostered a narrow and distorted view of East German poetry which is, happily, now being corrected. Much Western scholarship is focusing on the entire spectrum of DDR poetry.

Bobrowski saw almost none of his poetry published until the 1950s. Of his relationship to Brecht, he writes, "I have no very strong relationship to Brecht. Of course, I like him a lot, especially as a lyric poet. Otherwise I am not an enthusiastic admirer." Contrast this reserved position with that of Biermann, who is quoted as having stated, "Whoever writes anything useful in Germany today has been influenced by Brecht. The weaker writers honor this colossus in the form of rejection."[4] One doubts that Biermann is totally dismissing poets like Huchel and Bobrowski, but these two statements mark the extreme positions on Brecht's impact: in the one case, denigration; in the other, celebration.

There have been three separate generations of poets active in the DDR. The first of these is Brecht's own generation, already active and recognized before the Third Reich, including Becher, Weinert, Leonhard, Arendt, Huchel, Maurer, Kuba, Fürnberg, and Hermlin. These poets came to the DDR relatively late in life, already convinced socialists, and all but Arendt, Huchel, and Hermlin are now dead. Brecht's influence on this group was minimal. Of course, the fact that they were not much like Brecht does not make them lesser poets; it only renders them of less interest for this study.

The second generation was actively involved in the transition to socialism; these poets, such as Cibulka, Fühmann, Werner, Deicke, Wiens, Gerlach, and Berger, were born during the twenties; Bobrowski (*b.*

1917) was slightly older. They began their active literary careers after World War II, most of them after settling in the DDR. They, too, had generally developed mature styles before Brecht's influence was strongly felt, and there is little Brechtian impact on their work. The poetry of this generation is still receiving, with few exceptions, very little foreign attention.

It is the third generation that has been influenced most demonstrably by Brecht and his poetry. Many of these poets are acquiring Western reputations in addition to their domestic popularity. They include Günter Kunert (*b.* 1929), Heinz Kahlau (*b.* 1931), Reiner Kunze (*b.* 1933), Rainer Kirsch (*b.* 1934), Sarah Kirsch (*b.* 1935), Karl Mickel (*b.* 1935), Wolf Biermann (*b.* 1936), Kurt Bartsch (*b.* 1937), Peter Gosse (*b.* 1938), Volker Braun (*b.* 1939), and Bernd Jentzsch (*b.* 1940). I have chosen only the most widely known but do not mean to imply that they are the only talented representatives of this generation. Only Kunert, Kahlau, and Kunze had poems published before Brecht's death in 1956. Several of them worked with Brecht in the Berliner Ensemble and regarded him as their mentor. John Flores calls them the "Brechtians" but points out that "they are all different, having learned slightly different lessons, but they all learned most from Brecht, and they constitute his 'posterity' (*die Nachgeborenen*) in the country where he spent the last years of his life."[5] Now dominant in the East German literary circles, all of these poets are convinced socialists who believe in their country, and one does well to keep this in mind when discussing the nature of political dissent in their poems. Kunert, Kahlau, Braun, Kunze, and Jentzsch have been subjected to sharp attacks in DDR literary journals, mainly for the "formalistic" tendencies of their work.[6] A number of these poets now live in forced or voluntary exile outside the DDR.

There is no unanimity of opinion as to which period of Brecht's poetry has been most widely imitated or reacted to by his posterity. Heinz Piontek maintains: "The poets schooled their dialectics on the model of Brecht. But the slightly scuffed-up classicism of his middle period—for instance in his sonnets—also is imitated." Peter Demetz agrees, but with a reservation: "Brecht's impact on the younger poets (who imitated his ballads and the lean verse of his middle period rather than the imagist style of his last years) was an ambivalent blessing." On the other hand, Michael Hamburger sees Brecht's late poems as most influential and asserts, "It is the more laconic of Brecht's later poems that were of seminal importance to almost all of the younger poets."[7] Kunert, Kahlau, Kunze, and Bartsch have all devoted considerable attention to the aphoristic "minimal" poem (as in the *Buckow Elegies*), whereas Biermann and Braun have written numerous ballads in a *Hauspostille* mode.

Demetz states that some poets "prefer the young Brecht and themselves write like his Baal, taking the sterile conflict between experimental and committed art in their swinging stride." One cannot know precisely which poets Demetz has in mind, but the statement seems to contradict what he says elsewhere in the same essay about Brecht's "middle period." Though there may be something of a Baal-like thirst in the work of younger poets such as Thomas Brasch (*b.* 1945), the high spirits and forceful language of Braun and Biermann, as for instance in Biermann's "Wire Harp," differs from Baal's Dionysian nihilism. Demetz overstates the so-called sterility of the "conflict between experimental and committed art," which Hamburger views in a more balanced manner: the poets "are beset by doubts as to whether the writing of poetry can be useful or meaningful in a social order which has done away with the poet's earlier use as a luxury product for the privileged, leisured, and well-educated."[8] How to make poetry relevant in the building of socialism and just what function it should have in the depiction of socialist reality is an issue that troubles this generation of poets. Kurt Bartsch approaches the problem in a five-line poem called "Poetry," which is also a good example of a brief poem in the Brechtian style:

> the men at the power plant
> light their morning cigarettes.
> while I was writing at night,
> sweating, they fed my work lamp.
> they shovelled coal for a moon poem.[9]

The "moon poem" is used as a metaphor for traditional nature poetry. Bartsch stresses the symbiosis between the manual labor of the power-plant stokers and the efforts of the poet. They have "fed" his lamp, thus making the poem possible. Bartsch may have a guilty conscience, since poetry should have a relevance that justifies expenditure of socially useful energy, and it is not clear that his nature poem does. However, he is addressing the very real problem, which also concerned Brecht, of the role art should play in socialism.

Many contemporary DDR poets have discarded the tradition of nature poems in favor of "oppositional" poetry. I am reluctant to use the terms "protest" or "dissent" poetry because of the Western associations with such terminology, and because there are some fundamental differences between poetry of political criticism in East and West. Brecht, for almost all but the last years of his life, wrote his "oppositional" political poetry from a position outside socialism. His indictments of bourgeois capitalism, and the fascism and imperialism that he, as a Marxist, saw as the logical and inevitable extension of capitalism, by implication could affirm a positive goal only "when things have come to the point / that humans help humans" (9: 725). Brecht's affirmative poetry about the Soviet Union was written from outside that system. Moreover, there is an ambiguity to Brecht's affirmations of Soviet socialism which makes them open to variant interpretations, as in a poem such as "The Rug Weavers of Kujan-Bulak Honor Lenin" (see Theodore Fiedler's essay in this volume). This element of functional ambiguity is present in DDR poetry as well. Only after Brecht settled in the DDR was he able to experience the day-to-day reality of nascent socialism. His optimistic, energetic dedication to the task of building socialism and abolishing the militaristic strain in German culture was somewhat muted after the uprising of 1953, and much has been written about his uneasy relationship with his new country after that date.

The poets who dominated the literary scene in the 1960s and continue to do so into the 1970s have, from the outset, written from within socialism. The oppositional poetry they write is of a qualitatively different nature from Brecht's. They, too, attack the inhuman excesses they perceive in capitalism, but they also write oppositional or, more precisely, critical poetry that deals with their own domestic socialism. They criticize the means by which socialism is being implemented in the DDR, rather than the end itself. Western critics have had difficulty appreciating that Biermann, for example, the most controversial poet of such critical views, can express vociferous dissent against what he terms "betrayal of the revolution" and still be fully committed to communism and the DDR. Biermann makes clear, however, that he is attacking the party bureaucrats who, in his opinion, stopped striving because they now believe that the battle has already been won and are intent upon consolidating their power positions. As Brecht would view it, now is the time for the long march through the institutions; but in Biermann's view, the march has been brought to a standstill. This unconscionable stagnation is the opposite of progressive socialism. The revocation of Biermann's DDR citizenship in November 1976, while the poet was in the Federal Republic on tour, is the latest measure in almost fifteen years of censorship and punishment and a fairly accurate indicator of the degree to which Biermann continues to infuriate the cultural bureaucracy and the leadership of the ruling party, the SED. Such punishment has in turn made him famous both in East and West. In the West he is characterized as a martyr (much to his oft-stated disgust); in the East he has become a rallying point for dissent, a role he also claims not to want. To be sure, Biermann's situation is much more extreme than Brecht's in the fifties. Party criticism of Brecht's *Lucullus*, for example, seems mild in retrospect.

The innate ambiguity of poetic diction further complicates the question of opposition and dissent. Speculative discussions of straightforward versus deceptively compliant language and the dubious practice of reading all poetry from the DDR as "code" are often the result. Nonetheless, it has been remarked that there is more dissent in poetry in the DDR than in any other genre. The explosive potential of poetry in the DDR is reflected in the ongoing heated debates and cases of censorship. Much of the character of current dissent arises from what one may regard as the fundamentally skeptical, questioning attitude that the poets have inherited, most of them consciously, from Brecht. They have grown to maturity in the DDR and take their national identity for granted. Their relationship to their country is more direct than it was for the older generation, and they are inclined both to expect and to demand more. Favorite forms for expressing their criticism and demands are the Brechtian "minimal" and more complicated but still succinct poems. An examination of Brecht's influence with this type of poem can serve as a means of measuring Brecht's influence in concrete terms.

Consider, for example, one of Günter Kunert's most effective aphoristic or minimal poems:

> As an unnecessary luxury
> forbade to produce what people
> call lamps
> King Tharsos of Xanto, the
> —from his birth—
> Blind.[10]

With Brechtian sophistication, Kunert uses a syntactic inversion to force the reader/listener to restate the thought before interpreting it. The unexpected line divisions contribute visually to the same alienation. In normal syntax, the single sentence would have to read something like: "King Tharsos of Xantos, blind from birth, forbade the production of what people call lamps as an unnecessary luxury." The blind king forbids the lamps for which he has no use. An unnecessary luxury is tautological, for luxury is by definition unnecessary, and this also provides a word play on luxury and *lux*, as light is a luxury to the king. But since the people are not blind and do need lamps, the king has imposed on the people an autocratic will that is blind to their needs. Although it may be plausible to suggest that an East German poet expressing this sentiment would not exclude the reading of "state economic planners" for "King Tharsos," the formulation is intentionally ambiguous. It could just as easily be read as an expression of either the inhumanity of the feudal past or the perversity of bourgeois historians who consider monarchs the makers of history. The poem gains in expressiveness through its ambiguity and should not be belabored by the insistence that it is nothing more than a thinly veiled reference to unfulfilled consumer longings.

More directly Brechtian is another of Kunert's minimal poems,

> Recommendation
> Not to bow down:
>
> The ship would not move forward
> Were not, steadfast in the wind, standing
> The sail.[11]

which plays against the motto of Brecht's *Buckow Elegies*,

> Were a wind to be blowing
> I could set a sail.
> Were no sail there
> I'd make one of sticks and canvas. (10: 1009)

The attitude expressed in the second poem is one of readiness, flexibility, adaptability to difficult circumstances in times of material scarcity, where one must make do with less than ideal conditions: an exemplary attitude in the DDR of the 1950s. By leaving out conjunctions and adverbs and starting each line with the subjunctive verb, Brecht draws special attention to the stance of readiness. Brecht's Western detractors, whose voices were loud in the cold war era, doubtless construed this gesture of flexibility as one of opportunism, of adjusting one's sail to the prevailing wind. Brecht, however, countered such attacks by emphasizing strategy rather than morality.

Kunert, dealing in 1968 with a different set of circumstances, advocates not adaptability but persistence. His admonition makes clear the relationship between the steadfast sail and the steadfast person. This may be read as an exhortation not to capitulate under pressure. If so, the pressure is adverse criticism of one's work; since the work is nonetheless useful in contributing to forward motion, one must stand fast. Kunert, like Brecht, stresses the subjunctive verbs and uses the sail image, but his poem expresses a sentiment quite different from the model.[12]

Like Kunert, Heinz Kahlau builds on a Brechtian short form to stimulate a critical attitude.

> This morning we read in the newspaper:
> A man was convicted.
> For whom and against whom?
> Who pronounced the verdict?
> For whom and against whom?
> The newspaper only reported:
> The man was convicted.
> Who owned the newspaper—
> and who owned the man?[13]

Where Brecht, in his "A Worker, Reading, Asks Questions," criticized the omissions of bourgeois history books with rhetorical questions, Kahlau, although preserving the inquisitive tone, is asking questions to which the reader can provide ready answers only if he has more information. Kahlau's poem is more ambiguous than his Brechtian model, and more disturbing. The newspaper reader wants to know who is served by an action such as this particular court sentence. Repeating a phrase such as "For whom and against whom" recalls one of Brecht's favorite queries and creates a sense of urgency.

A third member of this generation, Reiner Kunze, has specialized in minimal poems with a Brechtian tone, including a series of twenty-one "Variations on the theme 'the mail,'" many of them addressed by the persona to his daughter. Mail, for Kunze, is obviously an important link with the West (until his emigration in 1977, Kunze lived in the Thuringian town of Greiz, about two hundred kilometers south of Berlin, a train trip of a few hours at most), and many of the twenty-one poems refer specifically to this link.

Special Delivery / Express
Berlin (West)   20 January—1 PM
Greiz   26 January—9 PM

Letter
Berlin (West)   1 February—5 PM
Greiz   9 February

What
am I to tell my daughter
in the post museum?[14]

The comical sense of the poem derives from a depiction of censorship as an outrageous inefficiency in the postal system, where even a special delivery letter takes six days to travel two hundred kilometers and a normal letter still has not arrived after eight (and may never arrive). In a narrow reading, the poem is an implicit criticism of state violation of the mails or institutionalized chicanery designed to blunt intercourse between East and West which is veiled in an explicit concern, how can one explain to a child who has seen all the modern wonders of postal technology on exhibit in a museum how such things could be. In a broader view, the father (the poet) seeks a means to explain to his daughter (posterity) why modern technology (the socialism both the poet and his audience affirm) cannot function adequately. To the convinced socialist, such as Kunze, the new socialist reality, even when it seems illogical, is worth reforming. Kunze shares with Brecht the use of a child's amazement to point out what needs to be reformed. As is the case with the other poets, however, the problem that Kunze is addressing either existed in a different form for Brecht or did not exist at all. Brecht's principal experiences with problems in publishing his writing were first in Nazi Germany and then in American exile, and only very late in life in his new homeland. When Brecht was twenty-eight, he was writing in Weimar Germany; when Kunze was twenty-eight, the Berlin Wall was built.

From the initial stimulus of Brecht's poetry and his personal attitudes has developed, for each of the DDR poets now in their early forties, an individual style of confronting aesthetic and ideological problems. These poets have emerged from under Brecht's shadow. From Brecht, as a major influence, they borrowed or learned how to use formal poetic elements, diction, and devices, and acquired a fundamentally skeptical attitude. This skeptical attitude has caused friction between the poets and the literary establishment. Even if the DDR poets wished to do nothing but imitate Brecht, which they do not, they would have a difficult time duplicating the circumstances that formed and motivated Brecht. The temptation to equate the exile experience of Biermann or Kunze with Brecht's exile must be resisted, for it is an inept analogy. The reasons for exile and the circumstances of exile for these men are radically different, and the probable reception of Biermann's and Kunze's work in exile will surely differ from that of Brecht's work.

Brecht's influence on the DDR poets is a point of departure. They are his posterity, not his epigones. Most importantly, these poets are being read by a population that is increasingly distanced from its national "poet laureate," who wrote about a world they did not experience. Max Frisch's oft-cited dictum about Brecht's "ineffectiveness as a classic"[15] is, of course, an exaggeration, but it has some validity even in the DDR.

There is now a fourth generation of poets, and their work is notable for its distance from the birth pangs of the DDR. The work of a poet such as Thomas Brasch (*b.* 1945), for example, is striking in its use of vocabulary and viewpoints scarcely known in the DDR. The poem "Lovely Sunday" is an interesting illustration of this:

> "Picasso is dead now."
> said the dramaturge Barbara D. in the rockingchair.
> "Chaplin is already 84.
> In a few years Mao will be 90
> and we'll be left behind in the twentieth century."[16]

This short poem, which recalls Brecht's "Citydwellers" poems of the 1920s, is part of Brasch's "Paper Tiger" cycle. The irony Brasch expresses is a thinly masked critique of those who are oriented to the historical figures of the past. Brasch, like Biermann, Kunert, and Kunze now in Western exile, is perhaps less typical of his generation than his current position in the limelight suggests. One cannot know the effect that exile will have on these poets, on their poetry, and on the overall nature of DDR poetry. It is, however, clear that Brecht's importance as a major model for successive generations continues. Different poets focus on different aspects of Brecht's works for guidance in confronting a wide range of political issues.

Notes

1. Manfred Jäger, "Zum Selbstverständnis der DDR-Lyriker: Das Beispiel Volker Braun," *Text + Kritik: Politische Lyrik*, 9/9a (June 1973): 74–85; Klaus Schuhmann, "Brechtrezeption in der sozialistischen Gegenwartslyrik," *Untersuchungen zur Lyrik Brechts: Themen, Formen, Weiterungen* (Berlin: Aufbau, 1973), pp. 149–211; Klaus Werner, "Zur Brecht-Rezeption bei Günter Kunert und Hans Magnus Enzensberger," *Weimarer Beiträge, Brecht-Sonderheft* (1968): 61–73.

2. Among the most useful studies of DDR poetry are: John Flores, *Poetry in East Germany* (New Haven: Yale University Press, 1971); Konrad Franke, *Die Literatur der Deutschen Demokratischen Republik* ("Lyrik" pp. 208–307) (Munich: Kindler, 1974); Horst Haase, ed., *Geschichte der deutschen Literatur*, vol. 11; *Literatur der Deutschen Demokratischen Republik* (Berlin: Rütten and Loening, 1976), esp. pp. 74–116, 423–91, 710–80; Peter Hamm, "'Glück ist schwer in diesem Land . . .': Zur Situation der jüngsten DDR-Lyrik," *Merkur*, 19, no. 4 (April 1965): 365–79; Gregor Laschen, *Lyrik in der DDR* (Frankfurt: Athenäum, 1970); Fritz J. Raddatz, "Eine neue Subjektivität formt die neue Realität," *Traditionen und Tendenzen: Materialien zur Literatur der DDR* (Frankfurt: Suhrkamp, 1972), esp. pp. 167–211.

3. Cf. Liselotte Gumpel, *"Concrete" Poetry from East and West Germany* (New Haven: Yale University Press, 1976); Gumpel's very broad definition of "concrete" includes not only the visual-concrete of the West (e.g. Mon, Heißenbüttel, Gomringer), but also what she calls the "exemplary" poetry of the East (e.g. the "minimal" poems as in this study), and although she makes this distinction quite clear, her title is still misleading.

4. Johannes Bobrowski, *Selbstzeugnisse und Beiträge über sein Werk* (Berlin: Union Verlag, 1967), p. 78; Wolf Biermann quoted in Reinhold Grimm, *Bertolt Brecht*, 3d ed. (Stuttgart: Metzler, 1971), p. 104.

5. Flores, *Poetry in East Germany*, p. 272.

6. Raddatz documents these attacks in *Traditionen und Tendenzen*, pp. 167–211.

7. Heinz Piontek, *Deutsche Gedichte seit 1960: Eine Anthologie* (Stuttgart: Reclam, 1972), p. 13; Peter Demetz, *Postwar German Literature: A Critical Introduction* (New York: Pegasus, 1970), p. 64; Michael Hamburger, ed., *East German Poetry: An Anthology* (New York: Dutton, 1973), p. xvi. Hamburger's collection of poems from twelve authors (including Brecht) from the DDR is one of the few sources easily accessible to the English-speaking reader. Another is the journal *Dimension* (ed. A. Leslie Willson, University of Texas, Austin), which, like Hamburger's anthology, has German texts and parallel English translations. *Dimension* has printed a number of recent DDR poems, see, for example, *Special Issue 1973, DDR*.

8. Demetz, *Postwar German Literature*, p. 65; Hamburger, ed., *East German Poetry*, p. xvi.

9. *East German Poetry*, p. 18.

10. Günter Kunert, *Verkündigung des Wetters* (Munich: Hanser, 1966), p. 21.

11. Ibid., p. 18.

12. Raddatz expresses a widely held view of the difference between the two poets with the observation: "Due to a certain aridity, a gnomic character of his poetry, Kunert was often compared with Brecht, which is wrong. Brecht was (or wanted to be) an activist, Kunert is an observer and judge. His poems do not have that invisible last strophe which is formed in the mind of the reader to restructure the message. They give a verdict which is explicitly stated, completely formulated" ("Eine neue Subjektivität," p. 176). Such an assessment, which is remarkbly perceptive, points up the need for more detailed study of individual poems. In this instance, an analysis of a single poem modifies Raddatz's general conclusion.

13. *East German Poetry*, p. 113 (translation by Michael Hamburger).

14. *East German Poetry*, p. 137.

15. Max Frisch, *Öffentlichkeit als Partner* (Frankfurt: Suhrkamp, 1967), p. 73.

16. Translation cited from *Cityscape*: Austin Theatre Group program for the world premier in November 1976 of Brasch's *Paper Tiger*. The poem was subsequently depoliticized and now reads

> "Picasso is dead now,"
> says the dramaturge Barbara H.
> "and Chaplin is already 84.
> Hendrix Joplin Morrison Cybulski
> Dean have rotted away."
> She leans back in her easy chair and reaches
> for the letter opener:
> "In a few years
> we'll be all alone
> in this century."

From *Kargo: 32. Versuch auf einem untergehenden Schiff aus der eigenen Haut zu kommen* (Frankfurt: Suhrkamp, 1978), p. 102.

The Reception of a Socialist Classic: Kunert and Biermann Read Brecht

THEODORE FIEDLER

Like many of their fellow East German poets who have come of age since World War II, Günter Kunert (*b.* 1929) and Wolf Biermann (*b.* 1939) have assimilated, adapted, or otherwise used Bertolt Brecht's poetry and attendant poetics in the course of realizing their respective aims as poets and citizens within the common framework of socialism in the German Democratic Republic. Significantly, their reception of Brecht spans not only their formative years through the early 1960s but extends into the 1970s as well.[1] Yet, if in earlier years both Kunert and Biermann were drawn to Brecht because of his insistence on the poet's critical stance and his attention to contradictions in individuals and their relations to one another whatever the cultural matrix, their recent response to Brecht reveals a different overriding concern—Brecht's canonization as the socialist literary classic of the DDR.[2] Exploring how each of the two poets comes to terms with Brecht's classical status in the 1970s can contribute to an understanding of two major East German poets and also demonstrate Brecht's continuing significance as a cultural force for change in the DDR.

[1]

Kunert responds most forcefully to the canonization of Brecht in the DDR with an essay prepared for the official commemoration at the East Berlin Academy of the Arts of the seventy-fifth anniversary of Brecht's birth.[3] Kunert provocatively joins the act of honoring Brecht to Brecht's own lyrical chronicle of one instance of the honoring of Lenin—"The Rug Weavers of Kujan-Bulak Honor Lenin." Kunert's purpose is to jolt his listeners into reflecting on their reception of Brecht in terms of Brecht's low-keyed commentary on the action of the weavers of Kujan-Bulak who, at the suggestion of one of their number, decide to honor Lenin not by erecting yet another plaster cast bust, as they had planned after receiving news that the day to honor Lenin was at hand, but by using their hard-earned kopeks to purchase oil to destroy the breeding grounds of the malaria-bearing mosquitos that plague them:

> So they helped themselves by honoring Lenin and
> Honored him by helping themselves and had thus
> Understood him.[4]

For Kunert, then, to ask how we are to honor Brecht in the light of Brecht's poem is to avoid the pitfall of secular idolatry; it is to ask instead what we are to do in order to show that we have understood him.

To dramatize the point of his query and to pursue his overall aim of deautomatizing the reception of Brecht as a socialist classic in a socialist society, Kunert questions the "realism" (in official DDR aesthetics *the* value) of Brecht's poem on both empirical and theoretical grounds. He insists, for example, that the weavers whose story the poem tells are fictions, that their decision to honor Lenin in a way different from the way he has been honored by others is merely an embodiment of Brecht's dialectical thinking, even though Kunert is aware that the poem evokes the real world as its frame of reference and that Brecht based it on an account of an incident entitled "A Monument for Lenin" which appeared in the *Frankfurter Zeitung* in 1929.[5] The weavers' decision, "a leap from emotional elatedness to incisive reason," is one, Kunert alleges, "which is truly thrust on the poor people in the poem, for we know only too well from history why such rational decisions tend to fail" (p. 468).

Yet Kunert is concerned far less with the "literal" realism of "The Rug Weavers" than he is with the underlying relation of the poem to contemporary reality, that is, its "essential" realism.[6] Identifying the alternative of emotionalism or pragmatism in human affairs as the content of the poem, Kunert argues that Brecht's overtly didactic treatment of this alternative simultaneously constitutes and suspends the essential realism of "The Rug Weavers." References to Brecht's didacticism notwithstanding, Kunert bases his paradoxical assessment of the essential realism of the poem on a particular conception of poetry. If Brecht's text is to qualify as a poem rather than as a set of directions for behavior in a real world context, Kunert observes, the alternative around which it is structured cannot be a real one but must instead be one invented for the specific instance of "The Rug Weavers." Moreover, Brecht's poem shares with all poems the distinctive trait of being "meaningful and, at the same time, meaningless," both "true" and "untrue" (p. 468). The specific truth of Brecht's poem results from Brecht's poetic suggestion that the reader arrive at rational decisions in conducting his or her life. The poem is specifically untrue, on the other hand, insofar as it asserts that such rational decisions are already a common historical phenomenon.

Kunert's conception of poetic discourse may or may not provide a valid basis for a discussion of the thorny issue of realism in lyric poetry. But, in the present instance, he has had to misread Brecht's poem in order to fit it into his scheme of things. Nothing in "The Rug Weavers" substantiates his contention that the poem is "untrue." Indeed, Brecht uses the poem to state a position directly contrary to the "untrue" and thus "unrealistic" view Kunert attributes to him. In the dialectic of the poem and, by implication, of history, the weavers, led by that embodiment of Lenin's theory of the vanguard, the red-army soldier Stepa Gamalew, appear to be the exception rather than the rule in honoring Lenin: they make rational decisions related to pragmatic ends instead of joining in the common idolatry that seems to be dictated from above. Brecht is careful not to valorize directly the emotionally seductive and officially sanctioned ways of honoring Lenin that he lists at the start of the poem. The words "Thus, however" (9: 666) with which he introduces his account of the weavers' honoring of Lenin in an out-of-the-way place in southern Turkestan are a sign to his readers that there is something radically isolated and infrequent, yet exemplary and very much in need of preserving about the weavers' way of going about the business of living while honoring the dead. Indeed, Brecht's poem dramatizes an incident counter to usual practice as a model of what the poet must have considered to be genuine Leninist socialist democracy in action.

Why does Kunert misread "The Rug Weavers"? I have already suggested that he pays far too little attention to the specificity of the literal level of the poem and thus overlooks the subtle dialectic, at once critical and affirmative, that structures Brecht's utterance and links it at least indirectly to the issue of socialist political practice as Brecht encountered it in the late 1920s in Germany.[7] Kunert's disregard for the detail of "The

Rug Weavers" is consistent with his devaluation of the literal realism of literary works in favor of their essential realism. This position, however, conflicts with his stated concern for the underlying relation of a work to its contemporary reality to such an extent that, given the problematic continuity between the political practice of the German communist movement in the later years of the Weimar Republic and that of the DDR leadership over the years, he might be suspected of avoiding the political ramifications that an assertion of the original negativity of Brecht's poem would entail in the DDR of the 1970s. Yet Kunert's disregard for the detail of "The Rug Weavers" and his consequent misreading of the poem appear to be due not to opportunism but to an aversion to Brecht's didacticism in both theory and practice, an aversion that goes well beyond his thinly veiled sarcasm on the subject in his brief essay.[8]

As early as 1965 Kunert observed in a letter to a West German scholar that the classical didactic poem with its direct transmission of a moral, as Brecht had practiced it, had become an impossibility. In its place Kunert posits a different class of didactic poems—"black didactic poems ... that open with a bad example, that show the negative as aim—but in such a way that allows one to draw from this 'moral' a counter moral."[9] More recently, in an interview published in 1974, Kunert articulated his conception of the utility of poetry in opposition to a fundamental aspect of Brecht's pragmatically oriented poetics—the notion of the poem as *Gebrauchsgegenstand* or useful object. In Kunert's view, the poem construed as useful object is condemned to futility because, in taking external conditions as its point of departure and its aim, it treats the reader merely instrumentally. Whether Kunert's characterization of the poem as useful object does justice to Brecht's notion is a moot point, but the relations of poem, reader, and world that Kunert finds implicit in that notion are clearly inverted in his conception of what a poem ought to do and how it ought to be used. For he views a reader's consciousness of self rather than of external conditions as the primary point of a poem. Why? "The reader already has consciousness of his external circumstances; since they are widespread he obtains it from many sources. He can learn of his internal circumstances from himself only if he dares to engage in a dialogue with himself: the poem ought to cause him to do so."[10]

Kunert's "anti-Brechtian" conception of the utility of poetry informs his critique of what he regards as the typical reception of "The Rug Weavers" as well as his assessment of the poem. What happens when we read Brecht's poem, Kunert asks his East German audience. We identify with the weavers, he observes, on both intellectual and emotional grounds— we concur in the rationality of their choice and we have an aversion toward monuments—and in our solidarity with them participate imaginatively in their revolutionary act. But we do so *only* imaginatively in an empty transcendence of self that has no personal consequences, one that does not lead to that confrontation with self that Kunert posits as the primary aim of poetry. Insofar as Brecht's poem allows its readers this reception, this "differentiated pseudoactivity" (p. 470), Kunert finds fault with the poem. Yet the moral that Kunert draws for his audience is not the rejection of a flawed Brecht but the need for a different kind of reading of Brecht, one that is both critical and self-critical: "One must question Brecht and demand of him what leads us to ourselves" (p. 470).

A number of poems in Kunert's book *The Small However* (1975) embody such a critical reading of Brecht.[11] Kunert's lyrical chronicle devoted to "Alexander Cumming the Great," for instance, is a half-serious, half-ironic, but certainly parodistic poem modeled on Brecht's chronicles. Like several of these, Kunert's poem presents one of the unsung heroes of human history, a matter Kunert underscores via the mock-heroic epithet "the Great." Unlike his namesake Alexander the Great, whose stature Brecht's reflective worker quietly relativizes in the chronicle "A Worker, Reading, Poses Questions," Alexander Cumming is hardly known, even though, as Kunert states in the opening stanza, as "inventor of the flush toilet" he is, in a very real sense, "everywhere." In the second stanza Kunert, in a manner reminiscent of Brecht, lends a kind of heroic significance to Cumming's seemingly mundane discovery:

> A bold stroke the idea
> of the doubly-bent drainpipe
> whose constant water content
> safeguards every household against
> the rising stench, disease and pestilence
> from the labyrinth of the sewers.

The remaining three stanzas abstract from the specific instance of Alexander Cumming to metahistorical and, by implication, metapoetical reflections on the role of the exemplary in human behavior. Thus, the third stanza, which initially thematizes our ignorance of the circumstances of

Cumming's breakthrough, relates Cumming's obscurity in recorded history to that of countless other unheroic heroes, implying that Cumming himself was unaware of his commonly shared fate.

> who can guess if he knew
> that he counted among the countless
> called to anonymous service
> after their own demise.

As if to conceptualize the critique of the historical record that informs Brecht's "A Worker, Reading, Asks Questions" the terse fourth stanza focuses incisively on the nature of that record, on its perpetuation of the Alexander the Greats of history:

> Transmitted are the names
> of heroes of futility.

Yet the moral that Kunert draws in the concluding stanza is decidedly anti-Brechtian in both its explicit and implicit meanings. The ambiguous opening phrase, translatable as both the "story" of Alexander Cumming and as "history itself," is identified as an example:

> . . . an example
> of the flawed utility of all examples
> that no one heeds.
> Oh Cumming!

Unlike Brecht, who in his chronicles represents seemingly insignificant individuals as historically exemplary and, as such, clearly worthy of emulation on the part of his readers, Kunert tells the story of Cumming and, indirectly, of history itself in order to focus his readers' attention on their negative implications. Kunert's readers are not only confronted with their failure as well as that of the rest of humanity to perceive and act on the truly exemplary, but the very efficacy of the exemplary is called into question.

Kunert's problematization of the exemplary and of our response to it within the framework of his overtly didactic poem with its various allusions to Brecht is hardly a matter of coincidence. Given the role that the exemplary plays in Brecht's poetic practice, Kunert's poem, whatever else it may try to achieve, is a continuation of his critique of Brecht's didacticism. Thus, Kunert exemplifies the concept of the "black" didactic poem that is to replace Brecht's "classical" version. The story of Alexander Cumming, not to mention the story of history itself, is the "bad example." And the "negative" is its "aim." Yet nothing about the poem prevents readers from drawing the "counter moral" that Kunert projects as the hidden aim of the new genre.

A second poem from *The Small However* that questions Brecht in order to "lead to ourselves" is "Self-Examination for Good Reason." Its tripartite division and several of its themes recall Brecht's self-critical yet ultimately apologetic poem "To the Descendants." Speaking as one of the descendants, Kunert engages in a critical dialogue not only with himself and his contemporaries but also with Brecht's poem and with the self-legitimizing use to which it has been put in the DDR. Like the persona of Brecht's poem, Kunert's persona takes stock of himself and his age, though on a greatly diminished scale and from a radically different perspective that takes into account the changes that have occurred in the nearly forty years separating the writing of the two poems, in particular the defeat of German fascism and the development of socialism in the DDR. Brecht's poem, written in exile in the mid-thirties, opens with the oft-quoted lament "Truly, I live in dark times!" (9: 722). Its anguished pathos sets the stage for the speaker's impassioned search for signs of solidarity in himself and others for the victims of these dark times. The authenticity of this concern is underscored by an acute awareness of vulnerability to the destructive forces that are about: "By accident I've been spared. (If my luck runs out, I'm lost.)" Kunert's poem, on the other hand, opens with an assertion of group solidarity with a new generation of victims only to call that assertion into question:

> We say we're affected
> before we start drinking beer
> although we aren't really
> (as we believe)...

Significantly, the poem by no means denies the existence of a new generation of victims that has fallen prey to, say, the fascist takeover in Chile or American operations in Viet Nam, two instances of political oppression that were widely publicized and condemned in the DDR in the late 1960s and early 1970s. At the very moment the speaker of Kunert's poem and his friends settle down to a round of beer, he surmises that their counterparts, "our doubles," are being murdered, maimed, and tortured. But Kunert's overriding concern in "Self-Examination" is to get at the reality of the group's response to the fate of these doppelgänger. Unlike Brecht's persona, who finds neither sufficient words nor feelings of solidarity, Kunert's finds too much said and too little honestly felt about the victims of contemporary dark times, if only because they are geographically distant "beyond the oceans and mountains," as distant as others once were from the beer drinkers when they were victims. "Words rattle around in us," he observes, and remain just that—words.

In the middle section of the poem, Kunert enumerates a series of obstacles impeding genuine feeling. The series culminates in an attack on the institutionalization of solidarity within the framework of socialism in the DDR.

> The feelings of rocks
> we feel and thus also
> the obligation
> to feel more: hence our discomfort
> our somewhat soiled conscience.
> (Happy is he who frees himself
> of that with a monetary contribution.)

Continuing the attack while alluding to the passage in part 3 of Brecht's elegy that expresses despair over the absence of outrage at injustice, Kunert, in a striking image, articulates despair over an outrage that has become an end in itself, thus diminishing both the victims and the professors of such sentiment.

> Our impotence develops splendid sentences
> cheap shrouds
> under which the victims disappear
> together
> with something of ourselves
> that has died.

The concluding section of "Self-Examination" is marked initially by the speaker's sudden retreat from the uncompromising public stance he had assumed in order to bring the problematicality of a particularly sensitive and opaque issue to the consciousness not so much of a couple of beer drinkers as that of the entire society these imply. But the gentle and intimate concern evoked by the fourfold repetition of the familiar imperative *come*

> come leave
> the autopsy of a long-past ethics . . .
> come into the open come
> into the freedom of joyful participation
> come onto the soccer field

turns out to be a deception. For the invitation to the soccer field is an invitation to experience the local version of reality *this side* of the oceans and mountains. The soccer field and the human activity it entails are emblematic of such local reality.

> Struggle, sweat and movement
> and the bleating
> from the brazen mouths
> of agitated bipeds:
> that is reality.

That rather than the unfortunately all-too-real "screaming of the martyred," "the mechanical death rattle of the dying" on the other side of the globe is the reality Kunert's persona wants his interlocutor to confront. At least in this confrontation there is a chance to experience a genuine feeling, some real pain—"You demand morality / and receive a kick"—and thus gain some firsthand knowledge about the upside-down nature, the *Verkehrtheit* of the world.

The fusion of revolutionary and elegiac pathos that marks Brecht's "To the Descendants" is conspicuously absent in Kunert's "Self-Examination." The heroic age of socialist struggle with fascism, depicted so forcefully in Brecht's poem, has given way to the problematic institutionalization of solidarity in a socialist society. Ironically, Kunert's central concern while speaking deliberately as one of Brecht's "descendants" is thus not the weaknesses of his predecessor's generation as Brecht had anticipated in the closing section of his elegy but those of Kunert's generation. And in leading that generation to itself—to paraphrase the fundamental principle of his poetics—Kunert is neither friendly nor considerate.

[2]

Wolf Biermann's continuing reception of Brecht is, like Kunert's, an attempt to actualize an influential predecessor in danger of becoming yet

another ossified socialist classic. But Biermann's motivation, as manifest
in *For My Comrades* (1972), is not Kunert's socialistically oriented Neo-
platonic dictum "Know Thyself" with its secondary political implications; it is an overtly political concern with the unfinished socialist
revolution in the DDR and other socialist societies.[12]

Given Brecht's commitment to Marxism during the conflicts between
socialism and capitalism in the 1920s and 1930s as well as his articulation
of the contradictions within socialism itself during the last eight years of
his life spent in the DDR, Biermann understandably sees in Brecht an ally
in his struggle against bureaucratic socialism. But what makes Brecht a
particularly useful ally for Biermann, who in the eleven years preceding
his expatriation in November 1976 was forbidden to perform or publish
in the DDR and thus had no official status of any kind, is precisely
Brecht's status as an accepted socialist classic. Indeed, Biermann deliberately plays on that paradox by choosing as the epigraph for *For My Comrades* an epigram in which Brecht, posing as the god of happiness,
cheerfully admits to what, from another perspective, is clearly a list of
damning charges, charges that DDR authorities have, either explicitly or
by implication, brought against Biermann at one time or another:[13]

> I am the god of happiness, collecting heretics round me
> Intent on happiness in this vale of tears,
> An agitator, muckraker, inciter
> And thus—close the door!—illegal. (*FmG*, p. 2; cf. Brecht 10: 894)

Not only does the pose of Brecht's god of happiness in all its ramifications
suit Biermann's cheerfully defiant self-conception as poet and citizen of
the DDR particularly well, but the epigrammatic point—the implicit il-
legality of the god of happiness (and thus of Brecht writing his poem in
exile in capitalist America!)—has in a very real and explicit sense been
true of Biermann in the DDR since December 1965. Biermann thus uses
Brecht's epigram and the official legitimacy of its author in the DDR to
relegitimize by association what DDR authorities in his own case have
declared illegitimate. Moreover, Biermann's use of the poem aligns his
socialist accusers with Brecht's capitalist ones as the common enemy. It
also raises the further paradox that Brecht, given the sentiments he has
expressed in the epigram and elsewhere, has become a socialist classic at
all under socialism in its present form.[14]

In his handwritten epigrammatic gloss to Brecht's epigram, Biermann

has the "Master," as he affectionately dubs Brecht, offer the use of his epigram as protection in full dialectical awareness that his self-proclaimed
utility has become, at least for the moment, a matter of his monumentality:

> Take
> this poem, a fig leaf
> can protect!
> I've been degraded
> to a monument
> and thus can be of use to you. (*FmG*, p. 2)

This tongue-in-cheek gloss underscores the need to break down the
official status of Brecht's work (its use by those in power as a "fig leaf")
and to reappropriate it to the critical tradition in socialism as part of the
ongoing struggle to revitalize the faltering, indeed betrayed, socialist
revolution.

Biermann pursues these objectives in "Brecht, Your Descendants"
(*FmG*, pp. 33–35), a bitter revision of Brecht's "To the Descendants" in
the tradition of Brecht's critical adaptations of predecessors. Unlike Kunert's "Self-Examination," Biermann's poem not only confronts Brecht's
poem head-on but also attempts a statement for the present generation
that is comparable in scope and force to the original. At issue in particular is the historical optimism of Brecht's elegy expressed in the opening
lines of its concluding section:

> You who will emerge from the flood
> In which we went under ... (9: 724)

Biermann quotes these lines as the motto of his ballad to measure his
contemporaries (rather than his predecessors as Brecht had feared)
against the brave new world these lines imply. Measured against that
world, that time, as the final stanza has it, "when human beings will help
one another" (9: 725), Brecht's descendants, at least in Biermann's view,
have failed to realize Brecht's hopeful expectations: "Those on whom
you based your hopes / With your hopes they perish." More concretely,
those whom Brecht had expected to do better under less trying circumstances than his own generation had in "dark times" excel only at
preempting the political emancipation of others: "Those who were supposed to do things better / Do other people's business better and better."
Furthermore, those who have betrayed Brecht's hope use his poem to

legitimize themselves and the new status quo: "In dark times they have set themselves up / Comfortably with your poem."

Biermann's attack on his contemporaries is not all-inclusive but restricted to specific groups within the new order of things. These groups, the new privileged classes under socialism in its present state, include the party elite and their supporters, the secondary bureaucracy and the opportunistic intelligentsia. After devoting the first one and one-half stanzas to the party elite, accusing them not only of political authoritarianism but also, in contrast to Brecht's generation, of waning anger and passion, Biermann takes on the remaining two groups in the second and fourth stanzas. The secondary bureaucrats, who, he observes, lack political substance, are "branded" by the tools of their trade, "tortured" by their privileges. Totally conditioned by their position and their circumstances, they are "as though blind from the darkness around them / ... as though deaf from the silence around them / ... as though dumb from the daily cries of victory." Their particular skill consists of inflicting and enduring ever more subtle pain. And in contrast to Brecht's generation, for whom the distant aim was clear, if unreachable (9: 724), they have not nearly reached their radically different end. To attack the opportunistic intelligentsia, Biermann reworks the image of shipwreck from Brecht's elegy. The good ship Revolution, dating back to the nineteenth century, has gone down, leaving nothing but its flotsam and jetsam to recall its past glory, to transfigure the revolutionary past at the expense of the turbulent present. Those who have indeed "emerged from the flood in which you went under" now see no land.

Directing his anger at all three groups simultaneously in a fifth stanza, Biermann speaks in "prose," that is, neither in the metaphorical mode of the previous stanzas nor in the harmonizing vein of the concluding section of Brecht's elegy, but in terms of the prosaic reality of the everyday DDR world. To get at that reality and the shortcomings of Brecht's descendants, Biermann inverts bits and pieces of the concluding section of Brecht's poem, pitting the present generation against the earlier one. Instead of making allowances for others, as Brecht had hoped, his descendants are lenient only with themselves. If Brecht's generation moved through class warfare changing countries more often than shoes, Biermann's changes its political stance with the same frequency. Biermann concedes that the voices of his contemporaries are no longer hoarse from protesting injustice; they no longer have anything to say. Similarly, their features are no longer distorted in hatred; they have become face-less. And in a double negation of Brecht's utopian expectation that human beings will help one another, Biermann concludes that humans have become wolves' wolves.

Despite the apparent finality of this bleak perception of reality, Bier-mann concludes with a self-assessment that avoids, in its sober intermin-gling of possibility and reality, both the closing utopian vision of Brecht's elegy and the unqualified pessimism emanating from his own bitter nega-tion of that vision. Biermann presents the possibility for change and his strengths in terms of his impact on his "guests," contemporaries who, having heard his excoriation of those subverting socialism, depart "in-toxicated by the subversive / truth of my ballads, set ablaze by the false logic / of my poems ... armed with confidence." Yet he also presents real-ity as presently constituted and his weaknesses in terms of his isolation upon the departure of his "guests." Just as Brecht's generation had taken on some of the worst characteristics of its age in combating the social evils of the age, so Biermann, in combating the social evils of his own age, feels himself, at least while in isolation, taking on the related characteris-tics of his own "dark times." Having charged certain of his contempo-raries with heaping the ashes of burned-out fires on his head, he now sees himself as "ashes of my fires." Like his detested contemporaries, he, too, has neither voice nor face. Like them, he has become as if deaf and blind, albeit for antithetical reasons that link his efforts to the revolutionary tra-dition betrayed by some of his contemporaries, but represented by his predecessor's generation in Brecht's poem—if it is read correctly. Worst of all, Biermann's isolation brings on his fear of his "own fear," a fear that is not just a general fear of reprisal, but the very specific fear, as refer-ences to it elsewhere in his writings attest, of being expatriated from the DDR. Biermann's fear, of course, has turned out to be a justified one. For in spite of SED General Secretary Erich Honecker's promising dictum of late 1971 that there could no longer be any taboos in the field of art and literature if the firm ground of socialism were the artist's point of depar-ture, Biermann was indeed expatriated some four years after his ballad was first published.[15]

Although "Brecht, Your Descendants" is one of the most dramatic and sustained instances of Biermann's critical use of Brecht's poetry, a num-ber of other adaptations of Brecht's texts warrant at least brief considera-tion. "Small Song about Constant Values" (*FmG*, p. 20), for example, is built around a revision of the sublime apocalyptic vision of Brecht's "Of Poor B.B." Biermann transforms the young Brecht's emphatic assertion "Of these cities will remain what went through them: the wind!" (8: 262) into a down-to-earth, chiasmically structured question and answer sequence: "and what—now what / will remain of them? / Of them will remain / what. . . . " This poem provides a human and usually humorous perspective on a series of seemingly overwhelming phenomena as well as one fragile one: "the great liars," "the great hypocrites," "the great despots," those who "glut truth's maw with bread," and "this sung-out song."

In a stanza of "Language of Language" (*FmG*, p. 17)—a pessimistic poem, at times angry, at times despairing in tone—Biermann once again challenges the historical optimism of "To the Descendants." The lines "Escaping the fires unhappily / we now rot in the bog / He who struggles, sinks faster" fuse the past and the future of Brecht's lines "The roads led into the bog in my time" and "Consider / . . . / Also the dark time / you have escaped" (9: 724) in Biermann's present and actualize the image of "bog" as well. In the same stanza Biermann also challenges the more guarded optimism of "Truth Unites," one of the many *Buckow Elegies*, written after the June 1953 uprisings in the DDR, that Brecht saw fit to keep to himself:

> He who has recognized his situation . . .
> is more lost than others, oh
> to the pressure is added
> the pressing consciousness of pressure.

The lines from "Truth Unites" which Biermann collates and transforms here are these: "Thus as Lenin: Tomorrow evening / We are lost, if not . . ." and "From our difficult situation / There is no escape" (10: 1011– 12).

Finally, Biermann's imposing "Eight Arguments for the Retention of the Name 'Stalin Avenue' for the Stalin Avenue" (*FmG*, pp. 41– 43) updates Brecht's fragment "To a Young Construction Worker on the Stalin Avenue" in which Brecht addressed some of the contradictions of the early years of socialism in the DDR. The fragment begins with the observation "Your avenue does not yet have trees" (10: 1003), a statement that captures both the possibilities ("*your* avenue," "trees") and the difficulties ("does not yet have") inherent in the new beginning—the "construction of socialism"—that the Stalin Avenue project represented in official DDR circles in the early 1950s. It goes on to encourage the young worker (and with him the working class) to stand his ground on what is now, after all, his *own* ground while dealing with his superiors. To quote one of several such suggestions contained in the fragment:

> To him who gives the order say:
> Orders are necessary, when there are so many in such great ventures
> With so little time
> But order me
> so that I order myself as well! (10: 1004)

Biermann's use of the image of the trees in the fourth stanza of his satirical attack on Stalinism in DDR socialism,

> And because graveyard silence
> Weighs on this street already
> At half past nine in the evening
> The trees stand in line

implies, however, that Brecht had, at best, mistaken one aspect for the whole. What really should have been at issue in 1952, when Brecht's poem appears to have been written, was the nature of the project as well as the decision-making process that led to it, rather than its mode of execution, in other words: Stalinism itself rather than one of its manifestations.[16] For the Stalin Avenue, long since built and renamed, has its trees now but not the manifestations of human community and sociability that were supposed to go with them. Instead, early in the evening it is deserted, indeed quiet in a way that recalls Stalinism at its worst, as trees rather than people stand in line. But that, as Biermann's argument goes, is precisely why the street deserves the name Stalin Avenue: "After all, for that reason, too, it's called STALIN AVENUE."

[3]

Whatever the closely interrelated differences in poetics and ideology between Günter Kunert and Wolf Biermann may be, and the foregoing analysis of their response to Brecht in the seventies suggests that these differences are substantial, both poets nonetheless share their predecessor's *critical* commitment to socialism. Each poet articulates that commitment in a manner that is also characteristic of his own critical actualization of Brecht—low-keyed, probing, more skeptical of fundamental assumptions in the case of Kunert; outspoken, alternately playful and impatiently angry, more affirmative of the revolutionary tradition in the case of Biermann. Yet, in spite of such differences, a common bond exists: the day after the Central Committee of the SED had announced the expatriation of Biermann, in effect making an example of its most outspoken socialist critic at a time of widespread dissension in the Soviet imperium, Kunert joined thirteen other well-known East German intellectuals in addressing to the SED leadership an open letter of protest over its decision. The letter called for nothing less than a rescinding of that decision in the spirit of a critically minded socialism as articulated by Marx.

This spontaneous and unprecedented act of solidarity, which subsequently was joined by more than 150 other cultural figures from throughout the DDR, seems to have caught the SED leadership by surprise. It demanded public support for its decision, a move that escalated the impact of the Biermann case by bringing it to the attention of a significant portion of the DDR population in a variety of public situations.[17] In the meantime, however, official order, to the extent it had been disrupted at all, has been restored through a series of arrests, interrogations, and other repressive measures. To note the most visible consequence, officially deviant socialist intellectuals have been emigrating to the West at a depressing rate since late 1976 as a result of economic, social, and political reprisals taken against them because of their support of Biermann.

By mid-1977 Kunert himself, having been expelled from the SED for his part in the "tragicomedy" in spite of his long-term membership in the Party, appeared to be weighing his alternatives in an open letter addressed to a fellow East German but published in the West German weekly *Die Zeit*.[18] Attempting to get at the causes of the Biermann affair without regard to the personalities involved, Kunert isolates three interrelated factors: the disparity between socialist theory and socialist practice that it was taboo to mention; the disparity between official consciousness, which is affirmative and functional, and that of the writer as type, which is existential and critical; and the structurally determined autism of administrators. The disparity between theory and practice, itself the result of a theoretically induced failure to acknowledge the empirical obstacles impeding the realization of a socialist utopia, gets exposed for what it is by the writer, who is concerned primarily with the tension between the ideal and the real. This confrontation between the writer with his Brechtian "pleasure in speaking the truth" and the established order leads to that order's "displeasure with truth," an aversion that Kunert glosses in terms of Brecht's characterization of those who never doubt in his "Praise of Doubt": "They don't believe the facts; they only believe themselves. If necessary / The facts get axed" (9: 627). Given the opposing modes of consciousness that this confrontation between writer and established order entails, it is hardly surprising that Kunert sees little hope for a dialogue. But he goes beyond that to dramatize the one-sided nature of the communication that does take place and ties it to his notion of the autism of administrators. Administrators, he observes, use language in disagreement primarily to stigmatize and not to establish matters of fact. Moreover, they have suppressed criticism and avoided the concept of contradiction for so long that every deviant opinion is construed as an assassination attempt with words. Kunert, in conclusion, captures his assessment of official behavior and his response to it in a quotation from the diary of another socialist literary classic, Johannes R. Becher: "He who doesn't know how to make friends of enemies will make enemies of friends." Speaking as an alienated friend, Kunert sounds a final warning in terms of the title of Becher's diary, *Such Great Hope of Another Kind*: "If such behavior continues, there is simply no hope of any kind."

That the present SED leadership will listen to Kunert's reasoned and reasonable plea for mutual understanding any more than it has listened to Biermann's far more pointed remarks is doubtful. Thus, in spite of his classical status or perhaps precisely because of it, Brecht's emphatic demand at the close of "Praise of Doubt" remains as far as ever from implementation:

> You who are a leader, don't forget
> That you are one because you doubted leaders!
> So permit those who are being led
> To doubt! (9: 628)

Notes

1. John Flores, *Poetry in East Germany: Adjustments, Visions and Provocations, 1945–1970* (New Haven: Yale University Press, 1971), pp. 275–92 and 301–13, has commented at length on both Kunert's and Biermann's reception of Brecht before 1970. For an East German account of Kunert's reception of Brecht before 1970, see Klaus Schuhmann, "Brechtrezeption in der sozialistischen Gegenwartslyrik," *Untersuchungen zur Lyrik Brechts: Themen, Formen, Weiterun-*

gen (Berlin: Aufbau, 1973), pp. 149–211, esp. pp. 154–81. Because of the official ban on Biermann in the DDR in effect since December 1965, Schuhmann silently excluded Biermann's reception of Brecht from consideration.

2. Biermann's expatriation on 16 November 1976 for alleged attacks on the DDR while on tour in the Federal Republic of Germany does not alter the fact that during the first half of the 1970s he read his predecessor within a particular East German context. Moreover, since his expatriation Biermann has continued to draw on Brecht in coming to terms with the DDR and its problems. See his "Westzucker und Ostpeitsche," *Die Zeit*, no. 5, 3 February 1978, pp. 16–17, which is a sympathetic critique of a "manifesto" authored by an anonymous DDR oppositional group and published in two January 1978 issues of *Der Spiegel*.

3. Kunert's remarks at the Academy of the Arts have subsequently been published as "Überlegungen zu den 'Teppichwebern' (und dazu, wie wir Brecht ehren)," *Sinn und Form* 25 (1973): 467–70, hereafter cited in the text by page number. All translations in this essay are my own.

4. Bertolt Brecht, "Die Teppichweber von Kujan-Bulak ehren Lenin," 9: 667.

5. Brecht's hand-marked copy of the account is available as item 936/11-13 in the Brecht Archives in Berlin (East). It has been reproduced in Gerhard Seidel, *Bertolt Brecht. Arbeitsweise und Edition. Das literarische Werk als Prozeß* (Stuttgart: Metzler, 1977), insert between pp. 226 and 227.

6. Kunert dismisses "literal" realism as "something from a children's picture book, something purely external" (p. 468).

7. Marsch, *Brecht-Kommentar: Zum lyrischen Werk* (Munich: Winkler, 1974), p. 279, indicates "The Rug Weavers" was written in 1929, a time when Brecht was periodically at odds with the German Communist party. The poem was first published in 1933 in *Versuche* 7 under the general heading of "Geschichten aus der Revolution." Its circulation was cut short by the Nazi takeover.

8. The German critical theorist Hans Robert Jauß employs the term *original negativity* in "Literaturgeschichte als Provokation der Literaturwissenschaft," *Literaturgeschichte als Provokation* (Frankfurt: Suhrkamp, 1970), pp. 144–207, to conceptualize those historically determinate aspects of "classical" works which initially make such works memorable but which are overlooked or suppressed later.

Kunert's long-term interaction with Brecht, going back to his own didactic poetry of the early fifties, perhaps could be explored in terms of the theoretical framework that Harold Bloom develops on the basis of psychoanalysis for the study of intra-poetic relationships in his book *The Anxiety of Influence: A Theory of Poetry* (London: Oxford University Press, 1973), though without regard for Bloom's obsessive mystification of poetry and the creative process. According to Bloom, one of whose major categories for coming to terms with literary influence is "poetic misprision" or misreading, poets misread influential predecessors in order to clear imaginative space for themselves. See especially his "Introduction," pp. 5–8, and the opening chapter, "Clinamen or Poetic Misprision," pp. 19–45.

9. Quoted by Gregor Laschen, *Lyrik in der DDR: Anmerkungen zur Sprachverfassung des modernen Gedichts* (Frankfurt: Athenäum, 1971), p. 95.

10. "Selbstausdruck und Gesellschaftsbezug: Interview mit Günter Kunert," in *Auskünfte: Werkstattgespräche mit DDR-Autoren*, ed. Anneliese Löffler (Berlin: Aufbau, 1974), p. 476. Elsewhere Kunert has insisted on the secondary social and political implications of the reader's primary act of self-recognition. See, for example, his "Manche, einige, gewisse und sogenannte," *Sinn und Form* 24 (1972): 1099–1104, esp. 1103, and "Günter Kunert," in *Meinetwegen Schmetterlinge: Gespräche mit Schriftstellern*, ed. Joachim Walter (Berlin: Der Morgen, 1973), pp. 88–89.

11. *Das kleine Aber: Gedichte* (Berlin: Aufbau, 1975). The two poems from this volume discussed below are found on p. 86 and pp. 67–69.

12. *Für meine Genossen: Hetzlieder, Balladen, Gedichte* (Berlin: Wagenbach, 1972), hereafter cited in the text as *FmG* with page number. Not all poems in this volume were written after the 1960s, but those discussed in this paper were written either at the end of that decade or in the early 1970s. CBS has released two Biermann albums, *Liebeslieder* (1975) and *Es gibt ein Leben vor dem Tod* (1976), that contain mostly songs written in the 1970s. I have not taken either album into account here, but for a discussion of one of the *Liebeslieder*, "Der schwarze Pleitegeier—oder: Eure Farben sind nicht meine Farben," from the perspective of Biermann's relation to literary and political tradition, especially Brecht's overall stance and his poem "Die haltbare Graugans" (10: 1081–82), see Silvia Volckmann, "Die ästhetische Form als politische Aussage," *Wolf Biermann: Liedermacher und Sozialist*, ed. Thomas Rothschild (Reinbek: Rowohlt, 1976), pp. 99–100. Biermann has conceptualized his political position and his related role as poet-singer in a series of interviews over the years. For an English translation of two recent interviews, see Biermann, "Two Interviews," *New German Critique* 4 (Winter 1977): 13–27.

13. See especially Erich Honecker's "Bericht des Politbüros an das 11. Plenum des ZK der SED: Kein Platz für spieß bürgerlichen Skeptizismus," *Neues Deutschland*, no. 46, 16 December 1965, reprinted with related pieces by various hands in *Dokumente zur Kunst-, Literatur- und Kulturpolitik der SED*, ed. Elmar Schubbe (Stuttgart: Seewald, 1972), pp. 1065–122. In his report, which provided the official justification for the ban by the Eleventh Plenum on performances and publications by Biermann in the DDR, Honecker singles out Biermann as a representative member of intellectual circles who were allegedly awakening doubt about the policies of the DDR and disseminating the ideology of skepticism by summarizing the DDR's failures, flaws, and weaknesses, thus jeopardizing "greater productivity and a higher standard of living" (p. 1077). Citing *Die Drahtharfe*, Honecker accuses Biermann of attacking "our social order and party" in the name of anarchistic socialism and of betraying not only the "fundamental positions" of socialism but also the life and death of his father, who was murdered by the Nazis.

14. As David Bathrick, "The Dialectics of Legitimation: Brecht in the DDR," *New German Critique* 1 (Spring 1974): 90–103, reminds us in connection with recent attacks by DDR cultural policymakers on Brecht's critical attitude toward the German classical literary tradition, Brecht's status in the DDR has had its ups and downs in the years since the author's return to Berlin (East) in 1948. Bathrick

attributes this state of affairs to the conflicting notions of culture—the one re-storative-affirmative, the other critically productive—that underlie Brecht's mature work and his function as a cultural figure in the DDR. Clearly, Biermann is as eager to actualize the critically productive strand in Brecht as his adversaries among the cultural and political functionaries are to negate it. Brecht himself, as his selective publication of his *Buckower Elegien* during his lifetime and similar instances reveal, was careful not to display more of his critically productive side than he calculated would be tolerated under a given set of circumstances. In this regard Biermann is much more open and daring than his predecessor.

15. Honecker's remark has been interpreted by one Western observer as more tactical than strategic in nature, as a move, given his new role in 1971 as head of the SED, to improve his image among artists after his central role in the prohibition of Biermann's work. Cf. Hans-Dietrich Sander, *Geschichte der schönen Literatur in der DDR* (Freiburg: Rombach, 1972), p. 267. To expose the catch in Honecker's remark one need only ask: Who decides on the basis of which criteria what "the firm ground of socialism" is?

16. Jochen Vogt, " 'Deine Allee hat noch keine Bäume': Zu Biermanns sozialistischer Kritik am Stalinismus," *Wolf Biermann*, ed. Heinz Ludwig Arnold (Munich: Texte + Kritik, 1975), pp. 114–30, draws attention to the connection between Biermann's poem and Brecht's, but he fails to see any critical implications of Biermann's use of Brecht beyond the observation that "trees as such don't help to build an unalienated socialism" (p. 129). Vogt overlooks the fact that Biermann's rejection of Stalin and Stalinism is categorical while Brecht's is carefully qualified, at times almost wishy-washy. Cf. Brecht's reflections on Stalin and Stalinism (20: 325–26), which at the start come uncomfortably close to a dialectical rationalization of Stalin and his legacy.

17. For an account of the related response by the Czechoslovak government to the Chartist movement, see Tom Stoppard, "Prague: The Story of the Chartists," *The New York Review of Books*, 4 August 1977, pp. 11–15. One of the Chartists informed Stoppard of an incident at a factory where the workers were asked to condemn Chapter 77. " '[T]he result was that they realized that a protest was actually a possibility in this country. So they made their own protest against certain work conditions, and won' " (p. 15). The long-term significance of such developments is unclear, however. Similarly, whether the Biermann issue has really "ripped open the social structures and has created new areas of social discourse and activity" in the DDR, as was editorialized in *New German Critique*, 4 (Winter 1977), in reference to the regime's unwitting escalation of the issue, remains to be seen.

18. *Die Zeit*, no. 33, 12 August 1977, p. 10. The designation "tragicomedy" is Kunert's. In October 1979 Kunert had to take up residence in the Federal Republic.

Enzensberger and the Possibility of Political Poetry

WULF KOEPKE

In the late 1950s critics accustomed to Gottfried Benn's concept of self-centered and purposeless poetry were provoked by the political dimensions of Hans Magnus Enzensberger's *Defense of the Wolves* (1957) and *National Language* (1960). Enzensberger seemed to be an angry young man and a Rousseauistic Luddite. Conservative politicians in the Federal Republic were incensed by the lack of patriotism in the poem "National Language." Such criticisms were muted upon the appearance of a volume of "pure poetry," *Braille* (1964), a work that the author himself later ascribed to political resignation. Indeed, for some critics in the 1970s none of Enzensberger's poems is political enough. This wide spectrum of criticism reflects an evolving political climate rather than basic discontinuity in Enzensberger's texts. The reception of his work demonstrates the complexities of the author-reader relationship and the precarious and experimental nature of political poetry. Enzensberger justly rejects the dichotomy *poesie pure* and *poesie engagée* which a number of critics used against him early in his career. One can understand the nature and intended function of Enzensberger's poems by reference to his relationship to Brecht as it appears in his statements on poetry and his use of Brecht quotations.[1]

For a young poet of the late 1950s Brecht was the logical model for socially and politically relevant poetry, of which he was considered the unsurpassed master. Sometimes he was even seen as the only poet who could fuse the poetical medium and the political message. And yet, even Brecht's work was often divided into "poetry" and "propaganda," a distinction Enzensberger observed in his earlier poetics and poetry. Brecht cast a long shadow over Enzensberger's generation, and it may not have been easy to realize that a Brechtian concept of political poetry would lead a writer living in divided postwar Germany to write poetry essentially different from Brecht's. In the late 1960s, Enzensberger even came to doubt whether poetry was at all possible for his generation, whether the poet had a function in society and whether poetry was significant for political action.[2]

Thus the paradox evolves that the Brechtian concept of poetry leads to a radical questioning of the possibility of socially relevant poetry. Each poem, then, becomes an experiment: an exploration into the question of whether poetry is still or again possible. If it is, which types of readers can it reach? Is the usefulness of poetry to be equated with a measurable effect on a large readership? In other words, does poetry have to be "popular"? Enzensberger's poetics focus on this question: is socially relevant poetry feasible today, and if so, how can it be created?

In the early essay, "Knife Sharpeners and Poets" (1961), Enzensberger quotes and rejects Benn with categories derived from Brecht. "Poems are not pure products" (p. 146). The objects that poetry has to treat are "hot." It is the function of poetry to demonstrate how things are in a way that more facile methods cannot. Poems are supposed to change the reader's consciousness: "Poems are thus not commodities but rather means of production with whose help the reader can produce truth" (p. 146). The pleasure that poems produce is anything but simple; poems are written for "patient" and sophisticated readers. The real touchstone is not the poet's political stand but whether the poems are useful. Poetry must generate socially relevant truth, be useful, and develop its form from the interaction between the subject matter and the reader. Enzensberger wants to appear objective, "cool," and factual. In another essay, "Poetry and Politics" (1962), Enzensberger insists on the social content of all poetry; no poetry is apolitical. Modern poetry, he maintains, does not support or praise those in power; it is by nature critical, if not subversive. Enzensberger supports his argument with Brecht's "Changing a Tire," an open-ended poem in which any affirmation is left to the readers and their responses. Both affirmative propaganda and reactionary "pure" poetry are objectionable. A fusion of social content, critical attitude, and poetic form is required.[3]

The main topic of Enzensberger's early poetry is the one-dimensional insensitivity of "you" (the reader) to the dangers that threaten our society. "They" (those in power, the government and/or corporations that control our society) are dangerous; "they" steer "us" into an ultimate

doom, destroy the environment and our civilization. Enzensberger repeatedly attacks the consciousness industry as the real enemy and continues to do so even today. The poet must use a full array of rhetorical
devices to get the reader's attention and to undercut the consciousness
industry: allusions, puns, quotes, parodies, montage. Such multiple-mean-
ing devices are didactic by nature and an intellectual challenge: they are
designed to combat the one-dimensional propaganda created by tabloids.
The poem "Tabloid" outlines in three parallel stanzas the false hopes created by *Bild*, as the most widely read tabloid in Germany is known collo-
quially: "you'll be rich"—"you'll be beautiful"—"you'll be strong." The
futility of these longings is stressed by allusions to one of Grimm's fairy
tales. The donkey of the Grimm tale from whose ears gold should pour
becomes for Enzensberger a symbol of stupidity and also a she-ass/girl
who must sleep with the producer to become a star. In another play with
words the worker who licks stamps for his retirement pay and who
punches the time clock becomes a "stamppuncher and timeclockpaster,"
thus punching his own future and taking away his own job. Though the
ambiguity and playfulness make the reading difficult, they nevertheless
activate the reader to political awareness. "You too you too you too" reminds the reader of pop songs and of election slogans like "You too, vote
C D U," but these attempts at creating a sense of solidarity within middle-
class society are countered by the phrase "will slowly perish." The message is straightforward, but a patient reader is needed, a reader who is
skilled and who understands literary allusions and the use of quotations.
Despite the difficulty of his poetry, Enzensberger writes "poems for people who don't read poems." *National Language* includes ironic instruc-
tions for use by readers who have problems handling this type of text.
The persona of the texts is the pessimist who would like to be proven
wrong. In "doubt" we read:

> What a triumph, Cassandra,
> to taste a future which would refute you!
> something new that would be good.
> (the good old things we already know ...)

The readers of these lines need to know who Cassandra was, but also to
recognize the allusion to Lessing's aperçu: "I saw many good and new
things at the theater last night. But the good things were not new, and the
new things were not good." With their esoteric quality, Enzensberger's

poems impressed primarily students, for whom these poems along with Brecht's were part of a political education.[4]

The dilemma of a limited audience is obvious. Another dilemma for the author who wants to undercut the consciousness industry by exposing its tricks and clichés, for the radical critic of capitalistic society who satirizes the contradictions of the consciousness industry and its hold on the public, is that he can be integrated into that industry and its ideology of free expression and thus be rendered harmless. Enzensberger, a "demolition worker in the superstructure" (Yaak Karsunke), was always aware that he might be used to maintain that very society he wanted to change.

Poetry as an instrument of social change, with its usefulness dependent on its effect on readers, seems for Enzensberger at times an exercise in futility. The persona of the early poem "Into the Sophomore Reader" (which reverses the message of Brecht's "My Young Son Asks Me") advises "don't read odes, my son, read timetables: / they are more exact," a poetic metaphor that helps us understand Enzensberger's political essays and the title of his cultural and political journal *Kursbuch* [train schedule]. Odes are not very useful, says the writer of odes in an ode. In the late 1960s Enzensberger stopped publishing poems, and the irrelevance of literature became a central theme of his essays—and poems. In "Commonplaces on the Newest Literature" (1968) he argues for a radical new beginning from point zero and recommends prose works of a documentary nature such as Wallraff's *Industry Reports*. Literature is still dominated by bourgeois values and traditions; a "new" literature has not yet emerged. The cool, analytical, and realistic doubts about the possibility of such a literature stand in contrast to Enzensberger's search for symptoms of a beginning. Reinhold Grimm characterizes this dichotomy as "pessimism of intelligence, optimism of will." Enzensberger sees Brecht's "To Posterity" as an optimistic evaluation of the usefulness of poets and poetry in the context of history. Enzensberger's skeptical mind would not allow him to say, as Brecht does, "But those in power / Ruled more securely without me, I hoped." He would stop and pause at Brecht's words "The Goal / Was far away. It was clearly visible, though for me / Scarcely to be reached." His pessimism should not, however, be opposed to Brecht's optimism, since Enzensberger is the skeptical idealist who does not believe that the ideal will ever be realized. This is not to say that he is a moralistic critic without a historical perspective.[5]

The poem "Expansion" from *Braille* reverses Brecht's address to future generations in the poem "To Posterity": "You, who will rise up from the flood / In which we've gone down" becomes "Who's to rise up any more from the flood / when we go down in it?" "Going down," Brecht's metaphor for political defeat, becomes the final disaster in which humankind drowns, a customary image with Enzensberger. Doomsday is one of the central themes of *Braille*. Whereas Brecht's persona describes the problems of his generation for a future society, "When it will come to the point / That humans help one another," Enzensberger's persona warns the present generation that there may not be any future. Enzensberger's poem gains an added dimension through reflecting on Brecht's vision, one which is not realized. Enzensberger then satirizes the capitalistic notion of progress, "a bit of progress or so more / and we'll see what happens," a notion that is of no consequence for the future, as we see in the verses

> who's to remember us
> and make allowances?
>
> that'll come out
> when things have gotten to that point.

(Cf. Brecht's "Remember us / And make allowances.") After this bleak rejection of vision, the poem degenerates into clichés of reassurance from the consciousness industry, followed by the harsh negation "no posterity / no allowances," which is predicated on the fatal consequences of our failure to change. While skeptical, this statement neither denies the possibility of historical progress nor ignores it as Benn did. The poet has the moral duty to warn against dangers. Enzensberger's generation is not Brecht's group of exiled friends fighting with little success for a better society to come, but a part of capitalist society that can expect neither allowances nor posterity unless it changes now. In Enzensberger's reworking, Brecht's ultimately confident lines are fragmented, his words are subjected to a new scrutiny that brings out hidden difficulties, and his implicit belief in progress is criticized. Enzensberger's text leaves much in doubt and asks the reader to assemble and organize the fragments. It reflects the self-destructive society that it criticizes and expresses awareness of humankind's fatal alienation from nature and from society. Brecht's message, insofar as it implies an understanding of historical change, is uplifting. Enzensberger's warnings, on the other hand, burden his reader with moral responsibility.[6]

In the poem "Two Mistakes," Enzensberger offers another example of the use of allusions to Brecht. The lines in "To Posterity"

> What times are these when
> Discourse about trees is almost a crime
> Since it contains silence about so many misdeeds! (9: 723)

are transformed into

> Sleeping, breathing, writing poetry:
> these are almost no crime.
>
> Not to mention
> the famous discourse about trees.[7]

(Brecht's *Schweigen* [silence] is echoed in the idiom *ganz zu schweigen* [not to mention].) Writing poetry—a term that is suspect for Enzensberger—is as natural as sleeping and breathing, and so it is (almost) no crime. Enzensberger continues with material not derived directly from Brecht, but in a Brechtian tone:

> I admit, in my time
> I've shot with sparrows at cannons.
>
> That that did not result in direct hits
> I recognize.

The startling reversal of the idiom "to shoot at sparrows with cannons" suggests the persona has tried to fight the establishment with unsuitable weapons, like poems. If poetry is judged by its usefulness for social and political change, the effect is minimal. But the resigned conclusion does not imply a complete negation of poetry:

> On the other hand, I've never claimed
> that now one should mention nothing.

Poetic expression is natural, and it will go on, useful or not.

> Cannons at sparrows, that would be
> to fall into the opposite mistake.

One should neither expect too much from poetry nor condemn it as an ineffectual weapon. The contrast with Brecht, who intimates that beauty and the relaxed "discourse about trees" would have to be left to future generations, must be recognized by the reader of "Two Mistakes" if the poem is to be understood as the author intends. Brecht implies that "pure" (i.e. socially irrelevant) poetry is desirable but impossible in his day. He saw himself as a poet of a "dark age" who realized

> Even detestation of baseness
> Distorts one's expression.
> Even anger at injustice
> Makes one's voice hoarse. (9: 725)

A generation later Enzensberger asserts that contemporary poets with their "hot objects" still cannot turn to the relaxed discourse about trees. Nevertheless, Brecht becomes, in Enzensberger's view, both the prophet and the poet of beauty; his poems represent an almost untainted universe.

"Two Mistakes" demonstrates that for Brecht and Enzensberger a concept of a "true" poetry exists which combines beauty and social meaning in a positive way and which cannot be written under the given historical and political conditions. For both authors, poetry aspires to change the consciousness of the reader and necessarily reflects the depravity of the time. However, Enzensberger sees in Brecht's poems a positive poetry that poets could write if they believed in a true progress of humankind. Enzensberger's reduced expectations seem more modest, even "realistic."

Positive poetry presupposes a communication between the author and the reader which Enzensberger cannot assume. Brecht intended his poems for an audience that included reading workers: he believed or wanted to believe in the revolutionary potential of the common people. Enzensberger believes that revolutionary change is effected by an elite. Poems like "On the Difficulties of Reeducation" and "The Force of Habit" present common people as incapable of any revolutionary action.[8] A society lacking common sense and addicted to the values of industrial civilization, whether working-class or middle-class, is open neither to change nor to the message of the poet. Irrelevant poetry reflects a society that is not accessible to revolutionary transformation and is in some way not worth a revolution. Enzensberger's readers are not the proletariat in whom Brecht placed his hope, but intellectuals, especially students. Brecht's readers generally need not recognize his literary quotes and allusions to appreciate his poems; Enzensberger's must.

Enzensberger's poems are monologues, and he, as an individualist attracted by anarchism, distrusts institutions. Thus even the dictatorship of the proletariat is no certain ideal. Within a framework of historical dialectics where antagonistic conflicts do not find ready solutions, the poet's significance is modest, but not altogether negligible.[9] In *Mausoleum* (1975) Enzensberger reiterates his conviction that the primary agent of historical change is the individual and not the group. However, it is questionable how much an individual can really achieve and what historical progress means. Progress is treated with irony. Each ballad in the volume is titled by the initials of a "mover" of history—some of the thirty-six figures presented are well-known, others obscure. Stereotyped notions about history are called into question. For example, the subject of the ballad "N.M." (Macchiavelli) seems an unlikely candidate for true progress. Yet this ballad begins with a laudatio:

> Niccolò Niccolò five-hundred-year-old brother
> I press this wreath of dry words on your hard skull
>
> Just between you and me we have every reason for admiring you
> dry and limited and eaten up by theories

followed by a list of negative qualities, a description of a more than questionable life, and the conclusion:

> Niccolò, rascal, poet, opportunist, classic, hangman:
> you're the proverbial Old Adam, and thus I praise your book.
>
> Brother Niccolò, I'll always credit you with that, and since your lies
> so often tell the truth, I curse your crippled hand.

Enzensberger's reader has to be alert and knowledgeable: Macchiavelli's *Prince* describes the old ruler, not the "new man" of whom the Renaissance talked so much. In the light of recent events, Macchiavelli looks more contemporary, and his positions, long considered false, seem to have become viable. A curse overshadows admiration. Did Macchiavelli advance truth? Does he stand for progress? The author's attitude is ambivalent. The reader is asked to decide.[10]

Enzensberger also includes a ballad on G.W.L. (the German philosopher Leibniz), who argued that this world is the best of all possible worlds and made significant advances in mathematics, developing the fundamental theories on which much of computer science is based. The beginning line of the ballad is: "We don't know his feelings"—and this lack of knowledge intrigues the German counterintelligence agency, the CIA, a scientific commission, and the Office of Inquisition of the Catholic

Church. These agencies all agree Leibniz must have been an automaton, a robot used by extraterrestrial spirits, or a computer. In this way his optimism can be explained. The poem ends with the words:

> An anonymous someone *maintains he occupied himself*
> *during his final days deciphering the language of the angels.*

In the eighteenth century one would have said Leibniz was a higher spirit and/or in communication with higher spirits, such as angels, and one would have considered men to be machines like clocks. These two ideas as they are misinterpreted by bureaucrats of the twentieth century present a distortion of Leibniz that calls into question the concept of humankind and understanding of optimism which ultimately derive from Leibniz and his age. Can one believe in progress in the form of a continuous movement toward perfection (i.e. in perfectibility) as Leibniz and his followers did?[11]

Enzensberger's history lessons are further removed from direct comment on contemporary political issues than his previous political poems. They are ballads, accounts of past lives and events which do not call for immediate action. They represent a detachment from direct action, a wider perspective, and a resignation. They invite a comparison with Brecht insofar as they regard the present from a historical perspective, but also the past in the germs of the present. *Mausoleum* presents antiheroes and misconstrued heroes. The effects of their ideas or inventions contradict their intentions. According to Enzensberger, they are remembered for the wrong things. In a complex, ironic, and learned way Enzensberger raises fundamental questions about human actions in a historical framework, but he is still a "demolition worker in the superstructure" of our pluralistic society. His ballads are more factual and less destructive than his earlier political poems, but they are just as critical and skeptical.[12]

For Enzensberger, writing poetry is still a frivolous, and yet inevitable, attractive activity no matter what the historical conditions. Compared to Brecht's hope that poetry might affect the course of human history, his expectations are drastically reduced. He creates poetry that survives despite itself, despite political ineffectiveness on a mass level. Brecht, who demonstrated the unique combination of commitment and skepticism and whose poetry was both popular and nonsimplistic, was the great model for Enzensberger's generation. Measured against the unique synthesis in Brecht's poetry, Enzensberger's must appear esoteric and overly intellectual. This difference, however, has less to do with political poetry per se than with the political realities these poets seek to confront in their verse. The form and complexity of any political poetry correspond to the political constellations it addresses. The Third Reich evokes more clearly defined responses than do the divergent and multivalent contours of Enzensberger's world. During Brecht's lifetime, the phrase "the bad people" clearly characterized Fascists; Enzensberger, in a world in which politicians are technicians, cannot permit himself the luxury of an unspecified villain. Thus, because of the specific historical conditions that inform political poetry, one must accept an author like Enzensberger in a contemporary context, eschewing unfavorable comparisons with Brecht, the classic.

Notes

1. Reinhold Grimm, "Bildnis Hans Magnus Enzensberger: Struktur, Ideologie und Vorgeschichte eines Gesellschaftskritikers," *Basis* 4 (1973): 141–43, 173; Alfred Andersch, "Ein zorniger junger Mann," and Hans Egon Holthusen, "Die Zornigen, die Gesellschaft und das Glück," now in *Über Hans Magnus Enzensberger*, ed. Joachim Schickel (Frankfurt: Suhrkamp, 1970); Werner Weber compares *Blindenschrift* to Brecht's *Buckower Elegien* in *Über Hans Magnus Enzensberger*, p. 99; Hans Magnus Enzensberger, "Gemeinplätze, die neueste Literatur betreffend," *Palaver, Politische Überlegungen* (Frankfurt: Suhrkamp, 1974), pp. 41–54; Walter Hinderer, "Probleme politischer Lyrik heute," *Poesie und Politik*, ed. Wolfgang Kuttkeuler (Stuttgart: Kohlhammer, 1973); Enzensberger, "Bescheidener Vorschlag zum Schutze der Jugend vor den Erzeugnissen der Poesie," *German Quarterly* 49 (1976): 425–37 and his introduction to his anthology *Museum der modernen Poesie* (Frankfurt: Suhrkamp, 1960).

2. Albrecht Schöne, *Zur politischen Lyrik im 20. Jahrhundert* (Göttingen: Vandenhoeck and Ruprecht, 1965), p. 42; Ulla C. Lerg-Kill, *Dichterwort und Parteiparole* (Bad Homberg: Gehlen, 1968), pp. 6–38.

3. Hans Bender, *Mein Gedicht ist mein Messer* (Munich: List, 1961), pp. 144–48; Enzensberger, *Einzelheiten* (Frankfurt: Suhrkamp, 1964); translation now in *The Consciousness Industry*, ed. Michael Roloff (New York: Seabury, 1974), pp. 62–82; for the reception of the poet Gottfried Benn, see Alexander Hildebrand, "Selbstbegegnung in kurzen Stunden: Marginalien zum Verhältnis Hans Magnus Enzensberger—Gottfried Benn," *Text + Kritik* 49 (1976): 17–32.

4. Hans Magnus Enzensberger, "Entrevista 1969," trans. Reinhold Grimm, *Basis* 4 (1973): 122–30; Wulf Koepke, "Mehrdeutigkeit in Hans Magnus En-

zensbergers bösen Gedichten," *German Quarterly* 44 (1971): 341–59; Reinhold Grimm, "Montierte Lyrik," now in *Über Hans Magnus Enzensberger*, pp. 19–31; Gotthard Wunberg, "Die Funktion des Zitats in den politischen Gedichten von Hans Magnus Enzensberger," *Neue Sammlung* 4 (1964): 274–82; Enzensberger, *Landessprache* (Frankfurt: Suhrkamp, 1969), p. 97; the first rule is: "these poems are meant to be used, not to serve as some sort of fancy gift." Rule five, which classifies the readers, is especially revealing. Yaak Karsunke talks about the student movement, "the politization of which began with reading Brecht and Enzensberger texts, including lyric ones," "Abrißarbeiter im Überbau," *Text + Kritik* 9/9a (1973): 17.

5. Brecht, 9: 818; Enzensberger, "Ins Lesebuch für die Oberstufe," *Gedichte 1955–1970* (Frankfurt: Suhrkamp, 1972), p. 13; "Entrevista 1969," pp. 129–30; also "Gemeinplätze," pp. 51–52; Grimm, "Bildnis," p. 174; Theo Buck, "Enzensberger und Brecht," *Text + Kritik* 49 (1976): 14; Klaus Werner, "Zur Brecht-Rezeption bei Günter Kunert und Hans Magnus Enzensberger," *Weimarer Beiträge, Sonderheft Brecht* (1968): 61–73.

6. Brecht, 9: 724; Enzensberger, "Weiterung," *Blindenschrift* (Frankfurt: Suhrkamp, 1964), p. 50; an example of drowning: "Schaum," *Landessprache*, pp. 35–44; examples of doomsday: the section "Blindenschrift." In addition to the title poem, see "Middle-class Blues," "Purgatorio," "Prähistorie," "Doomsday," "Countdown," "Die Verschwundenen." See also my article, "Mehrdeutigkeit," p. 355. For Brecht and Benn, see Werner, "Brecht-Rezeption," p. 69.

7. Brecht, 9: 722; Enzensberger, *Gedichte 1955–1970*, p. 162.

8. Enzensberger, *Gedichte 1955–1970*, pp. 128–29 and 164–65.

9. Theo Buck, "With good reason Enzensberger sees in lyric poetry an elitist form with the character of monologue," "Enzensberger und Brecht," p. 12; Grimm, "Bildnis," pp. 161, 165; it is also informative to compare Enzensberger's *Der kurze Sommer der Anarchie* (Frankfurt: Suhrkamp, 1972).

10. Enzensberger, *Mausoleum* (Frankfurt: Suhrkamp, 1975), p. 11.

11. *Mausoleum*, p. 27.

12. In opposition to Theo Buck, I fail to see a "synthesis" of Brecht and the earlier Enzensberger in *Mausoleum* (p. 14). His present detachment and resignation may be followed again by a period of activism, as it has been in the past. See also Michael Franz, "Hans Magnus Enzensberger: Mausoleum," *Weimarer Beiträge* 12 (1976), who sees the *Mausoleum* poems as "lyrical paraphrases of Brecht's *Life of Galileo*" (p. 132), and applauds the newly acquired "objectivity" in contrast to "subjective protest" (p. 139). This change, which would correspond to the detachment discussed in this article, may be more resignation than "objectivity."

Afterword

Literary Practice: Literary Heritage

FRANK TROMMLER

"At the end of it all," John Willett remarked a few years ago, "we come back to the poet, because you cannot really appreciate the playwright Brecht, or even perhaps the theatrical director, let alone the theoretician, without realizing that he was a poet first, last and all the time."[1] Quite aside from the fact that in making this statement Willett may have been promoting his English edition of Brecht's poetry, we must admit that he helped keep open an approach to Brecht as a writer in our times. Willett supported his view with Ernest Bornemann's sardonic remark about the negative reviews Laughton's *Galileo* had received: "The truth, of course, is that Brecht never bores those who are at all susceptible to his lyricism: but he bores almost everyone else." What Willett accepted as an argument has, to be sure, been hotly debated. A long time has passed since Bornemann's remark, and I have the impression that just the opposite is true now; that is to say, Brecht is stimulating and controversial for those who are interested not in his lyricism but in all sorts of other things, especially in his political comments and aesthetical concepts. Even in England and the United States many scholars today are concerned with those aspects of Brecht which the critics have decried as boring. What was disparagingly referred to as "typically German" in Brecht has now acquired a contemporary relevance.

The essays in this volume provide an instructive commentary to this state of affairs. They show how intensely Brecht is respected on the basis of his political thought and aesthetic theories, to what a large degree his work is used as a vehicle for contemporary concerns, to what extent he is cast in the role of a guru for artistic intellectuals. I have reservations about what seems to me the exploitation of Brecht for the furtherance of one's own ideas. However, these reservations are outweighed by the vitality of the ongoing debate on the relationship of art and society, which approximates Brecht's intention more closely than would a treatment of his works in well-rounded, exemplary, "classical" interpretations.

What Efim Etkind says about Brecht's epoch-making effect in the Soviet Union after Stalin's death provides especially good arguments for the public "utility" of Brecht's works. Up to the present day Brecht has served in communist countries, particularly in the DDR, as a catalyst for the discussion of what is modern in literature. And his utility is no less important in Western countries. Here Brecht challenges us to take a stand on Marxist criticism of prevailing conditions within capitalism.

If we examine more closely how and by what means Brecht has made an impact, we must take into account historical and social conditions—in this case those of the 1960s and 1970s, with increased political activism in intellectual circles. During this period one facet of Brecht engaged the interest of the younger writers, theater people, and intellectuals. This facet is neither form nor theory but his stance or attitude. Brecht represented and inspired a specific stance with respect to reality. Manfred Wekwerth, who worked with Brecht in the Berlin Ensemble in the years 1951–1956 and who, as a successful director and theoretician, has never hidden his debt to him, described this attitude as follows:

> Brecht left us with exciting ideas, and a lifetime is not sufficient to bring them to fruition. But one thing, I believe, was essential: the critical attitude that Brecht recommended to us. It is anything but a negating attitude, it has nothing to do with Adorno's critical theory. Brecht considered meaningful only that criticism in which negation was joined by negation of the negation, i.e., resolution that produces progress and nothing else. That does not mean that the criticism Brecht directed at certain phenomena was not harsh, impatient in the face of unreasonable behavior. Assuming a critical stance for him never meant, however, getting mired down in criticism. Brecht's recommendation of a critical stance is the recommendation of a fundamentally politically productive stance which can be measured by its results, by a visible improvement of society, of the environment, but also concretely: in the factory, in the theater, etc.[2]

In his polemical demarkation between this attitude and the critical theory of the Frankfurt school, Wekwerth follows the position taken by Brecht, who poked fun at the "Frankfurtites" as "Tuis," as representatives of an intelligentsia both opportunistic and divorced from practice. Whether Brecht was himself really so far removed from these intellectuals has been debated. He has been accused of limiting himself to a critique of existing conditions rather than developing an image of what should come. Indeed, it is perhaps no accident that Brecht's influence became noticeable in West Germany at a time when the Frankfurt school reached the high point of its effectiveness.

It cannot be denied that Brecht remained not just a figurehead hero of literature and theater for the younger generation but also part of an intellectual dialogue. He became a cult figure, whether several gathered together in his name or an individual recluse brooded over tracts and poems. When the students and artists attacked the institutions and traditions of their day, they found more in Brecht's works than pure arguments. They sought and found themselves; they identified with Brecht. In a period of antiauthoritarian attacks, he offered the possibility of a "legitimate" appeal to authority. It was a critical authority—some spoke of a superego—and this authority often led one astray, to an authoritarian critique. Positive and negative results lay in close proximity: on the one hand, a strengthened self-awareness, a critical consciousness, criteria for the political utilization of art and literature; on the other hand, a dogmatization of dialectical thought, embalmment of Brecht's forms and formulas in an antiquarian framework.

In the 1960s Brecht played a greater role in sparking interest in Marxism than many of the "classical" authorities of socialism. After all, he was a writer and practitioner of the theater, and a good portion of the political and ideological interest of the students is a redirected aesthetic interest. The radical rejection of literature at the end of the 1960s, when Enzensberger and other contributors to his *Kursbuch* proclaimed the "death of literature," demonstrates how deeply radical thought was rooted in the realm of aesthetics. Most of all, however, a type of Marxism became relevant through Brecht's critical stance. An alternative was offered to the precipitous decline of the socialist movement since the end of the 1920s. Brecht's critical distance from Marxism as practiced in the 1930s and 1940s in the Soviet Union—a Marxism for which some, using typically aesthetic categories of thought, tried to hold Georg Lukács responsible—lent his observations not only ideological but also historical weight. Although the younger generation generally, especially in Germany, tried to stay as far away from history as possible, they were not able to push the historical dimension in Brecht's works aside. For many he became the only link to the past, to the struggles of the 1920s and the 1930s, to exile and Stalinism. Here, too, it was less a question of the soundness of the arguments than of the intensity of identification.

Brecht's indelible imprint on the last decades can be seen in three areas. The first: his part in shaping Marxism as an instrument of the intelligentsia since the cold war—to be sure, a type of Marxism for which concepts such as proletariat and class struggle play a key role, but in which the workers themselves participate passively at best. After the defeat of socialism by the National Socialists in Germany, in which the workers exercised their power only reluctantly, Brecht's efforts (his work in the theater in the DDR, at first rather isolated) affected primarily the intelligentsia. His notion of freeing thought from preexistent aesthetic and political determinants conveys intellectual satisfaction, not practical, organizational knowledge.

The second area, closely related to the first: Brecht's engagement as Marxist *and* writer. In a period when the roots of this intellectual satisfaction in the aesthetic realm were increasingly denied, he continued to attract attention as a writer. He seemed to many to be an ally in the dissociation of politics and lyricism despite his being a poet. The interpreters groped, detouring by way of his theoretical comments, toward the central theme, toward the question of the legitimation of literature in a nonliterary social order and in a nonliterary political movement. Brecht served as an authority to be cited by everyone who did not reject art and literature as an escapist manifestation of bourgeois decadence but rather sought to incorporate them constructively in the process of social change and thus to justify them. Citing Brecht in this manner remained for the most part within the confines of intellectual satisfaction and rarely entered theatrical practice. All too frequently the discourse about literature and theater appeared to be far more advanced than the laborious trundle of Thespis's cart. The reality of Brecht's plays seemed suddenly to limp along far behind his efforts to create a new political (Marxist) art.

The final area: artistic practice. That this category is mentioned last is not surprising in view of the comments above. What actually happens in the theater, whether particular acting techniques of Brecht's are still viable today, whether they attract a present-day audience, and where the problems of directing are to be found—these problems are at present of little interest to most theater practitioners and of less to literary scholars. The Brecht boom in German theaters has diminished in the last decade and only gradually has an image of Brecht's impact become clear. Whoever wishes to circumvent the frustrations of tracing theater history should keep in mind Wekwerth's stress on Brecht's critical stance which has become the most fruitful element for dramatists and directors. Whoever engages in a modicum of theater history will discover that even in the 1920s Brecht's fame rested to a considerable degree on his capacity for critical adaptation.

The paradox discussed around 1930—that Erwin Piscator as a director influenced primarily dramatists and Bertolt Brecht as a dramatist influenced mostly directors—sheds light on Brecht's contribution to drama and theater after 1950. He was not really instrumental in introducing new topics (no more than in the 1920s) for the stage. In East and West Germany other, mostly younger, authors did this. He did not to any great extent provide German theater with plays on National Socialism and war, the persecution of the Jews, and the development of socialism. His contribution was the increasing readiness to tackle burning problems as theatrical ones. In 1930 he had already tried, in collaboration with Hanns Eisler, to systematize the acquisition of existing works which Piscator had been attempting. The concept of the potential of existing works as raw material for political statement was appreciated by dramatists and directors of the 1960s, and this new appreciation was not accidental. They, too, rejected—if it served their purpose—the idea of intuitive poetic creation, of the primary value of originality. They understood literature and theater to be a part of the system of modern communication and mass media. It was not by accident that Kenneth Tynan, Brecht's advocate in England, answered the question as to whether he saw traces of Brecht's influence in English authors by stating that the stronger influence could be found among the directors. Brecht does not necessarily aid in providing a model for the presentation of reality as dramatic material, but he is of great help in making theater relevant to reality.

Brecht's influence on poetry—in the East and in the West—was more direct and is well represented in this volume. Here, too, Wekwerth's comments about Brecht's critical stance are pertinent. Lyric poetry is the genre in which this stance is translated most directly into linguistic expression. Innumerable poems were written under the influence of Brecht which reproduce this stance toward contemporary life. The events of the day do not necessarily provide the insights for the poems; like a drama on the stage, the linguistic expression of the poem acquires its own justification, its own dynamics, and overpowers everything else. In this respect

Brecht's poetry is comparable to that of other great poets, in that later poets are tempted to continue in the tone of the original and sometimes overshadow their model. The model, even overshadowed, retains its own luminescence. The difference between Brecht's poetry and that of his "posterity" may lie in the fact that Brecht's poetry needs no sun. Perhaps Willett is correct, after all, when he attributes Brecht's appeal to his lyricism.

Translated by Hubert Heinen

Notes

1. John Willett, "The Poet beneath the Skin," *Brecht heute—Brecht Today: Jahrbuch der Internationalen Brecht-Gesellschaft* 2 (1972): 88.
2. Manfred Wekwerth, "Brecht. 75 Jahre: Ein Gespräch mit den *Weimarer Beiträgen*," *Schriften: Arbeit mit Brecht* (Berlin: Henssel, 1973), p. 400.

Notes on the Contributors

Notes on the Contributors

MARGARETA DESCHNER (Southern Methodist University, Dallas), who has published on such writers as Böll and Dürrenmatt, is preparing a longer study of Hella Wuolojoki.

EFIM ETKIND (University of Paris at Nanterre), a translator and literary figure who formerly lived in Leningrad, has published studies on European literature, including Brecht. A recent book is *Unblutige Hinrichtung—warum ich die Sowjetunion verlassen mußte*.

IRING FETSCHER (Johann Wolfgang Goethe University, Frankfurt), an authority on Marxism, has authored numerous books and articles on literature and political philosophy, including *Karl Marx and Marxism*. Among his most recent studies is *Terrorismus und Reaktion*.

THEODORE FIEDLER (University of Kentucky, Lexington), the author of articles on Hofmannsthal, Trakl and Hölderlin, and Ingarden's theory of the reading process, as well as a comparative study of Brecht and Cavafy, is investigating problems in the history and theory of literary criticism.

HENRY GLADE (Visiting Professor, 1979–80, University of Cologne), a specialist on German theater and Soviet-German literary relationships, has published widely in these areas; he is the author (with Peter Bruhn) of *Heinrich Böll in der UdSSR*.

HUBERT HEINEN (University of Texas at Austin), who is predominantly a medievalist, has also written on modern German, English, and American literature, primarily on poetry.

DOUGLAS KELLNER (University of Texas at Austin) has edited several volumes and is conducting research on politics and aesthetics in theater, film, music, and the broadcast media. His concern with political philosophy led to his *Karl Korsch: Revolutionary Theory* and *Herbert Marcuse and the Vicissitudes of Critical Theory*.

WULF KOEPKE (Texas A & M University) is noted for studies on such varied authors as Jean Paul, Borchert, Thomas Mann, and Enzensberger, as well as on German culture and exile literature.

GEORGE LELLIS (Coker College, Hartsville, S.C.) wrote his dissertation on Brecht and the *Cahiers du Cinéma*; he is the author (with George Wead) of *The Film Career of Buster Keaton* and has published film criticism in numerous journals.

IAN MCLACHLAN (Champlain College, Trent University, Ontario) is poet/novelist/dramaturge and a student of comparative literature.

KLAUS-DETLEF MÜLLER (Christian Albrecht University, Kiel) has published numerous books and articles in the field of German literature. His best-known volume on Brecht is *Die Funktion der Geschichte im Werk Bertolt Brechts: Studien zum Verhältnis von Marxismus und Ästhetik*; his latest work is *Autobiographie und Roman*.

RICHARD RUNDELL (New Mexico State University) wrote his dissertation on Brecht's use of aphoristic formulations.

WOLFGANG STORCH (Schiller Theater, Berlin) has worked with numerous theaters as dramaturge and director. At the Fourth Congress of the International Brecht Society in Austin, he assembled an exhibit and prepared a catalogue on productions of Brecht plays in West German theaters, 1968–1976. In conjunction with the Fifteenth Exposition of the European Parliament, he edited *Stücke der zwanziger Jahre*.

ANTONY TATLOW (University of Hong Kong) teaches comparative literature and is the author of *The Mask of Evil: Brecht's Response to the Poetry, Theatre and Thought of China and Japan*.

FRANK TROMMLER (University of Pennsylvania) has published widely on nineteenth- and twentieth-century German literature; he is the author of *Sozialistische Literatur in Deutschland: Ein historischer Überblick*.

BETTY NANCE WEBER (University of Texas at Austin) published on German theater and literature and worked with experimental theater groups producing original scripts. Her study of the chalk circle plays, *Brechts Kreidekreis: Eine Interpretation*, was one of the volumes chosen to commemorate the eightieth anniversary of Brecht's birth. She was killed in an automobile accident on 10 January 1979.

Index

Index

The following list of Brecht's works, divided by genre, includes passing references as well as thorough discussions, since the range of interest in a given work is significant.